APOCALYPSE
The Book of Revelation

JACQUES ELLUL

APOCALYPSE

The Book of Revelation

TRANSLATED BY GEORGE W. SCHREINER

A Crossroad Book

THE SEABURY PRESS · NEW YORK

1977
The Seabury Press
815 Second Avenue · New York, N.Y. 10017

Library of Congress Cataloging in Publication Data

Ellul, Jacques.   Apocalypse.
Translation of L'Apocalypse, architecture en mouvement.
"A Crossroad book."
Includes bibliographical references.
1. Bible. N.T. Revelation—Criticism, interpretation, etc. I. Title.
BS2825.2.E4413   228'.06   76–54322   ISBN 0–8164–0330–9

CONTENTS

APOCALYPSE
The Book of Revelation

INTRODUCTION

Presuming to write on the subject of the Apocalypse is ambitious, rash, and unacceptable. Ambitious in the presence of thousands of existing commentaries (what could we claim to add?) and of scientific research, which abounds during these last years. In addition, I am not an apocalyptist, a specialist in the study of apocalypses. Rash, above all, because of the final warning, "to anyone who adds or takes away something from this book of the Revelation . . ."; and how write or preach on its subject without changing this Revelation? But also because there never has been a book provoking more delirium, foolishness, and irrational movements, without any relationship to Jesus Christ, as if this book contained the possibility of a temptation actually demonic. Oddly, this text which has been placed by the Church at the end of the Bible has continually been interpreted as an introduction to a third part—that of the Holy Spirit. It is well to recall that even balanced theologians who have begun the study of the Apocalypse upon true foundations have progressively gone astray. But, moreover, in our day a reflection upon, or proceeding from, the Apocalypse is unacceptable—at least if it is not a work of pure exegetical, historical, or structural analysis. And it seems to me we encounter here three criticisms. One, certainly, is inspired by the memory of all those spiritual or gnostic vagaries of which I spoke. With good reason the symbolism—the occasion for false judgments and false hopes renewed at each epoch, and responding to a frenzied imagination—is feared. If on the one hand it can be said that the development of scientific thought today must reject the symbolic and gnostic mode of thought, on the other we must note well that there never have been so many seers, divines, and astrologers, a reversion to that sorcery which can reutilize the Apocalypse. It is expedient, then, to observe great prudence. But must we for all that give up seeking a meaning, and restrict ourselves to the so-called scientific work of exegesis in order not to fall into delirium? A second criticism expresses a true theological reservation: too often the Apocalypse shunts us off toward the examination of detail. What is the meaning of the Beasts, of the number 666, of the delay of three and one-half years, etc., which has only a very secondary importance but excites our curiosity, unbridles our imagination, arouses our appetite for mystery, and finally hides from us the central truth which ought to be revealed. But one is then tempted to say that, after all, this truth reduces to that of the Gospels—and then prudently turn away from the Apocalypse and its image-making. Finally, a third criticism issues from the apparent pessimism of this revelation. We generally attempt in modern Christian milieus to validate history and the efforts of man, to diminish the decisive character of sin, to show the positive aspect of human achievements in politics, technique, work (fulfillment of the creation); we seek to attenuate the rigor of Christian morality and the presence of the Judgment; we yield to the optimistic logic of progress, and we live with the assurance of a progressive approximation of the Kingdom in history, not an end given by God, but work accomplished by humankind. After a theology of the total No upon the work of humankind (puritanism), we have entered into a theology of the Yes of God upon the world and humanity. In this perspective the Apocalypse, with its plagues, its judgments, its lake of fire, and its catastrophes, is unacceptable. One can easily extricate oneself by ascribing it to a localized, historical current, the result of a stereotyped procedure, of ready-made images, which are to be found everywhere in the apocalyptic writings for at least two centuries before the redaction of the text under consideration. In these conditions one can consider it a cultural product, enlightening us concerning the mentality and ideology of certain Christian groups at the end of the first century and upon their reactions confronted by political problems. But no more. Certainly, no more! No question of finding here an actual meaning, an eternal message. And one can, in order to fortify this reservation, this skeptical attitude, recall that the Apocalypse was from the beginning in the Church a marginal book. It had not been easily integrated into the canon and had not been accepted by all the churches. With the Epistle of James it is a suspect book. It is receiving a strictly relative rehabilitation during these last years because of the perception that it was a political book. The political reading of the Apocalypse enters well into our presuppositions: on this condition it can be tolerated. But we go no further.

The Question of Method

It is then necessary for me to attempt to delimit my undertaking. I do not seek here to make an exhaustive commentary. Given just this immense literature (including the modern) to which I have made allusion, twenty volumes would be required. And not even a readable commentary for the use of the faithful: there are some very good ones, those of Feret, of Allo, or of Brütsch, for example, which do not appear to me obsolete, and which there is no point in replacing. I do not seek either to produce a scientific work enumerating the multiple interpretations of each passage, confronting the arguments, or again working on a purely historical or structural reading. I do not abandon the search for a meaning. But, of course, I will not engage in the deciphering of symbols, in cryptography, in a study of conundrums and puzzles. This is not very useful. I will attempt to discern the specificity of the Apocalypse, avoiding as much as possible what has been said. I will not make, for each text, an inventory of sustained or possible interpretations: this so common method can again only involve us in detail. Now, and I will attempt to demonstrate it, I maintain that the Apocalypse must be read as a whole, of which each part takes its import by relation to the whole: in other words, the Apocalypse cannot be understood verse by verse. It matters little whether the symbolism of the two prophets or the dragon is deciphered, in itself, or even in a short sequence: each has its role in its relation to the totality. And it is that, moreover, which makes possible the avoidance of the detail of figures that hide the forest. Each of the symbols is a tree of the forest, but it is a matter of grasping the forest as such. And this whole is characterized by a movement. The problem is less that of comprehending a section of the book than the movement which effects passage from one section to another (and which is visible in the transitions). It is necessary to attempt to restore this movement: the Apocalypse is not an immobile and definitive architectural whole, but it is in itself movement, which goes from a beginning to an end.

Its title also evokes this: a revelation is not a once-for-all established fact. It is not something inscribed, a thing, an object: revelation is an act, and it is only revelation as act.[1] It is not the effects, the consequences that are important, it is the act itself. The error is expressed by Péguy: "When the effect has passed you seek the cause." If the Apocalypse is revelation, that means an act of God who intervenes in the course of history, and the book is not the description of this intervention, contrary to what it has too often been considered, nor is it a potential revelation that the Holy Spirit could come to animate (as all the rest of Scripture). As revelation, the book is propelled by an internal movement and the attempt must be made to recover this movement. I am going to proceed then outside the scientific, exegetical method. I will make a "naïve reading," but not completely naïve: the naïveté of the one who, having known the interpretations fairly well, takes up everything again with an eye he wishes were new. That which I will try to guard against is redundance. In these conditions I must situate myself between the total message and the analysis, whether that analysis be symbolic (and become insignificant by the accumulation of details that are no longer related to the central purpose of the text) or whether it is historico-exegetical (and thinking to explain a book because it succeeds in restoring it to its time or even cuts it up into pieces emanating from sources or several authors, capable of explaining precisely the origin or the occasion, but not at all the meaning). But at the other extreme it is necessary also to beware reduction to a universal message. When the narrative has been stripped of its poetic splendor, of its digressions, its images, or its specific structure, the Apocalypse certainly can be proclaimed a book whose purpose it is to revive the hope of a Christian community in danger, or, further, a political book directed at, contesting, the power of Caesar; but how can we fail to perceive that reduced to these broad banalities the uniqueness which produces true vigor is lacking! The central question is not answered. If it were as simple as all that, then why would not the author make a frontal attack and speak of hope, in a brief text. If we are before such a masterful construction, it is not in order to make the account entertaining for the readers, nor to fashion some crossword puzzles around a banality; the form of the whole and the wealth of themes utilized require a meaning. And that is totally lacking in seeking a general idea. Not that there isn't one. But it takes its force and fullness only if the totality of expression, by means of which it has been formulated, is comprehended. It is then this middle ground that I will attempt to occupy. And just as, in writing *The Politics of God and the Politics of Man* I have attempted to explicate the dialectical position I have in regard to politics, between the modern concrete political reality and the reading of an *example* (not at all a doctrine of the Old Testament), in the same way here I attempt to set forth the dialectical position I can have in regard to society, human works, and especially technique, for the confrontation between the sociological reality and the reading of an *example;* here again because the Apocalypse is the unique example (and not the doctrine) of the meaning of the work of humanity and, equally, of its nonmeaning.

This Apocalypse has been written in certain given historical circumstances (one or the other of the great persecutions of the first century; but today it is universally referred more readily to that of Domitian, particularly since more recent authors have begun to doubt that there had in fact been any persecution under Nero; but this appears to me very overstated). It is then generally considered a text probably clear for the readers of that epoch, perhaps directly so or written with a certain popular symbolism and in a certain political and cultural context. But I am not at all sure that it was easily readable on the basis of the characteristics of contemporary apocalyptic. It is not the author's utilization of traditional symbols and images of apocalypses that in itself made possible the effective comprehension of the meaning that he wished to give his text: because he had another objective, another purpose than the ordinary apocalyptists, and like many other biblical authors, he utilized a certain idea, a certain poetic image, a certain fragment of myth in order to make them say a wholly different thing from that which was generally heard. I believe, and I will attempt to show, that the Apocalypse of John is a text carefully constructed in function of a complex and unique message, which makes the elements of construction different by their insertion in a totality, and incomprehensible if one tries simply to interpret them by reference to the formally identical elements of the multiple other apocalypses. In other words, it is a matter of discerning both this unique structure and at the same time the meaning to which this totality refers.

Thus this Apocalypse cannot be understood on the basis of the traditional images of apocalyptic or of a general idea (gnostic or Christian) but solely on the basis of the meaning itself. But then, if it were already hermetic for the readers of the epoch, how much more today! Even so, could one necessarily consider that it no longer contains anything discernible or interesting? Always susceptible of inflaming the imagination by the intensity of its images, it would be in other respects only a text totally obsolete. It is necessary in any case to understand that it remains efficacious in its direct apprehension, in the transmission of visions which still respond to a lot of archetypes present even to modern man. And each religious reawakening even today is nourished anew by these images. But the Apocalypse specifically is not a text capable of being understood directly. Every supposed immediate comprehension is false. It is a discourse extraordinarily sophisticated, which can be understood only by the indirect mode: it functions by the play of mirrors and the reality to which it refers can be grasped only by a kind of triangulation of these inverse images. It requires then a reading both naïve and knowing, but knowing by being situated at the very interior of the system that the author has built. This can be clearly perceived by an application of the structural method. But if it is useful the latter cannot be applied completely, at least to the extent that certain of its theoreticians consider it necessary to eliminate the meaning, assuming that the text is an "object-out-there" which must be analyzed as such without any problem of meaning being posed. It is obvious that this text had been written by a man who had an intention, the purpose of transmitting something accurately; but certainly it does not suffice to seek out this intention, to examine the psychology of the writer, nor to assemble the cultural elements that he had been able to utilize. Certainly also, the structure itself of the text reveals a certain number of realities of which the author was not conscious. But I remain very certain upon this point: the author had not been a mere writer of "something," of a text, but he had an *intentional meaning*. And even more he had also desired to convey meaning by the construction itself, by the organization, by the plan and structure of his work.

Then, of course, to inquire into the psychology of John, or his primary purpose, is of little value: it is really possible for us to know only that which he has said, not that which he meant to say. But the existence of this purpose makes it impossible to avoid the problem of the text's meaning. It is the expression in a certain direction, and producing a statement with a certain meaning, which appears to me to be essential, and that is exhausted neither by the historical context, nor by the cultural content, nor by the reconstruction of its origin. The author has of course powerfully experienced the events of his time, but he has not limited himself to reflecting them. The symbolism, the distancing, the construction to the second degree show that the Apocalypse is neither a writing of circumstance nor a reflection of events. We interpret it thus because we impose our own practice. In case of persecution we would write somewhat pious letters of consolation, and we would take the precaution of speaking with disguised words. But are we really here in the presence of a pietistic text? Clearly not. It is a matter of strong theological construction, which speaks hardly at all to the "soul." And in the same way because there is the question of martyrs, etc., we immediately relate it to the "persecutions": *this is not impossible.* But the latter is actually all that can be said from the historical point of view, for did a man such as this author have to be plunged into persecution in order to comprehend that the death of Jesus and his condemnation would be enough to condemn as enemies of the emperor of Rome those who openly called upon His name? It was evidence itself. We can admit the relation with a certain persecution without that being decisively explanatory. The reasoning upon which that rests can be seen, apparently scientific but actually faulty: there is the question of martyrs in the text. In the primitive church those who had died during the persecutions had been called martyrs. Then the text had been written during or after the persecutions. So its major emphasis and objective is to console and fortify the persecuted churches. And thereby a conclusive deduction is made concerning this book as well as an interpretation of the less clear passages; and the philosophy of history of the Apocalypse is fabricated or the taking of a certain theological position is explained *on that basis.* And it is this that troubles me (much more than the attempts at fixing a date, which has little importance). Thus it is announced that if the author is hostile to Rome, and to political power, it is because a persecuting power is at issue (which is actually very simplistic). In reality, all results from forgetting that for the first prolonged Christian generation, after the theological construction of Paul and the first years, the authentic Witness, the Martyr upon which all else depends, was Jesus Christ and that it was enough so to consider him in order to comprehend what the political power was and the true situation of the Church in the world. I maintain then as much more certain scientifically that the Apocalypse, in its theological intention, is not a reflection of the concretion of historical or ecclesiastical circumstances. Of course, it had been written on the occasion of concrete events; it is related to them. But it is neither a reaction to circumstances, nor a justification of positions already held, nor a utilization, nor an (awkward) essay of response and explanation, of these occasions. For the apocalyptist the concrete is only an *opportunity* for saying something fundamental for the faith of the Church. It is a vestment expressive for an abstract thought. A set of symbols can certainly be found in the concrete to better interpret the thought, but the historical or liturgical elements, the ecclesiastical problems, are nothing more than material transposed to express something totally different, which has no *direct* relation with that which is said. A whole work of symbolization and distancing is carried through (which properly speaking is the creation of the author) where the historical material loses its specificity to serve as the means, the contingent intermediary, for expressing a thought abstract and fugacious. There is then construction of another reality, integrating, however, the historical concrete, but not dependent upon it.

And consequently we are here at the very heart of the uniqueness of the apocalyptic work: a certain reality-truth relationship. As we have often said, in our epoch, because of the activity of science, there is a confusion of truth with reality. To schematize, in the Middle Ages there was an opposition between truth and reality (and this opposition is found already, for example, in John, between the world, which is reality, and the Kingdom of God, which is truth). But in the Apocalypse there is a close relation between the two: the real provides the truth with the means for expressing itself, the truth transfigures the real by giving it a meaning that it obviously does not have in itself. This is thoroughly fundamental, and we will see the decisive interpretive capacity that taking this position provokes.

Another current tendency to which we are also opposed, from the point of view of method, is that of "fragmentation" of the text. As I have already indicated, it is now a tradition to cut texts up into fragments in order to discover the sources. This is a possibility, not without interest, but which rarely explains anything. I do not deny that the author of the Apocalypse could possibly have used one or another text already written, but that provides us with absolutely nothing. On the contrary, what appears to me basic is to consider the totality of the book in its *movement* and *structure*. It is there, actually, that the meaning is situated, in the relationship of part to part, in their connection, their progression. We must consider the text in its final state, because that has a value as such completely superior to the bits and pieces that compose it.[2] But everything depends upon the end sought: if one can succeed in cutting the text up into primitive elements, to arrive at a date, in an investigation of the milieu in which the text could have been produced, before the last redaction, that is perfectly legitimate, but definitely limited. In fact, two barriers must be imposed to such an inquiry. First of all, the meaning does not depend upon an *Ur-Sprung,* upon an origin: the oldest is not linked more closely to the truth. The primitive is not the more important (one yields unconsciously to this mythology, which arose during the century of the enlightenment, of the good savage, the primitive expressing the true state of man). In the second place, the text can be partially clarified by knowledge of the cultural milieu where it had taken birth; but I have already expressed elsewhere many reservations about the importance of this cultural classification, particularly because it can never really be known, and in addition the text is never actually in direct dependence upon this milieu, and could as well be a reflection as a contradiction.[3] Therefore the classic historical exegetical research is certainly not useless, but it illuminates the meaning very little. And if the latter is sought, the taking of other more complex ways must be accepted, without neglecting, however, the results of these works when they are sufficiently assured.

As far as the Apocalypse is concerned, there has been some

wavering. After a hypercritical period, when its composition was pushed up to A.D. 150, and when a puzzle of disparate bits was seen here, there has been a return to more classic considerations. That there are some similarities of style between it and other texts attributed to "John" is emphasized; then, that this bit of bravura had been written probably in the surroundings of John the Evangelist is acknowledged; the date is set between 65 and 95. What is considered an enumeration of emperors in chapter 17:10–11 favors the first date; also it is thought that there is an allusion to the destruction of the temple at Jerusalem, which will be restored and be infinitely more grandiose. For the second, there is the testimony of Irenaeus of Lyon, and the creation of the cult of Caesar by Domitian, although I would have many reservations about this "cult."

It is necessary to recall again, as we have already noted, that the Apocalypse of John is inserted into a general current of apocalypses, that there had been, since about 180 B.C. and perhaps under Iranian influence, a "literary genre" of revelations of God. This appeared, probably in some mystic sects, with two usually recognizable characteristics: the "revelations" are supposed to have been delivered by some great personages of the past (e.g., the Apocalypse of Moses) and are related to some historical events of the present. They often make reference to a last judgment. Moreover among them, the popular apocalypses (more nationalistic, political, and often deriving from the Maccabean wars), the rabbinic apocalypses (very theological), and the "transcendent" apocalypses (in which a celestial future of glory is opposed to a terrestrial humiliation) can be distinguished.[4] Jewish apocalypses are also found again in the first century A.D. It is very difficult to know what their influence was, if they had a large audience, or if they were limited to certain groups or sects. It is clearly seen that they did not enter into the canon; they are then considered a pious literature, of edification or warning, but not a Word of God. Yet the apocalypses of Matthew 24 and of John are situated, as far as style, cosmic vision, presentation of events, and symbolism are concerned, in this apocalyptic current. Some other Christian apocalypses appear subsequently, from the second to the fifth century, but they are more and more fantastic, more and more romantic or literary, and their baroque accumulation holds less and less interest. I recall these banalities summarily as a matter of duty; all that will be found well detailed, well analyzed in all the introductions to the Apocalypse (see for example that of the Century Bible) and particularly in the specialized works on the Apocalypse.[5]

As I have already said, I do not have here any intention of presenting an "introduction" to the Apocalypse, and because of this there are some problems that I will not enter into, taking for granted most of the elements that I mentioned above.

Apocalypse and Prophecy [6]

On the other hand, a question which it seems ought to be clarified is that of the relationship and opposition between apocalypse and prophecy. It is known that a very superficial view can reconcile the two in the measure that a double misinterpretation is made. Prophecy would be a forecast of the future, and the apocalyptic would be also, with the difference that apocalyptic presents only the catastrophes that accompany the "end time"; that is, interpreted as the end of the world, and the apocalyptic is ruminated upon as meaning the possibility of prophecy of the end of the world: when you see these things of which the apocalypse of John speaks, then . . . , etc. It is known that on this rests all the delirious interpretations of the year 1000 and of the fourteenth century. For many years, on the contrary, the attempt has been made to show the difference scientifically, the radical opposition between the two. In the first place, in a comprehensive fashion, prophecy is analyzed as being always in three movements: a reminder of the past (this is what God has done for us), then a solid political analysis of the present (these are the relationships of the forces at present), and there is derived from that not a divination concerning the future but a kind of conclusion, implying an exhortation: if you do not repent, behold what is going to happen, for God will abandon you to the logic of history; if you repent, as he saved and delivered you at other times, in the same way now he will intervene to allow you to live. All that is completely foreign to apocalyptic. The latter does not speak of concrete political events that can take place in a kind of foreseeable unfolding of history, but of a brutal invasion of catastrophes of which nothing is said except that they will finally take place, are perhaps already present. Moreover, these events are situated in reality outside of historical time—the end time. But that cannot be identified with the years which precede the end of the world, the catastrophe of the destruction of our planet or of our galaxy. There is then a profound opposition in the relationship to history which schematizes the difference between apocalypse and prophecy. In apocalyptic it is said in general (and I report here less my feeling than that, very common, of the specialists who make of the Apocalypse of John a special case of generic apocalyptic) that there is an opposition between a bad present and a good future, which reflects a conflict between a cosmic Good and Evil, while in prophecy there is hardly ever reference to cosmic powers at war in heaven. Moreover in apocalyptic man is a spectator to events, while in prophecy he is an actor and called to be still more an actor: he must act to change the foreseeable. At the most in apocalyptic man is advised to flee or hide. But there is also (which is less often noted) an opposition of comprehension: the apocalyptist is first of all a seer while the prophet is a hearer. Of course the prophet also has visions, but what is important, decisive, are the words which are spoken to him. Of course, the apocalyptist also receives words, but he is first of all the one who sees the personages, the scenes, the scenario of events. The break between these two modes of appropriation is fundamental. And it is known at what point this dictates two types of behavior, two different relations to the real. I do not insist upon this. As for the seer, he receives an announcement of the end, in such a way that the resolution of the dramas, disasters, and sins is situated outside of history: heaven or the celestial Jerusalem, in any case an *other* world, is the only "place" where all will be resolved, while prophetic

thought is that of expectation of a response in history; it follows the route of the design of God in this history. It implies
a duration, a continuity, not at all a rupture for an incommen-
surate new beginning: so much so that prophecy is always
situated in a very concrete, very local plane (even if its teaching
is finally universal), while apocalyptic is situated upon a universal plane and because of this fact abstract, at all times and
everywhere. Not at all (at first sight) *hic et nunc.* Other differences are related to this, the major one. In apocalyptic use is
made of symbolism, allegory, the secret cipher, while these are
practically never found in prophecy: the latter is not a secret,
mysterious message. But on the contrary, completely clear and
explicit. It is a text (usually) exoteric, while an apocalypse is a
text for the initiated, esoteric. One is addressed to a believing
people, and to the faith of this people, the other to anyone, but
initiated into the mysteries and their deciphering. This communication of a secret knowledge has for its aim to furnish
signs of interpretation, a warning, while in prophecy a concern
for exhortation is encountered, an appeal for conversion. In
one case, the announcement of punishment is inevitable, in
the other the disaster is not "in itself"; it is suspended for the
repentance of obduracy of humanity. And reciprocally in
apocalyptic it could be said that there is, mechanically, the
necessary, inevitable triumph of God, which, for people, implies only a commandment, that of perseverance; while in
prophecy the act of God is always finally his return to the
Covenant which has been concluded, always a remembrance
of fatherhood, of the act of God entering into history and
going with humanity, and of the fact that what is expected of
humanity is its conversion in order that it may enter, in turn,
into the history of God, and its faithfulness which is the condition for maintaining the Covenant. Apocalyptic could then be
considered to sketch a comprehensive movement covering the
totality of the present eon (under the domination of evil powers) and of the future eon (under the exclusive domination of
God, obvious and without obstacle), while prophecy is inscribed precisely in the first, which is less simple, less schematic than the apocalyptists say it is.

One would be tempted to say that there is a much greater radicalism in apocalyptic thought: the total exclusion of evil powers, the impossibility that there could be continuity between the actual eon and the future eon, that there could be any reconciliation whatever between the world and God (in which case the thought of the Gospel of John is also an apocalyptic thought). But certainly as much can be said of prophecy: there is no possibility either of any reconciliation between God and the idols, or the false gods: the combat is just as radical, just as decisive. But it takes place with humanity, with human initiative and participation, while in apocalyptic, it unfolds above humanity's head. It is the exclusive affair of God (and this, then, obviously makes this "genre" suspect with the good theologians of the Incarnation: at this moment in fact it recalls too much the oriental or hellenistic cosmogonies). But the true opposition, and there is always a return to history, is that apocalyptic radicalism holds to a break between history and a beyond history, while prophetic radicalism occurs in a conflict *hic et nunc* which produces history. Apocalyptic is, it will be said finally, ahistorical.

Undoubtedly all this is correct, but not completely: for the Apocalypse does not know an unfolding with diverse possibilities, it does not express a wide range of possibilities open before us; it expresses a totalizing knowledge starting from a specific view of the end time, which is a kind of "eternal," immutable vision, not at all of the order of things, but of the order of time, and consequently, contrary to what is often thought, it is not at all concerned with the future because in fact there is no future. (Of course, the Apocalypse does not leave us without *any* vision of the future.) Everything is already accomplished, realized, inscribed at the same time. The enrolling of a magnetic tape in a tape recorder is not a future even if we have not yet heard, and not at the same time, the totality of its recordings: the Apocalypse is in some way this totalization of what God has recorded. But on the other hand, it cannot be denied that the Apocalypse is inscribed in the present with utmost force; this is why I cannot totally subscribe to the idea that this is a type of metaphysical, mystical or demobilizing book. It is written in terms of political events, it tends to act upon the reader, well inserted in history; it seeks to disclose to him the "mysterious riches" of the present, the hidden dimension of this world in which he finds himself. Certainly this present is not shown as the result of the temporal act of God, but there is rather a more profound, more essential reality than that which we see immediately, and this reality can be comprehended only starting from a consideration of the end time. It is starting from the ultimate fulfillment (and not the graces of the past) that we are able to grasp this other modality of the work of God, this reality perfectly present and perfectly hidden. Undoubtedly, the Apocalypse is concerned only with the "last things" but it is certainly right to consider that this does not mean the last moments of our galaxy. Only that which is last in the decision, the ultimate in Tillich's sense. And these last things are present, actual; it is in terms of them, from now on revealed and so discernible, that we have to read our actuality. Thus, prophecy describes for us a moment of history in showing us its insertion in the totality of the design of God and in calling us to make history. The Apocalypse does not describe a moment of history but reveals for us the permanent depth of the historical: it is then, one could say, a discernment of the Eternal in Time, of the action of the End in the Present, the discovery of the New Eon, not at the end of time, but in this present history, the Kingdom of God hidden in this world. It reveals then, on the one hand, the core of the problem, the insoluble core, and does not just summon to passivity but to the specific work of hope. It reveals to us, on the other hand, the actual presence of the end, with its two possible meanings: it shows the *telos*, that is to say, the goal, which is here, and the conclusion, the limit which is included in history. And in thus starting from the end, the Apocalypse remains conformed to the scheme of Hebrew thought: it thinks starting from the end and not from the beginning ("there was evening and there was morning: the first day"; but it is starting from the morning and from the Light, which is final, that the whole must be viewed and comprehended). To take a formula incorrect by its reference to succession, but correct as representation, we can say that it is the light which comes *after* that clarifies that which was *before*, which brings about comprehension, which shows that the chaos was chaos, that the abyss is the abyss, that the obscurity is obscurity. Thus the end enables us to seize and apprehend what history is and also, at the same time, actuality. But it is not a matter of a temporally successive end: it is a matter of an absolute end. From there (and only from there) are we able to say what history is.

The depth of today is not the mechanical consequence of yesterday and the day before, but it is the presence of the end in this time of living. The Apocalypse does not yield to causal thought, it does not seek an origin, it does not locate the explanation in a genesis from which the rest unfolds logically. For Jewish thought the origin is neither cause not explanation. Nothing is put in place by a temporal development starting from a first cause. What is important is the goal, the end, the access toward which the movement drives. And this the Apocalypse gives us. But it is exactly this present that the end explains. Therefore, the contrast between apocalyptic and prophecy is perceived to be a little less simplistic than the popular interpretation and less schematic. In fact, we should at least take seriously the prefatory declaration of the text where we see at verse 1, "Revelation [Apocalypse] of Jesus Christ," and at verse 3, "Blessed are those who hear the words of the *prophecy.*" Obviously, it can be said that the author uses a language totally corrupt, and the word "prophecy" for him, in the first century, has already taken the meaning that it will take in the Middle Ages: prediction of the future. But that seems to me very improbable on the part of a writer who elsewhere manifests great precision in style and vocabulary.

Certainly one would be tempted to keep this popular reading, because at verse 1 we read, "To show to his servants what must soon take place." But still it would be a misunderstanding to think that there is here a description of historical realities to come; in fact, what is announced here, as verse 3 reveals to us (the Time is near), is the theme of imminence. It is not the "what must come" that is essential, but the "soon." Actually the Apocalypse is a book of imminence, of urgency. But not an imminence that is counted in days: it is not an interval during which extraordinary events will happen. It is the imminence of God in time, it is the "clash" between two irreconcilable and unimaginable dimensions, that of Eternity and Time if one wishes, that of the Wholly Other and the Similar, that of the Not Yet and the Already, that of the Absolute and the Contingent. That which must come soon will not be incidents calculable upon the tables of historians and chroniclers (in which case the apocalyptist would be precisely a chronicler); it is the emergence of what is so deeply hidden that only by refractions and symbols can it be discerned. And consequently if the contradictions already noted between prophecy and apocalyptic are correct, they are not completely correct: because starting from the theme of urgency, of emergence, there is something of the Apocalypse in every prophecy, and there is prophecy in the Apocalypse, as verse 1 and verse 3 of chapter 1, brought together, recall. And from this fact it does not appear to me correct to say simply that the Apocalypse is ahistorical. It proceeds according to a different historical course.

But the two meet at the point of hope: we know that for Jürgen Moltmann hope results from the specific movement of prophecy: the promises and their fulfillment, which produce a reappearance of the promise. But hope is also the central theme of the Apocalypse; we will have to return to this with the comprehension of the work of the end in this present. But if there is hope, it cannot be said that the seer calls the reader to passivity: the Apocalypse is not a spectacle but a deciphering. And the one who understands is not only encouraged to persevere but to become himself a witness of this truth, an actual sign of this emergence. Then these are not at all passive roles but a participation in history in taking into oneself the present end. Therefore, the Apocalypse takes very seriously both the role of mankind and of history but in a way which is not familiar to us and which is based upon a specific conception of time. The time of the Apocalypse, is, on the one hand, the intermediate time (between the creation and the re-creation), and, on the other hand, the time of the end. The first must properly be considered in its fulfillment; it forms a unity in spite of the vicissitudes and the events of politics and of existence. Time is throughout the same; it is one, not at all in unimportance but in the absence of progress because the encounter between the "time of heaven" (where the lamb reigns) and the time of earth no longer supposes any progress. But a tension that could be called dialectical between the reign of Christ and the possession of the Antichrist. And it is not at all a matter of "combat" between the celestial and the demonic forces (although in fact the image is found twice in the Apocalypse of John). Rather, at issue is a crisis which is precisely the characteristic of the historic time of the emergence. And this crisis, in the etymological sense, discloses an *egress* from the radical closure of the present time. In other words, it is a misunderstanding to interpret the Apocalypse as a banal hypothetical consolation turning to a "beyond." We must say emphatically that the banality to which the commentators often reduce the Apocalypse (things are going badly now, but be consoled and hope because it will be well in heaven, or in Paradise, or at the end of the world or in the beyond) this banality is not that of the Apocalypse but of the commentators, historians, exegetes, and theologians themselves. The Apocalypse is infinitely more rigorous and decisive: it is the discovery of the egress of history, which implies a possible emergence for the present time.

And because of this it includes a structure and a movement. The difficulty is that of grasping both at the same time as they are in the Apocalypse itself. Most works insist upon destroying the Apocalypse by reducing it to simple unities. For example, it is often said that there are repeated descriptions, more or less similar, of the plagues and the judgments. Thus the plagues of chapter 8, the woes of chapter 9, the harvest of chapter 14, the bowls of chapter 15, the catastrophes of chapter 18 are found greatly to resemble one another: there are then repetitions; in the same way there are several judgments of God. But if this were so, it should be noted that there is an indefinitely repetitive discourse. (And then why not ten, twelve visions, why stop at a particular moment? Even if the author has sewn together several fragments, he surely must be dragging along some others that he ought to add: in other words, in this "scientific" hypothesis it would be necessary to explain at least why the discourse stops.) And on the other hand, the discourse is incoherent, since there are contradictions among the fragments which are repeated. But above all, that implies that there is no *progression:* we will show that there is precisely progression from the beginning to the end of the book. As elsewhere, a naïve and cursive reading fails to notice it. The passage from one septenary to another implies precisely this progression: it expresses in its internal movement the fact that it is directly engaged with history. But it does not reflect history; it does not narrate it. Nor is it written to disclose future events, nor to make possible the interpretation of a present event in its immediate historicity (nor to reveal mysterious events that take place only in heaven). All that is the unhealthy curiosity of the reader who introduces it. We said above that it concentrates history in a point (but history does not cease to be history for that), and it reveals history, by a true developer* (in the photographic sense). It is this revelation of history, of what history is fundamentally, essentially, which is in itself the crisis of which we spoke. At the same time as the disclosure of the reality of history is brought about, the crisis, that is to say, the rupture, is provoked.

Consequently, we see in what way there is similarity to and difference from prophecy, in a totally other manner than by the banalities mentioned above: prophecy and apocalyptic are "crossed" revelations of the work of God in relation to the history of people. But to arrive here, at the explosion of the temporal category in its contact with eternity, we are brought into the presence of a double way (exactly that of the processive movement and that of the structural). There is a constant reduplication of the two factors, which are treated at the same

---

*Translator's note: French *révélateur*, "revealer," "developer" (photography).

time, and it is that which creates the extreme difficulty of this book. There is, on the one hand, the discovery of the significance of the historical event in relation to the eternal (which does not mean time in relation to eternity); on the other hand, the confrontation of the structures issuing from the sociological (and that are denoted by means of a code) with the constants of the meaning (which issue from the divine purpose revealed in Jesus Christ). There is then a dialectic that is established between these two pursuits (or tendencies), and it is this dialectic that makes possible comprehending at which point the Apocalypse is a theological book. Its central theme is neither the political (of course, it is *also,* accessorily, accidentally, a political book) nor piety or consolation (of course, it is *also* secondarily a book that can inspire hope), nor still less a book of forecasts. Curiously, it is that which it ought to be! That is to say, a book which speaks of God, of the Action of God, and of his interaction with the creation. But the exegetes do not take account of what the book that they study claims to be. They reduce it to their categories. I claim that to do serious scientific work in these domains, it is necessary to begin by accepting that the text studied corresponds to its declared intention. And letting oneself be guided by this objective, one discovers a much more correct meaning, which is excluded by the other presuppositions. I would have nothing against this attitude, if it did not claim to move from so-called historical exegesis to the meaning. And if it did not attribute to the text a meaning deriving from the work carried out. If we take the text in itself, we find a meaning much more complex, much more subtle, much richer, and which there is no right to exclude under the pretext that it does not result from the modern exegetical method. If there is contradiction, it is this method which finally must be put in question.

Thus we are obliged to ask ourselves where most of the errors come from that we have taken up on the subject of our text, and very particularly in the opposition between prophecy and apocalyptic. We have seen to what degree things are simplified, and finally the Apocalypse is made to say what it does not say at all. I believe that essentially the errors are based on the assimilation of the Apocalypse of John to other texts that are considered as belonging to the same literary genre. The process is very near the following. In a series of texts there are visions, plagues, bowls, trumpets, lakes of fire, angels, etc.,— all that marks a literary genre, the genre of apocalyptic. The book of Patmos contains these factors and many others (for example, style) which relate it to one or another book: it belongs then to this genre. Therefore, the general categories, or the characteristics drawn from the other books of this genre are applied to the book of "John." Then an opposition is established between prophecy (in itself) and apocalyptic, without taking account of the fact that there is a world of difference between the Apocalypse of John and the others. It must be realized that there is a qualitative difference and an opposition of intention. That the apocalypses of the first century before Christ were books of piety I admit, but that of John proceeds to a genuine transmutation of the genre. It does not present two phases of time, or a species of time, but two orders: the historical order and the eschatalogical order. It does not adopt any of the rules of the genre tied to a *hic et nunc* response to a historical problem (for example, antedating, pseudonyms). It does not give any indication concerning dates, concerning the occurrence of events that we are able to follow, nor about the arrival of the day of the Lord. (Of course, I know that it is used in that way; but this is again the corrupt intelligence of people which puts in the Apocalypse that which manifestly is not there!)

The transmutation of the genre, which is unique to the book of "John" among all the others and prevents interpreting it as "an instance of apocalypse," rests on the fact that it bears a relation with the one who is named as Messiah by the Gospels: that is to say, the Apocalypse is not a book in itself, it is a book in relation to Jesus the Christ. It cannot be interpreted for itself (or for ourselves) but as clarifying an unknown visage of this Jesus. It cannot be separated from *his person*. It has no meaning apart from that. It is then, as Jesus himself, a book *in* history, and not outside of history. But it expresses well the ambiguity of this person. And its theological theme could be summed up in the revelation that Jesus Christ is master of history: it does not at all contrast a bad present with a good future; it reveals the *present* work of God, it shows the *present* victory of Jesus Christ. It does not propose any flight into heaven, nor hope in the miracle of God to save us historically, but the accomplished triumph. The new era is inaugurated by the reign of Christ, but the advent of the Kingdom is brought about in mystery. It does not provide then an explanation of objective history that would be acceptable to every person. That which it says is conceivable and comprehensible only through faith in Jesus Christ. But insofar as it discloses how Jesus Christ reigns and saves, what the fullness of his reign is, then in fact consolation, hope, etc., can be derived from it. But this is neither the end nor the objective. And this is evident in the fact that we are in the presence of a writing rigorously theological; that is to say, leaving little room for human sentiment and for the immediacy of religious sensibility. It is truly a writing in the "second degree" and when understood is situated in the mosaic of writings about Jesus Christ, with its specificity but intolerable by itself, and the knowledge of which poses a certain number of major difficulties concerning the Incarnation. To comprehend to what degree we are here before a theological work, and not at all before "visions" or explanations about the end time, or political proclamations, it suffices to consider the importance of the "I." All through the text, it is Jesus Christ as Lord, and the God of Jesus Christ, who speaks in the first person either to tell us who Jesus Christ is ("I am the Alpha and the Omega": the proclamation which opens the Apocalypse) or to tell us what he does ("Behold, I make all things new": the proclamation which closes the Apocalypse). And in each section it is not the spectacular which is important: the latter is only environment, or illustration, or parable, or allegory of who the Lord is and of what he does. In the seven letters it is not the Church which is the center of interest; it is the Lord of the Church, who guides it and judges it. It is not the cataclysms in the world that are the revelation, but that God is the one who "kills and makes alive." It is not the destruction of the power of the world which is significant, but rather the fact that God is more powerful than all the powers; it is not the heavenly Jerusalem which ought to interest us, but the love that God shows for his whole Creation by fulfilling it in that Jerusalem. In other words, because we have an unhealthy curiosity, a deficient comprehension, because we are always attracted by the spectacular and the emotional, in the Apocalypse we generally become interested in what is only an envelope; and when many commentators have employed the allegorical method they have not been completely wrong, since in fact there is allegory, but they have been deceived as to its object: the whole Apocalypse is an allegory of God and of his work; nothing more!

A theological writing, that means a writing ordered, thought out, reflective. If we are trying to comprehend this book, we must abandon the conception of an ensemble of tumultuous, explosive visions, of cataclysms and disorder at the end of the world. It is clear that even the use of this word itself exposes the usual error: apocalypse, understood as an aggregate of frightful disasters. This is all that has been retained. During bombardments we speak of an apocalypse of iron and fire. Of course, the meaning "revelation" has been totally forgotten. *Apocalyptic* means the same as frightful visions, delirious situations, ventures in which people do not find their way again, in a word: anguish and terror. All that which in the Apocalypse is adoration, praise, proclamation of salvation and of the love of God, all that is completion in the marvelous manifestation of the new creation, all that is hope and promise has been completely lost from view. The popular meaning shows clearly what we are always tempted to retain and to forget. But objectively the content of the Apocalypse is not the former. If we are interested in numbering the verses related to a certain theme, we find about 150 verses of consolation, adoration, and hope; about 120 verses directly concerning God and the Lord; and 150 of cataclysms and disasters. In reality we ought not to read the Apocalypse as the book of Judgment and Calamities; its sole purpose, finally, is to manifest by means of a synthetic recapitulation all that has been successively revealed in Old and New Testament history about the Lord God.

The symmetric construction of the Apocalypse corresponds to that of Paul's approach: the latter effected the resumption of interpretation on the plane of the intellect, and I could say of philosophy (but he spoke of nothing other than Jesus Christ, and Jesus Christ crucified). The author of the Apocalypse effected the same resumption on the plane of images and symbols: but he does not at all replace the center of interest, and we must not think that because it is a matter of vision, the enterprise should be more incoherent: on the contrary, it is carried out by the hand of a master, with a rigor, an exactitude, a precision, a coherence, a care for the adequacy of images, a progression which will appear, I hope, in these pages, on condition that one is entirely willing in fact to treat the Apocalypse for what it is: a theological book.

It is perhaps necessary to add an explanation concerning a method of interpreting apocalyptic symbols. I believe that the utilization of references to related symbols in the Chaldean or Hebraic or cabalistic traditions, or in cryptographic and other texts, and comparisons with other apocalypses are not useless and can shed light secondarily. But it is also what has caused the most disorientation in the comprehension of our text. We must not forget that the biblical tradition is dominated by the Word; the God of Israel is a God who speaks. Though we cannot develop it here, the gods who show themselves *(eidōlon)* must be contrasted radically with the God who speaks. Every theophany is suspect in the Bible. But the Apocalypse seems to be opposed to this current: it is a book full of visions: one sees. However, it must be clearly understood that the vision is, biblically, characteristic of the end time. "You have believed because you have seen; blessed are those who do not see and who believe." The intermediate time, which runs from the election of Israel to Jesus, then again from the resurrection of Jesus to his return, is a time of the word and of listening. Not at all of sight and of manifestation. Vision is tied to the sight that we will have when we see face to face, knowing as we have been known. So to speak of vision means all that is related to the end time. Insofar as the Apocalypse is the book of the last times, the vision is in some way both adequate language and also authorized by the God of the Word. Then in fact "our young men will have visions and our old men will dream dreams." But we cannot seize upon these visions and symbols as if they were part of our present universe and consequently as if they were *directly* comprehensible and readable. We remain in the time between the times; we remain in the universe, where *only* the word conveys to us something on the part of God (and it is perhaps this which caused an uneasiness among the first Christians at the reading of the Apocalypse and provoked reticence concerning its acceptance). In other words, we cannot comprehend visions and symbols in themselves, by a direct reading, nor by parallelism with other visions and symbols: only the word can enlighten us regarding their meaning.

And moreover, we must in fact observe clearly that most of the visions are accompanied in the Apocalypse by spoken explanations. So the symbols must not be interpreted by other images, nor by our images, but by means of a correct reading of the word which relates to them. It is necessary then to go back from the text to the symbol and not study the symbol more than the text: the former is only the occasion for the latter. For example, what is told us concerning the two witnesses (power, death, resurrection, etc.) must be analyzed accurately in order to know who they are before fixing upon the fact that there are *two witnesses.* That is the least important. In the same way attention must be given to what is said of the action and work of the four horses or of the two beasts rather than to the description of the vision itself, its colors or the number of horns. Then the symbol is clarified by the word and becomes comprehensible, and generally there can hardly be only a single solution, only a single interpretation. But then, is this to say that the symbolic is totally useless, that it could be ignored, that the spoken discourse would be fully sufficient, that the vision is purely folklore? I definitely do not believe so. Because once, by means of what is said in the text concerning the symbol, its subject has been grasped in a contemporary interpretation (and for us it is inevitably modern) then we also perceive a distance between the symbol itself and the reality that it discloses and that it hides. If we say that the first beast is the political power, we comprehend that, in interpreting the discourse that is given us on the theme of this first beast; but still everything is not said: we know to what it refers, but at the same time, it is the matter of an image which in itself then says more. This is to say that the word is the sole means for encompassing and defining the subject (in other words, we must interpret the text exclusively by the text itself: the white horse cannot be understood by external references, by example, to another white horse, but by reference to the text of the Apocalypse itself). But once the matter is known, the symbol obviously goes beyond its definition: a distance appears between the real and the deciphered symbol. And this distance enables us to discern a reality *more* than the real, in its turn deciphered by the symbol. The word has a full and entire primacy for the revelation of the vision, but the vision makes it possible for us to apprehend another dimension of the real. When we look at a cube, we can see only three or four faces among the six. The word explains to us that it is a matter of a cube. But the vision permits us to apprehend the six faces, discloses to us what the two or three faces are, naturally hidden from our view. Taking account that we are not able to comprehend it and that we can proceed only by approximation. This is then the course that we will attempt to take when we are in the presence of apocalyptic visions and symbols without, moreover, being preoccupied above all with their deciphering, because these are always only illustrations of a central theme; and if the certain interpretation of 666 is lacking, that is of no importance in relation to the message that primarily must be clarified in all its facets. When one of them is lacking, the light is nevertheless sufficiently reflected.[7]

·1·

A STUDY OF THE STRUCTURE

The Axes of a Dynamic

We have said that the extreme difficulty of the Apocalypse is caused finally not by the obscurity of its symbols or by its mysteries, but by the fact that it is at the same time the static of history (reduced, we said, to a point) and the dynamic resulting from the presence of the end in history. The secret of the Apocalypse is the relation between these two conceptions (or even two existences). But it translates this contradiction by being at the same time a structure, a truly monumental architecture, and a movement from the end toward the present, from the present toward the meaning inscribed in its very texture. It is this double aspect that we wish to illuminate here. When this has been grasped by means of an understanding of the groundwork, the subsequent interpretations of the text will follow very simply.

A first indication is furnished us by what is generally called the "septenaries," which is to say that from all evidence there is a process of division in the Apocalypse because the events are related to the opening of seals, to the sound of trumpets, or to the overturning of bowls. There is a superficial way of taking this (although claiming to be scientific). The division by septenaries is a well-known reality: it is found in other apocalyptic writings; it is a stylistic artifice; and here very particularly where the text is thought to be made of bits and pieces, it is a framework for enclosing the fragments of the puzzle, and so need not be a matter of much concern. But I still believe that what is written there is not just an artifice of style. That the meaning of the symbols and the division by septenaries are traditional and that our writer has not used them differently from the others goes without saying; yet these significations must at least be recalled.

There are no difficulties concerning the number seven: four in this language is the number of creation; three is the number of God. Seven, it has been often said, is the number of plenitude or of totality. I believe that in reality it is the number symbolizing the union and even the unity of God with his creation, the indissoluble relation of the creation to God; and consequently in this sense it is clearly the number of totality. But this is particularly important in a book such as the Apocalypse because it is precisely the book of the reintegration: the creation and humanity are separated from God, they are distant from one another; there has been a rupture resulting in the autonomy of humankind and now we are at the reunion, the reconciliation, the "recapitulation." And the Apocalypse reveals to us the conditions of these rediscoveries, the obstacles and their disappearance, the transcendence of the old situation, the rupture of the autonomies and of the ancient crystalizations. Thus in this book the number seven is fully significant. Therefore, that the author had taken this number because it was traditional and currently employed in this genre of writing, that he had utilized it like anyone else because it was at hand or because he was conformed to the cultural milieu, is an idea that fails. In fact, this number seven corresponds perfectly to the content of the book and at the same time expresses that content. But then the division into septenaries is no longer something stylistic and circumstantial; we must believe that it is, on the contrary, a fully voluntary and intentional construction. Moreover, we are told of seven seals, seven trumpets, seven bowls. And there again I am amazed to observe that with many commentators either no account is taken of these objects, or the allegorical meaning is given vaguely without seeking further, as if the author could just as well have written seven boxes, seven dishcloths, seven pins. But in reality it is well known that the seal plays an essential role in society and in symbolism. It is at the same time what forbids knowledge and what guarantees it: that which closes the letter addressed to a single personage who has the right to receive the information, and that which attests, authenticates that information. It is a barrier for all except one, but to that one it guarantees that the text delivered is genuine. Moreover, it assures the permanence of the document: the sealed letter is the letter that is kept until it is possible to open it. Symbolically, it is the expression of the secret of God and of his veracity. But it is in addition the mark of appropriation: it is specifically I who have written this. I attest that what is written here is true, or conformed to reality. It is my truth which is there, because I bind myself; at the same time what is said there belongs to me. By extension, one marks with his seal all that belongs to him. It becomes the exterior sign in order that each can recognize that a certain object, a certain animal, belongs to a certain master. The sealed letter, as long as it remains sealed, is always the property of the one who has closed it. The seal cannot be broken except by the one to whom the letter is addressed and, at this moment, he becomes its owner. The secret which was in the letter becomes his secret. He now has title to it, he divulges the information and becomes himself the guarantor of its truth. The seal must not be confused with the reality, that is to say, it is a form and, even in the concrete, a symbolic factor. There is then a sort of reduplication of the symbol in its allegorical utilization. But at the same time the secret under cover of the seal is obviously not the person himself, it is not the secret of that person's *being;* it is strictly information that he transmits and which is exterior to him. In the same way when the seal attests ownership, there again it is not a matter of the person himself: it is his domain of action, that upon which he can act, that of which he can dispose; it is not the internal, but the external. And when in this series of seven seals (chapters 5, 6, and 7) the sealed book appears, the events which happen at the breaking of each seal do not then convey a revelation concerning God in himself but about his domain and the place of his power. But the fact that the letter is sealed attests that he is precisely the one who holds the secret of this domain; and the breaking of the seals entails the transfer not only of knowledge, information, and the secret of this power, but also of the power itself. Now we will see that this corresponds perfectly to the significance of chapters 5, 6, and 7. The choice of the seal then is not by mere chance; on the contrary, it is the apt symbol (quite obviously in the symbolism of the first century).

If we take the second septenary we find the same suitability. It is a matter of trumpets. The trumpet is the instrument which sounds before the king, before the general, before the powerful. It both calls and musters; it concentrates the forces in a point, which is going to be the crucial point. It is the signal for decisive actions. From the military point of view it musters the soldiers and launches the action. Then it is also a transmitter of information but of a different order, since now it sets the action in motion while in the preceding case there was a transmission of knowledge. Finally, the trumpet is the instrument of the proclamation of glory. It sounds to mark the victory, and before the victor. It proclaims the victory after the combat. In this septenary of trumpets we are here in the presence of the longest and most complex part of this book, from chapter 8 to chapter 14. And there can be the impression of a certain incoherence. We will have to return to this at length. But for the moment we observe only that there is here clearly a launching of violent action, a sort of concentration of powers, a decisive combat (the woman and the dragon), and the gathering of all the factors of the rupture with God, both the combatants against God (the dragon and the beasts) as well as all the combatants for God (Michael, heaven and earth, the two witnesses). And that manifests the glory of the Lamb. Consequently, the trumpet here plays its role perfectly. It is definitely a matter of central combat and triumph. It is both the appeal to combat and the herald of victory. From this fact, here again the choice of the symbol is not at all by chance; it corresponds well to the content and to the end sought.

The third septenary is that of the bowls. But here we are in the presence of a symbol sacred and holy. The bowl is of course that of the banquet, which is passed from hand to hand and which symbolizes the union of the guests. So inevitably it is the cup of communion. But it is also, and this is not contradictory, the cup of libation which is associated with sacrifice: a portion of the wine is poured out on the ground as an offering to the gods. Therefore, it is, from the Christian point of view, a participation in an unacceptable act. And here the ambivalence of the sacred comes into play. The sacred-bowl factor of a communion or of a sacrifice is positive, but every sacred is at the same time bearer of blessing and of curse. These are really the two faces of the sacred: it is at the same time *tremendum et fascinans*, terrible and adorable. It is necessary to enter into the sphere of the sacred to encounter the gods, but at this moment one becomes a curse to other men. Thus the bowl is at the same time that of communion and that of rejection (Judas who flees at the moment of the Last Supper), the sign of blessing and the sign of curse, the cup of reconciliation and the cup of wrath. The wine in the bowl fulfills the same function. But in addition, wine in the Old Testament is recognized as the symbol of life, and there is no remaining fixed in the ambivalence of the sacred. There had been in the Old Testament both an acceptance and a transmutation of the Canaanite sacred, and that derives essentially from the character of progression in Israelite thought and from Israel's conception of life and of the world. And it could be said, if one wished, that it is from the historical or dialectical character of this thought. In any case that means that we do not remain in fixed structures, in a constantly renewed repetition. God who chooses Israel engages in an enterprise. But the ambivalent sacred of which we have spoken remains a structure: the sacred *is* such, and one remains there. While in Hebraic thought there is inevitably an emergence, an issue, where things do not remain as such. So much so that the equilibrium of the ambivalence of the sacred is found broken by a result, a positive reality which changes everything. This is exactly what we find in chapters 15 to 22. The bowls are actually bowls of participation both in God and in the demons. They become in reality the bowls of the wrath of God, and wrath all the more radical, final, since it is related to what could have been the fulfillment of the grace of God for the salvation of man signified in the cup of communion, attestation of the promised life. Consequently, the symbol of the bowl is perfectly coherent with the meaning of these last chapters concerning the judgment and the new creation.

Before continuing, an incidental remark must be made: there is in other passages of the Apocalypse the evocation of the number seven. For example, in 10:4 seven thunderbolts are mentioned. Certain authors find this number again in the addition of the three woes and the four angels (chapter 11). But what must be emphasized is that in these cases the sevens or threes or fours, keeping their symbolic value, have no common measure with the septenaries, which suppose not a designation of a numerical element but an unfolding, a succession, a periodization. For example, there would be a septenary if for the seven thunderclaps we were told: when the first sounded, there happened . . . etc., which is not the case. This periodization separates then the designation of the seven seals, trumpets, and bowls from the other sevens.

After this remark we take up the development. Since in each of these three passages there is correspondence between the symbols and the content of the chapters included in the septenary, that means that each section is very specific: the trumpet signifies something precise and gives the general tonality of the text, which in fact in its development corresponds to it very well. But this very certain observation entails two major consequences: the first is that the different sequences of the Apocalypse are not repetitions one after the other. I know that for certain exegetes, who believe that a parallelism between the diverse parts of the book can be established, there is no succession (again the succession of visions would be a literary artifice): there would be always the same message, repeated with different images and renewed illustrations. But I am certain that there is a message, and only one, in the Apocalypse; but it is not repeated: which means that it is the totality of the book with its specific structure that gives it to us and never just one of the passages. On the other hand, I do not mean that the succession of visions in the account is an actual temporal succession. But the succession implies a *progress,* a movement *in the text.* It is not a repetition of the same message, and there are good grounds for saying that there is a "first of all" and a "subsequently," but this is not a passage of time: it is a pattern of the totality of the Revelation.

The second consequence that can be drawn is that the correspondence between the dominant symbol and the content of the text implies that the septenaries are then clearly divisions of construction of the text itself, and not at all superfluities, embellishments. In other words, these septenaries must be taken as actual partitions of the text. Today we would no longer say, for example, "I saw seven angels with seven trumpets, etc.," but, for example, in chapter 3: "Manifestation of the glory of God." And we would no longer say, "When the first angel blew the first trumpet, etc.," but: "First paragraph, first manifestation, etc."

Up to here we have spoken only of the three septenaries that are always dealt with, but I am very surprised that it is practically never envisaged that they are preceded by another nevertheless obvious one: the letters to the seven churches (chapters 1, 2, and 3). Certainly there is a difference: in the septenaries there is a gesture, an act effected by an angel and an appearance of temporal succession in the series of seals or trumpets, while here there is only the fact that, successively, and under the dictate of the Lord, John writes to the seven churches. Nevertheless I believe that we are really in the presence of a septenary equivalent to the others, not only because of the number seven according to which this first part is arranged but above all because the internal structure of this part is identical to that of the others, which we will see subsequently. But what is less evident is that the end of the Apocalypse, chapters 19 to 22, is likewise constructed according to a septenary. Here it is not the symbols that are brought forward, because the new creation is itself presented in a symbolic fashion, and because, on the other hand, for what happens at this moment there is no traditional, suitable apocalyptic symbol. But the division into seven is very clearly punctuated by the sevenfold repetition of "Then I saw" (which begins at 19:11; then: 19:17; 20:1, 4, 11; 21:1, 10). This part is also structured like the others and what is more, it corresponds exactly to the first, which is to say that everything rests upon the order that John receives to *write* (1:19 and 19:9), and on the other hand, all the titles and designations of the Son of Man in the first part are found again exactly in the last. We will have to analyze precisely how this last septenary is organized, but we can acknowledge for the moment that the Apocalypse is constructed specifically in five parts, determined by the septenaries.

This is confirmed by the fact very easy to observe that the construction of the five parts is always identical. Each time we have an introduction containing the vision of a personage: vision of the Son of Man (1), of a powerful angel (5), of the angel with the censer (8), of the Lamb with the seven angels (14), and of the angel who gives the order to write (19). Then in each part after this visionary introduction, there is the body itself: the seven letters, seals, trumpets, bowls, visions, and finally the closing of each is affected very normally by a canticle glorifying God, a doxology, an action of thanksgiving and praise: chapter 4, chapter 7 (beginning with verse 10), chapter 14 (1–5), chapter 19 (1–8). Thus the arrangement and division of these five parts is perfectly clear and visible. However, one point must still be stressed. These five chapters are not completely separate one from the other, that is, we are not in the presence of a division as rigid as that of chapters or sections. In fact, each movement is attached to and inserted in the preceding. The thing is perfectly visible in the three middle parts. Each one can be accounted for by the system of connections: the seventh act produces what engenders the following part. There is the opening of the six seals, then a doxology; and the opening of the seventh seal does not produce anything equivalent to the first ones. The seventh seal provokes the vision that introduces the following part: "when he opened the seventh seal there was a silence, and I saw, etc." Nothing is attached directly to the seventh seal except entry into the period of the trumpets. It is the same for the latter: the seventh trumpet introduces a long development where the mystery of the real is disclosed. This is like a mysterious interlude in which everything is condensed, and which leads directly to the seven bowls. In the same way the seventh bowl provokes the destruction and the judgment, but as a sort of necessary passage to the last part: that of the new creation. All of which seems to me to signify that each of these episodes cannot be separated from the others. And the art of the construction, as well as the difficulty, is that each forms a very complete whole, with an introduction, a body, and a conclusion. But at the same time each is found grafted by a sort of overcoating, by a repetition, to the preceding. All that happens in this series is defined by what happens in the preceding, and serves in its turn as support for the part that follows. Then the one must not be interpreted without the other, nor, however, can a logical line be drawn; but there is implied by this very remarkable method of connection a sort of fundamental ontological line from one part to another. This relation is fundamental and must be clearly understood: each sign launches the event, and the seventh sign launches the series that constitutes the section of subsequent events. What makes the thing especially difficult is that the seventh trumpet provokes all that announces the fourth and fifth series, and the seventh bowl provokes all that makes the occurrence of events in the fifth part both possible and necessary. The relation between the five parts is then secured not in a narrative, linear, successive fashion, but in a truly essential way.[1]

To this must be added the device that we only indicate here to call attention to something found throughout this study. We have referred to it as the "preparatory allusion." Toward the end of each part we find a verse which does not relate to what is announced here but which gives a kind of résumé of the following part; it is integrated into the preceding section as what could be called a point of attachment for the later development. It is then not only the formal method of connection but also the utilization of these preliminary allusions internal to the text, which continues to affirm rigorously the unity of the whole and to show how the passage from one development to another is brought about; by example, 19:7–8 is the connecting point of chapters 21–22.

We now reach the structure itself of the book, that is, the significant arrangement of the five parts. To comprehend that there can be a significant arrangement, it is necessary first of all to realize to what extent these five elements overlap each other. It appears at a glance that the first part is dedicated to the word of the Lord addressed to the Church. That is said clearly and it is unnecessary to insist on it. In the same way it is also very clear that the fifth is related to the new creation, the celestial Jerusalem, the Kingdom of God. It can be perceived next that there is a relationship between these two fragments: the first shows us what the body of Christ is upon earth, with its faults and particularisms; the second reveals to us what the fullness of the body of Christ will be. The first, a mediated relation between the Lord and the Church, the second an immediate relation. The first contains the promises, the second their fulfillment. The first shows the contingency of the inscription in history, the second the constancy acquired in the Kingdom. The first implies the little flock, the second universality. The first is under the sign of the "already—not yet," the second under that of the "yes—amen." But one corresponds to the other and it is clear that to the Church upon earth of the first part corresponds the People of God in heaven of the last. With most commentators there is now agreement, with some nuances, concerning the second part: it includes the four horses, the prayers of the martyrs, the development of the temporal plagues, and the existence of the Church, again, it seems, in its temporal framework. All this likewise characterizes history as it is envisaged in Scripture. It is not imprudent to say that this part is consecrated to the history of humanity upon earth, and we will have to justify this at length in chapter

3. But then, if now we refer to another part whose meaning is evident, the fourth, we see that here we are in the presence of the "end of the world," of the "Last Judgment"—to keep the traditional terms—that is to say, the act at the same time eternal and temporal (as we have indicated in the preceding note) by which God puts an end to history. In other words, we again have two symmetric parts: the second, which is history; the fourth, the end of history. Not at all its fulfillment but, in some way, its rupture. And in the second there are "forerunner signs," "premonitions": the prayer of the martyrs, various plagues, the existence of a People of God set apart. But this presence of the end in the course of events participates in this history; while on the contrary in the fourth sequence we are before a closure and an irreversible radicalism: temporality is no more. In other words, the first and second parts are found in temporality, in the world of mediations; the fourth and fifth outside that temporality and in immediacy. But if there is thus correspondence between one and five and between two and four, that means that we are in the presence of a construction by symmetry, and that consequently the third part constitutes the axis of the whole, the place where the Temporal and the Eternal, the Accidental and the Proclaimed, the Mediated and the Immediate encounter and engage each other.

We have before us a "Christian" book, written by a "theologian." What is for him the axis of all things? It is quite evident that this is, and can only be, Jesus Christ. But we must pay close attention here: because the whole beginning tends to affirm that Jesus Christ is the Lord of the Church and of history; the end, that it is in Him that all is re-created. But at the center, there is no longer any question of the Lord: what makes the break between history and the Judgment, between the Church and the Kingdom; the break and at the same time the line; what brings about the entrance of the end of time into this time, the Eschaton into the Present; what causes "the Kingdom has come upon you," "is in your midst," is not the fact that Christ is Lord, but the Incarnation, the Death and Resurrection, that is to say, the historicity of Christ, the conjunction of Jesus and the Christ.[2] That is the axis, the center,

by relation to which all the rest is organized. Thus the Apocalypse is oriented around the Incarnation (chapters 11 and 12).
But we then encounter another problem: it is evident that the
writer of Patmos is a seer. In other words, what he relates is
an ensemble of visions and not at all a historical account. But
the birth, the life, the death of Jesus happened upon earth.
And it is of this terrestrial life that the Gospels tell us. John
does not tell of this life; he does not write a fifth Gospel which
claims to relate some other events of the life of Jesus. But if
Jesus is truly the Messiah, if he is truly the Son of God, if he
is truly God himself, how could we fail to comprehend that the
terrestrial events of the life of Jesus had had their correspondence, or rather their repercussion, in "heaven"?[3] We have
occasionally some allusions to this aspect that is hidden from
us: thus, during the death of Jesus, the darkness that covers the
earth, or the opening of the tombs, which burst asunder and
cast out the dead. Again, when Paul tells us of the triumphal
chariot of Jesus to which are attached the powers, thrones, and
dominions as vanquished. And further, the decision according
to which the act that condemns us has been in fact nailed to
the cross with Jesus (Colossians). We have there an allusion to
that profound reality, which is not visible, which does not
appear in the domain of the historic, but which constitutes the
divine mystery of the act, of the terrestrial life of Jesus. The
Apocalypse is centered entirely above: it no longer speaks
except by allusion of the earthly life of Jesus; the divine mystery is the theme of the Relevation. And we find here another
totally new aspect of the Apocalypse by comparison to the
current apocalypses. It is not a matter of visions of what will
come to pass later upon the earth. It is not a matter either of
apocalyptic events, which unfold in the heavens as thousands
of theosophical or mythological writers report to us. At issue
is a relation between that which has happened upon earth with
and around Jesus, and then the celestial domain, the world of
powers, thrones, dominions, angels and demons, but above all
the secret of God. What chapters 9 and 14 teach us is that in
reality *the terrestrial event provokes the celestial event.* What happens
in the divine world is defined, determined, provoked by the

venture of Jesus upon the earth. We are not told that the crucifixion and resurrection happen upon earth as an after all minimal consequence of an arbitrary decree of God the Father from all eternity. We are not told that the Incarnation itself is the result of a kind of intra-divine deliberation. And we know well that we approach one of the most unfathomable points of theological reflection. Is the Son the Son from all eternity? But even if we say yes, does that mean that the man Jesus was the Son from all eternity? And is the virgin birth the birth of a God? Or is Jesus the Son adopted by the Father (for example, at the moment of baptism—adoptionism)?

We need not enter here into these insoluble mysteries, but only consider the way the Apocalypse speaks of it. From all evidence it reveals to us that everything is oriented around the terrestrial crucifixion and the resurrection upon earth. Jesus is the one who in his life, told by the Gospels, determines what happens in the world of God. He is liberty itself, and what he decides upon earth is what unfolds in heaven. He creates the divine venture. Not that that means God does not exist! But this God, who is fully love, has delivered himself in Jesus, and has kept nothing of his power, so completely that in an unbelievable fragility all was truly risked in the moment and person of Jesus—all, including the supreme power of God. And what happens in heaven is not a fictional adventure; it is truly the combat and victory of Jesus. But this happens only upon earth. And what the Apocalypse discloses to us, among other things, is that the Incarnation is seen in this celestial world only after the crucifixion. "After" does not signify anything, since we are outside of time, but we, in our life that is in time, must think in terms of "before" and "after" (as we said above for the spatial). Now what concerns the Incarnation is told us in chapter 12, while what concerns the crucifixion is told us in chapter 11. There is no before and after in heaven, but that means that we must "read" Christmas in the light of, and beginning with, Good Friday. The little child who is born at this moment *is* the crucified. We cannot consider the life of Jesus according to the normal development of a human life, which begins at birth and ends at death: the Apocalypse teaches us that "in heaven" the crucifixion comes first, and the Incarnation is defined by that. Upon the cross, *All* is truly accomplished. And the Incarnation itself is accomplished there. And the fullness of the love of God for his Son.

But a decisive remark must be made here: this description of celestial events in the Apocalypse gives us a schema opposite to what is seen in all the other religions. In fact, in the Chaldean religion, the Egyptian, and in the Greek of the Homeric epoch, everything unfolds in a very clear fashion: the world of the gods is full of the gods' adventures: they love, hate, are jealous, make war, join forces, are afraid, become angry, etc.; and as more or less negligible consequences, the "fallout" of the divine adventures has repercussions upon the earth. A certain hero is favored by a god, who is detested by a goddess, who is going to instigate a whole network of difficulties for the hero in order to embitter the god, etc. The events of human history are reflections of the divine misadventures. But Israel had completely detached this relation, on the one hand by the invention of the creation, and also by the discovery that God desires one man free from the other. God reveals himself as liberator; and the creation, because it is the object of the *love* of God, is not a mechanized object. But the Apocalypse following this movement goes still further and reverses completely the situation described by the classic religions: it is what happens on earth, in human historicity, that becomes the source of what takes place in heaven, in the world of powers and angels. History has become the affair of man in Israel (but there remains nevertheless a mystery of history, which the Apocalypse treats). And the Apocalypse completes the reversal begun in Genesis: "the history of God" takes place upon the earth. The Apocalypse closes what Genesis had opened; it is impossible to go further. Then it is an error to imagine that it furnishes us completely mysterious and unassimilable information about God. It does not tell us anything about God *ad intra*, because we can say nothing about it. It remains remarkably discreet about "the one who is upon the throne." We know nothing about the matter. It refers only to the one who has been upon earth, and shows how the sphere of the divine has been totally defined, transformed, by the crucifixion. It clearly establishes a relation between the celestial and the terrestrial, but opposite to the other religions and mythologies. This is why the Apocalypse is at the same time completely different from the allegorical stories and imaginary deliriums of *all* the other apocalypses, incoherent series of visions and verbal ecstasies, and also from the myths related in the mythologies: *it is not mythical because it is subordinated to a very definite history.* And it even shows how a factor that can be considered mythical in the Gospels (the virgin birth) depends upon the history of the cross, and consequently, from this fact itself, ceases to be truly mythical.

Thus, to sum up, we are able to comprehend the structure of the Apocalypse; there is a central axis, the crucifixion of Jesus Christ (11); around this is organized in the central part (the third) the dramas of the separation of the creation from the Creator (8 and 9) and the proclamation of the gospel (10); then the Incarnation (12) and the fury of the powers as a consequence of the work of Jesus Christ (13).

Around this central part we have, symmetrically, a first part concerning the Church, to which corresponds a last part on the new creation. Then a second part on history, to which corresponds, as the fourth part, the judgment and the destruction of evil and of the powers. We repeat that we are not in the presence of a temporal succession. There are five themes, each one coordinated to the others, tied together by an essential relationship, but not a progression either causal or historical. We have already said that if the judgment comes into our lives after history, this does not mean that it is situated at the end of history; we re-find it ceaselessly, the judgment is constantly present in history. That the new creation comes after the judgment does not signify a succession in time, but implies that the last word is not left to destruction and death. The *truth* is not that of nothingness; it is life, it is the world related to God, it is the transcendence of death. But the arrangement implies in reality that the Church comes first, placing man before his responsibility; and the fulfillment in the Kingdom is brought

about through the Mystery of Jesus Christ in heaven. In the
same way, we must be told what history is in the light of
revelation in order that its judgment be revealed to us; but,
beginning from the moment when all is seen from the perspective of the crucifixion, this judgment is no longer that of the
individual. History, in some way, stripped to its profound reality (chapters 5 to 8), passes through the prism of the venture
of Jesus and from this moment we see the sole temporal conclusion, which is disaster, collapse, death. But paying careful
attention that it is by means of the death of Jesus that we
discover it; that is to say, that the whole work of death is
effectively accomplished upon the cross: the judgment of the
world is the judgment of Jesus himself. That is why one cannot
speak of this judgment before having spoken of the mystery of
Jesus Christ in heaven.

But if the relationship of the five parts, one to the other,
explains perfectly the arrangement of the text, it must also be
said that each includes and implies the others. We say, by
example, that if we read what is told us of the Church, and if
we attempt to combine it with what is told us subsequently of
history, that leads inevitably to pose the Incarnation. The Lord
of the Church who is at the same time the Lord of history is
not a God far off, inaccessible and incomprehensible; he is the
one who speaks to his Church, he is the one who lives in
history by a people; then he is necessarily the God who has
assumed the condition of man. But in the same way, if we
combine the second and third parts, history and the hidden
mystery of the Incarnation, then that leads necessarily to the
Judgment. Because this history—of which certain aspects are
well described as harrowing and desperate, in which "the
good" is represented only by the martyrs who pray, and a
Church turned toward its Lord, without any power—seems to
be able to go only toward catastrophe. But there is no other
catastrophe (save the plagues inherent in nature itself) except
that of the judgment of God upon God; and it is then that we
are able to endure, without having the experience of an absolute failure, the destruction of that which the power and grandeur of man has made, of what, rather, man had believed to

be his wealth and glory. It is when we have apprehended that the powers are conquered in Jesus Christ, that we can bear the proclamation of judgment not as a condemnation upon us, not as despair, but on the contrary, as the temporal comprehension which we can have of the defeat of Evil and Death. And finally: if we combine the third part relating to the Incarnation and the fourth part relating to judgment, then we are necessarily led to the new creation and the celestial Jerusalem. Because the Incarnation is the presence of God with men, it is the creation by Jesus and in Jesus of a new world, that of reconciliation. For what is the Incarnation except the total and definitive reconciliation of God with man, of man with God, of man with men, and of men with creation? But consequently it is not possible to remain with the judgment and condemnation upon the rupture and the explosion, the dispersion and destruction: by means of that the Incarnation must fulfill the plentitude of reconciliation. Then it can be said that each part is determined by the two preceding: it is the result, and each time it fulfills not the issue of what immediately precedes it but the antecedent. Thus the first part on the Church is explained and fulfilled in the third by means of the second. The second is explained and fulfilled in the fourth, but by means of the third. The third is explained and fulfilled in the fifth, but by means of the fourth. It is this resumption that the connections of which we have spoken signify. And it is that also which explains what has often been called "repetitious" and "doublets." One part constantly shows its relation to another by taking up a certain aspect of what has been said: the repetition (never totally repeated) is not a re-saying, a redundance, but a true re-actualization of the text by the text. Very far then from being an expression of negligence, it is the utmost artfulness. Under the circumstances, it is the exegete who is negligent! This shows us not only that the Apocalypse is not an incoherent series of repeated visions, nor a successive series, but a fundamentally dialectical movement. It is then at the same time, as we have said, an architecture (five parts organized symmetrically) and a progressive structure, and very specifically a dialectical process.

This dialectical organization of the Apocalypse we find again also in the detail. For example, we meet constantly contradictory formulations of which the contradiction can be understood only by the dialectical movement. For instance (5:6): a slaughtered lamb is raised up. It is both slaughtered (dead) and raised (victorious). This method of presenting synthetically two contrary realities is found constantly in the book. Reciprocally, in order that the dialectical process be possible we sometimes have a splitting in two of the same reality: it is in this way that I understand the *two* witnesses where there is obviously only one single being concerned (chapter 11). We will return to this later. But in a somewhat more profound way, we find the dialectical movement again and again in the division of forces which are combined. We will analyze only one passage from this perspective, chapters 6 and 7. Thus, the four horses: we have a relationship of contradiction between the first white horse and the three others. We will have to examine why the white horse is not of the same order as the others. But it is important to discern clearly the opposition between the one who is a conqueror and will conquer, and the others of which we are told precisely that they have only limited power and that they are never conquerors. In the same way, we see another dialectical relation in the making of history between the powers who act (the four horses) and the prayer or the testimony (corresponding to the fifth seal: the prayer of the martyrs as the making of history, causing the patience of God to intervene). Likewise, the people of God, present in history (chapter 7), are composed of two complementary and contradictory elements: the people of Israel whose number is fixed (both perfect and limited) and the multitude of the nations (whose number is limitless and not decreed). There again every reality, spiritual as well as terrestrial, is organized around two contradictory poles, in function of which the evolution of history is possible. We would be able to take up practically every section of the Apocalypse and show this same dialectical structure. It is not in conformity to fashion that I employ this word; I am profoundly convinced that from the beginning (that is seen clearly with Paul) Jewish thought, then

Christian thought, is, and *can only be,* dialectical. It is there, and not with the Greeks, that the dialectic is enrooted, and a biblical text cannot be understood except by inserting it in the network of contradictions, the crises and the historical resolution of the crises.

Has the Apocalypse a Content?

. . . or a theme? Most authors give a résumé that can be reduced to the following five points.[4]

First of all: the work of God has arrived at its term; the Christ has triumphed and his Kingdom is inaugurated. Jesus is the sole Saviour and Lord. We live in the last times, the prelude to the Judgment. Then: confronted by this reality, in this situation, men are divided into two categories: those who recognize the Christ and who constitute in him the people of God; and those who do not recognize him (the inhabitants of the earth), who remain under the control of Satan, doomed as he is to condemnation.

The third point concerns the Church: she is associated with her Lord; an elect community, redeemed by his blood, she inaugurates the Kingdom. Then we find all that which has to do with the association of Christ and the Church: Christ was prophet and witness (and the Church is now the sacred community who exercises in her turn the function of witness and prophet). Christ has carried his testimony as far as the Passion and has encountered the opposition of the world (and the Church in her turn knows combat and martyrdom). Christ is conqueror and risen (and the Church participates already in that victory; she knows the first marks of the resurrection). Christ is glorified, he is Lord (and the Church is already the priestly Kingdom; from now on she exercises her celestial function in the cult). Thus in the present time the Church lives the various aspects of the mystery of Christ. Finally, from this condition, from this reality of the Church, can be drawn a certain number of ethical and spiritual consequences: the Church must bear witness in a world that does not recognize God; she must then live in faithfulness. She suffers persecution, which is the test; but she has the assurance of glory, which implies for her, perseverance. She is in exodus, and not only in exile; she advances toward the heavenly Jerusalem and consequently she lives in hope.

Such are the five agreed-upon themes frequently recognized in the Apocalypse when there is the desire to avoid fantastic and esoteric interpretations. It is obvious that all this is correct. It is no less true that that takes account of only a small part of the Apocalypse: essentially the seven letters to the churches. But in addition we say that this reassuring and orthodox reading is fairly banal. Is it true that the author of the Apocalypse had only these well-known truths to transmit, which, for example, do not alter much what Paul had written? Is it true that the great production, the subtle construction, the play of images that are reflected reciprocally, the plurality of planes on which the text is developed, could be reduced to these rather sterile and abstract statements? It is not only the translation into dogmatic and intellectual terms, always carried out, which poses a question to me; it is the impoverishment, the static character of these statements, which disturb me. Certainly all that is in the Apocalypse, but is that what the author wished to convey? Is it not a kind of reading made in terms of the most orthodox theology, a kind of dissection of what had been written for movement, play of colors, multiple interaction, multiple meaning? It is in fact the movement itself that I do not find, and this is probably the most essential quality of the text. Now I do not say that another résumé, another synopsis, would be more successful; I believe that the idea itself of reducing the content of the Apocalypse to a series of propositions is incorrect. The Apocalypse cannot be reduced to some simple catechetical truths. It is not a question of more or less, of exactitude or inexactitude; it is the fact that every reduction of this text causes it to lose radically its existence. It simply ceases to be. And one can no longer speak of it except in banalities.

But instead of content does not the Apocalypse have at least a central theme, or an essential objective? For some, this would be the attestation without limit of the Lordship of Jesus

Christ, which is undoubtedly true. But when that has been said, everything remains to be said: how is that manifested against all probability, what is that Lordship not only on earth but also in heaven, what is its end and significance? and a hundred other questions to which the Apocalypse attempts precisely to respond not at all logically and theologically, but that it tries to imagine and integrate existentially. For we are in the presence of a book characterized by its vitality, its animation, by its adhesion to what exists, and, once more, it is just this quality which escapes. Yes, certainly, it has in its center the Lordship of Jesus Christ, but nothing has been said when that has been set forth. Because the how, the Mystery, is everything.

For others, today more numerous, the Apocalypse is the great book of Christian hope. And without doubt that is equally true, but on condition of understanding hope as I have attempted to do *(Hope in Time of Abandonment)* and not confusing it with a human hope or with a theological formula. Human hope is what most commentators inflict upon the Apocalypse. Summarily: all is going badly now, but, be reassured, all will go well tomorrow. To reduce this book to that banal "consolation" is a fundamental betrayal. In the Apocalypse there is no kind of hope that things will turn better, no confidence in the future, no consolation drawn from a future victory. The contrast between a bad today and an excellent tomorrow is a simplistic invention of exegetes perfectly blind to the grandeur of a design which does not at all reduce to the petty difficulties that the Christians could actually encounter. (Even persecutions are petty difficulties.) In this case there has been exactly superposition of a rather simplistic hope upon the most intense formulation of hope. But the other confusion which must be avoided consists in reducing hope to being only a kind of theological armor of faith: we *believe:* the pardon, the resurrection of Jesus Christ and his return, and so the reality, the advent of the Kingdom of God. And because we believe, *then* we hope. Hope is, then, either the expectation that all that will be realized (but it is completely passive) or it will be reduced to a "I hope firmly that . . . ," but it is identified with the faith. To say that we believe in the resurrection is to say that we hope we will be raised. Therefore, hope does not have any particular dimension. Of course, it is true to say, because Jesus Christ is raised, we hope for our resurrection; or again; we believe the promises of God, and consequently we hope. But I would say that hope is then simply a *locus theologicus.* And I ask what else it furnishes. Hope can never be the object of a simple theological analysis because it can never be "cold," congealed, arrested. It *is,* or it is not. When it is not, upon the existential plane, it is perfectly unknowable, incomprehensible; because it is finally always *other* than what has been thought. All that can be said about it theologically is certainly correct, but it is not hope! And this is one of the difficulties of the Apocalypse: if it employs language that is mythical, or mystical, or full of imagery, it is to express something infinitely shifting, unknowable by a logical, rational discourse—something that cannot be known except in living it. If hope has an essential importance, it is because it must furnish what can be offered by nothing else—neither by faith, nor by an ethic, nor by an interpretation of events, nor by an irrational confidence in man or the future. When is hope necessary, radically other by relation to human circumstances and to spiritual certitudes? When is it the place of the All or Nothing? When can nothing be substituted for it? There are, it seems to me, two conjoined circumstances (and I have tried to develop this at length in *Hope in Time of Abandonment*). First of all, hope is, when the human condition is without issue; when there is not, from the human point of view, any means of escape; when there is not, in a reasonable expectation, any positive result; when there is no longer, apparently, any history still possible; when there is no longer any possibility in any sense; then hope is the affirmation of the "in spite of." Thus, in the presence of death, which is total, without illusion or consolation, without belief in a survival or an immortality of the soul, hope is the absurd affirmation of the reality of the resurrection. It is then the affirmation of a total risk, it is the step forward into the void, the step of the bearers of the Ark crossing the Jordan. It consists in making history when there is no longer any history possible. It is inscribed in the revolt that is the refusal of this impossibility (and not at all in the Revolution, contrary to our good theologian fathers of the Revolution who had not reflected sufficiently upon either hope or revolution). And in the second place, there is affirmation of hope when God is silent or has "turned away his face," when "the Word of God has become rare," when it seems to us dead. As long as the Word of God is living, spoken, believed, heard, received, hope does not have any reason for being; we are here in the domain of faith. And this is why Jürgen Moltmann is right to situate it in the play of promise and fulfillment: it exists precisely *in that interval.* The Word of God has been spoken and has brought a promise. But from this moment begins a period more or less long, in which we live with that promise of the past that our faith reactualized; and God does not repeat that promise at each instant. And it is precisely in this desert, in this silence of God, that hope continues to affirm that the promise is *already* fulfilled, that, even if we do not see it, there is no distance between a Word of God and an Act of God. Hope fills the void between what we have historically received as promise and what we expect historically as fulfillment. But when we have all, that is to say the relation of communion with God, we do not have need of anything: hope has no place. It is only in that interval of the already and the not yet that hope is situated, in what can be experienced as the silence of God, or dryness, when it seems difficult to continue to believe. The two central words of hope are those of Job who, having observed his unacceptable situation, concluded: "Nevertheless my Redeemer lives!" And that of Jesus upon the cross: "My God, why have you forsaken me?": the accent being placed upon "My God," that is to say, *You are my* God, even so. You cannot be the God who is silent and who forsakes. Such is the declaration of hope. It is, then, not resignation, the passive acceptance that God is silent, is hidden, forsakes; it is the demand before God that he reveal himself as the one he said he was.

Such are the orientations, briefly summed up, that I have attempted to give on the subject of hope. We see here very clearly the relation with hope (not at all the simplistic schema: all goes badly, but all will end well). Hope is the attitude of the Christian in a radical and last situation; beyond the absence of history, beyond the silence of God, there is nothing, and it is the presence itself of this last event of which the Apocalypse speaks. Hope, as we see it in the Apocalypse, implies the total rejection of the confusion between the Kingdom of God and any kind of politico-social system. It demonstrates even incompatibility, which is plainly the cataclysmic affirmation of the Apocalypse. But hope pronounces reciprocally the Yes of God upon a world which by itself merits only condemnation, destruction, and death. It is certainly not the Yes upon *this* world which would merit this Yes by itself, but the Yes upon a world perfectly unacceptable and radically evil, which can by no means be assumed as such by God, but which must be delivered from its captivity. Moreover, the Yes of God—it must be affirmed—as the Apocalypse ceaselessly demonstrates it, while God is turned away, is silent, while he is the great Absence, in spite of his indirect presence witnessed precisely by the mediation of angels. The bearer of hope thus pronounces the Yes, in the name of God, taking the unheard-of risk of speaking while God is silent (and this is certainly why also there has been so much nonsense spoken on the subject of the Apocalypse). The witness, then, like the seer, actually engages God, according to his promise. But it is not a matter of a Yes of validation upon that which simply *is,* such that it is; on the contrary, it is the Yes of destruction of the absence of possibility, of the absence of history, of the absence of issue. It is the combat against illusion, against sinking, against the shutupness in which man always situates himself, in order to *attest* that God himself assumes what was man's work of Nothingness and which from now on becomes a work of life. In other words, the "plagues," the "judgments" must be read as being the putting in question, the destruction, of that which annihilates and enslaves man and not at all the destruction of the greatness of man, nor, still less, of men themselves.

Further, as we have already said, the Apocalypse, like hope, participates in the end. I would say, schematizing, that while faith always participates in God's Already Done (remember Israel), hope participates in the real not concretely accomplished. It is the attestation of the last things in this present time; like the Apocalypse, the actualization of these last things. Therefore hope is clearly what the Apocalypse shows us: the affirmation of a counter-reality, but a counter-reality (not at all idealist or future) hidden in the present and of which hope can discern the signs, which never derive from a simple observation of an observable reality. Which signifies that hope is in itself the mark of the distance of the Kingdom (when the Kingdom is established, there will no longer be hope). Therefore hope, manifested in the Apocalypse, is always that which declares to the present: "No, it is not the Kingdom of God, nor the reign of Christ"; but it demands that the Christian be situated in the present in terms of this Kingdom. Thus hope is the positive act in face of the too evident absence, which hope measures and knows but also recognizes (in the passage from faith to hope). Therefore the relation between hope and apocalypse is fundamental, but in a totally different sense from the simplistic one which spontaneously comes to mind.

Certainly it must not be said that there is hope because one has an apocalyptic conception of history; exactly the opposite is true. The apocalyptic conception of history results from the apprehension of hope, from life in hope, of which it is the intellectualized expression. In the same way it is completely incorrect (and on the plane of a truly childish psychology!) to say that the Apocalypse had been written to give hope to the persecuted Christians. On the contrary, because a strong hope existed in that first Christian generation they had expressed it with violence in the Apocalypse. The latter is a writing of provocation and of defiance over against the world, and not at all consolation for the poor disoriented Christians. Hope affirms the impossible realized in a situation experienced as impossible by men. But we must pay attention: what impossibility? We have the impression that, because it is a question of persecutions and martyrs in the Apocalypse, the author is interested in the situation of the Christians themselves. But his view is not so narrow. He includes the entire creation in the movement that goes toward the new creation. The revelation does not have to do with what will become of the Christians, nor even with the Word of God in their favor, but with the Lord who gives meaning both to the persecutions and to the fidelity of the Christians as well as to the totality of history including the work of humanity as a whole in all its dimensions. It is an astonishingly egoistic and limited view which leads us to say that such an immense perspective has been conceived only for the encouragement of the Christians. It is then not the apparent impossibility of a foreseeable future for the Church or for the Christians that provokes the vision of this totality; it is, rather, the apparent impossibility of a future for all humanity. Because this humanity is far from God, but also because this humanity is found in a political crisis undoubtedly experienced as grave—the crisis of peoples conquered and made subordinate to Rome, but also the crisis felt at Rome herself concerning the future of the empire. It is known that in the first century there developed schools of political and philosophical thought for which the empire had entered into an irremediable decline. And I am often asked if the authors of certain texts of the New Testament (for example, the Epistles of Peter and the Apocalypse) were not aware of these doctrines and prophecies. In reality, it is in the face of this conviction according to which the future is either impossible or catastrophic that the Apocalypse developed. And it is this problem, not that of persecution, which is the object of this monumental construction (I say object deliberately, and not theme or subject, still less center and axis). But hope (that the Christians had to bear for all) supposes passage through judgment and the annihilation of the powers of seduction and aberration. And those who refuse this vision of a radical judgment, of a collapse of the world for its own redemption, for its new creation (but new creation of *this* world), for the recapitulation of history and of the work of men—those who deny the negative phase—express the absence of hope. It is not possible that the dialectical movement end without passing through the crisis provoked by the decisive negation. And the negation is decisive only if it leads to a radical destruction, only if it is borne by an absolute denier. But if there is no passage through this, there is no possibility of recapitulation and summation: then no hope. It is essential therefore to take account of the fact that the movement of hope in the Apocalypse has nothing to do with good sentiments, with pity, with a spirit of moderation, which would cause us to say: "But no, no, there are a whole lot of excellent things in our world that God will preserve"; or, "God, because he is love, cannot deliver us to such destruction"; or again: "The city of men is the beginning of the city of God, and the passage will be made by harmonious development, in continuity, in the manner of Teilhard or of Mounier." All that is actually the exclusion of hope to the profit of a mediocre consolation and a heap of good sentiments. Indeed, to conceive that history ends inevitably and normally in the Kingdom, by technical progress or by political revolutions; to conceive that God acts in history by the intermediary of the political actions of man, revolutionary or conservative, is the complete opposite of hope. Here lies the error of Moltmann, visible in his book on the political consequences of the Theology of Hope.[5] Why can I say that? Simply because, in spite of good intentions, there actually are epochs in which for men, for nations, for peoples, there appears from all evidence the impossibility of making another step, the impossibility of continuing; and when there is desire for change, whatever the way might be, that way is worse. The future of humanity is just totally blocked; then no explanation concerning the continuity of history can respond to the situation, nor satisfy. And it is then that hope comes into being. And it is then that the Apocalypse brings its authentic message: yes, the future is really blocked; yes, there is no longer any history possible; and in spite of that, here is the true future, here is the meaning, here is the break. Now very curiously for our theologians of Revolution, who are actually the principal deniers of the Apocalypse (changed into a simple political document), with their refusal of *this* hope in terms of this "Last" Judgment, there is a transformation of the Lord of History into a Vase

God. The avant-garde theologians have jeered at the stopgap God that has been utilized under all conditions to respond (fallaciously) to inexplicable questions. But they have done better: their God is actually the ornamental vase that one puts in a corner and says: "Let us make our revolutions and our history; it is we who are in charge, and you remain very quiet in your corner; we do not ask you to intervene; what we do is, moreover, your work." Strangely, Babel is repeated: "Let us make a name . . . ." And this position is exactly the opposite of that affirmed in the Apocalypse where it is God who fulfills the work of man, assumes it, and glorifies it. The Apocalypse very obviously is the inverse of the theology of the vase God: it is not by his revolutions nor by his science that man gives meaning to history or even fulfills it. This Apocalypse is in fact the great book of the constant affirmation of the liberty of God. In that it responds to Genesis (and we find once more this correspondence, this resumption). In the two books God as Creator and as Recapitulator is sovereignly free, conditioned in his liberty only by his love. Throughout the Apocalypse we must in fact consider not the power and terrible majesty of the living God, nor seek metaphysical qualifications, but the attestation continually resumed of his liberty encompassed and interpreted by the doxologies of the first four parts. Hope is precisely that work which provokes this living God to come and to reveal himself in his glory. Hope is truly that which is affirmed as the counterpoint of man to the liberty of God. It is the sole legitimate affirmation, the sole living and experienced expression of the liberty of man. The Apocalypse must then be read as the fabric made from the warp and the woof of the liberty of God and the hope of man, which *is* the liberty of man. Such is the sole possible significance. And if God is not free, as the Apocalypse shows him to be, then man can count upon nothing. It is Fatality, Destiny, who are the masters. And if man does not hope for the glory of God, then he is delivered over to destiny. And if man is not free in his work of hope, then God does not exist; and further, the whole work undertaken by God at the beginning, at the first day, is a failure, because there is no future. Confronted by these two agonies, the Apocalypse brings the triumphant Revelation. And we perceive at what depth hope is joined to the Apocalypse without being, however, either the theme or the purpose.

·2·

THE KEYSTONE
Chapters 8 to 14: 1-5

If we are not deceived in our study of the total structure of the Apocalypse, we must obviously start with that which is, in fact, the heart, or the axis by relation to which the rest is ordered. In reality it is in this sequence of six central chapters that we find first of all how the total ensemble is related to the end time. It is there also that the affirmation of the first two parts comes to be validated: that Jesus Christ is Lord of the Church and of history (in what sense and how is that Lordship possible?). And finally it is there that we must situate what follows: in particular the judgment, because the judgment and the end of the world cannot be read and understood except in terms of the judgment which has fallen upon the Son of God; and those who are condemned in the final destruction are not men but the rebellious powers who are described for us in the central section, upon whom men depend and whom men represent only figuratively. It is indeed the action of these Satanic powers that in every circumstance provokes death in the Apocalypse, and not at all, never directly, the action of God upon men. It is the Satanic power that God destroys, which very obviously entails also human disasters, since man is deeply attached to them and profoundly possessed by them. We will have to return here for a more lengthy treatment.

The series of trumpets appears in general singularly difficult to the degree that it is extremely composite. It has often been interpreted as the judgments of God, but then it would be necessary to admit that there is a doublet with what follows chapter 15, where we find, in fact, the description of *the* judgment of God. Sometimes these texts have been reduced to the description of the judgments of God in history: after the description of history, there would be the intervention of God's judgments in that history. This cannot be accepted because our texts are very clearly symbolic or allegorical and do not refer at all to the historical. It has been possible to present as present, temporary judgments that which would be only a prophecy of the Last Judgment. But that really has no meaning in an apocalypse (where, if there is reference to a present event, the latter is only the pretext for a permanent and fundamental revelation). There cannot be any prophecy at the *interior* of an apocalypse envisaging that which is going to be *said* subsequently. Finally, I do not think that an interpretation can be accepted that sees God unleashing the evil powers, the powers of the Abyss. Certainly it is there, but not at all in itself, nor in a central fashion. And this interpretation presents other difficulties: there had been already in chapter 7 the intervention of the powers, and above all, it is impossible to explain by this theme the series of chapters 10 to 14: there is clearly something else.

What appears to me to be at the heart of the problem and the difficulties is that this book of the Apocalypse, in spite of its great proclamations concerning Jesus and the visions of the Son of Man, would be hardly Christian, since, if there is a question of Christ in glory, there is never a question of the Incarnation; if there is often a question of the judgment upon men, there is never any question of the crucifixion of Jesus Christ (where the judgment of men has certainly taken place, but at the same time is entirely assumed by God). Two such enormous lacunae can be comprehended only with great difficulty. We do not have the right to say that this is an aspect which the author has not retained in order to concentrate upon the glory and the Lordship: there cannot be one without the other. It is then before the impossibility of such a lacuna that I have been led to rethink these chapters in terms of the Incarnation and the crucifixion.

But we can also arrive at this point by considering the universality of the events described to us in these chapters. We find eight events: the series of cosmic catastrophes—figurative, symbolic, or allegorical (chapter 8:6–13); the series of catastrophes concerning humanity, massively delivered to death, but which of course must also be interpreted, equally, in an allegorical or symbolic fashion (chapter 9); the revelation of the *hic et nunc* by a scroll (chapter 10); the apparent victory of men over the witness of God (chapter 11); the fulfillment of the prophecy of Isaiah by the victory of a little child over the dragon (chapter 12); the surging up of the two beasts who are the new power and temptation in the world of men (chapter 13); the victory of the one who is only the Lamb (14:1–5); which borders upon the "Last Judgment," the seventh trumpet having sounded.

If the eight elements that we have referred to are synthesized without excluding anything, we perceive very clearly, but in silhouette, the person, life, and work of Jesus Christ. And it is all the more interesting that, while very explicitly in the first and second section Jesus Christ is abundantly described (Son of Man, Lion of Judah, etc.; there he is truly the one who determines and provokes the revelations and events), and while we expressly find him again in sections 4 and 5 (chapters 19 and 22); here, on the contrary, in this central section, he disappears, except in chapter 14, but the latter is only the result of preceding developments. While in all the other sections Jesus Christ is determinative, here he seems to be absent. Consequently, we must admit, if there is unity and coherence to this ensemble, that Jesus is designated *otherwise:* here he is not the Lord of Lords, the head of the Church, the Master of history. He is the God who is stripped of being God, and consequently here it is no longer possible to speak directly of

God. In fact what is very interesting in these six chapters is that there is just no longer any question, as elsewhere, of the Throne of God, of the one who sits upon the Throne, nor of his environment. There is something like an absence, at the same moment when it is announced to us that when the seventh trumpet sounds then the Mystery of God will be fulfilled (10:7). But what is this mystery of God? When the seventh trumpet sounds there is the ark of the celestial covenant, the woman and the little child. Thus we are led to interpret all as being the illustration, and, it could be said, the cosmic imagery, of what takes place during the Incarnation, death, and resurrection of Jesus Christ. That which happened in heaven, as spiritual event, but also in the cosmos during this venture, is a parable of the profound reality of Jesus Christ, of what has been changed, transformed in the world and in heaven by these terrestrial events. It is the breaking of the powers and of history. We will see later that the opening of the seventh seal, and all that accompanies it, is essentially ambiguous. But the double fact signified (Judgment of God falling upon humanity and intervention of salvation) is fulfilled precisely in the ambiguity of the Incarnation, of the death and resurrection of the Son of God. And the general catastrophic disturbance, described to us as cosmic plagues, is the allegory of the disturbance of the world, of its perturbation because of the fulfillment of this intolerable mystery of God. It is intolerable, impossible, that God in his fullness abandon himself, cease to be God and become man. It is intolerable, impossible, that God die in Jesus. It is intolerable, impossible, that a man truly dead be raised and that death be conquered. It is this triple impossibility that brings about the general upheaval of all creation and the celestial powers. If we would come to take seriously for a moment this unbelievable mystery of the Incarnation, this cataclysm that can mean "God is no longer God, he has abandoned himself, he has delivered himself up, he has stripped himself, he has reduced himself to being only a man," then the cataclysms described in chapters 8 and 9 would appear to us benign. They are really the allegory of this incomparable, incommensurable event, and by means of them we perceive the meaning of this mysterious decision of God for the whole creation: if the Creator is no longer there to put a check upon the powers, then they are unchained. Which our text actually describe to us. If he is no longer there to maintain order, then disorder reigns and there is chaos, the abyss, the risk of a de-creation. And this is clearly what is described to us in chapter 8, to which we will return. If he is no longer there to protect man, then the cavalry of death is unleashed, as in chapter 9. And we can understand that while we can speak of the "three woes" (chapter 9:12), these are not at all calamities in themselves. Because finally what greater woe could there be than that of the death of God? I do not speak of the theologies of the death of God, and the bombastic, vain, and pedantic declaration of man that "God is dead." No, but the true decision of God to submit himself to the ordeal of death. Then there, yes, is a woe, the absolute woe, the triple woe, the consummate woe, and the woe which, because it is *triple*, actually has to do with God. The traditional interpretation of the woes (plagues upon men) is impossible, because everything culminates in the third; now what is the latter? The fact that the woman bears a child who must shepherd all the nations; and this is the trial and *defeat* of the dragon. But how is this a woe? For it is clearly qualified as such: 11:14 and chapter 12. If we go back from this woe to the first two then we understand that in fact the three woes envisage God renouncing his power as absolute and intangible Creator, the Incarnation and death of the Son of God.

Everything begins with the seventh seal, the last of the series which closes the book of history (we will return to the interpretation in chapter 4). The seventh, after the first six are broken, is the one which at the same time consummates history, marks an end to it, and also permits the book to be opened (whether it is a scroll or tablets comes to the same thing). As long as the seventh is intact, the breaking of the first six is still of no use. It is only when the seventh is broken that the scroll can be read. Then can be understood what is within; in other words, the rest can be read only beginning with this. It is then beginning with the Incarnation, the death and the resurrection of Jesus Christ that history becomes readable. And it is also because this series of trumpets, chapters 8 to 14, is determined by this seventh seal that we begin our interpretation with it. In fact, the seventh seal sounds the seven trumpets, which permits for the sections that follow the comprehension of the judgment and the new creation *by means of the modality* chosen by God for his presence in the world. But, further, what characterizes the seventh seal is the silence of a half-hour. The truncated numbers—there is enough agreement on that—designates biblically a crisis. On the other hand, there is silence for a half-hour. In apocalyptic literature, quite often, silence is a sign of the end or the fulfillment of time. But in biblical literature, silence is the presence of the all-powerful Lord (Hab. 2:20; Zech. 2:13, for example). We have then a triple overlapped meaning: crisis/end of the time/presence of the All-Powerful. And I think that the three can very well be related to the death of Jesus Christ. Symbolic events in the Apocalypse nearly always have a double meaning. We find this again with the trumpets which are, as we said, the sign announcing the judgments of God (the day of Jahweh, the wrath) but also the call for the triumphant assembly of the elect, and for their liberation. In the same way the trumpets of Jericho destroy the city (the world) *and* assure the entrance of the elect people into the Promised Land.

Finally the act of the angel (8:3,5) is also composed of two apparently contradictory elements: there is first of all the presentation of the incense. The sacrifice of the altar symbolized at the same time purification and mediation; it is a very sacred place (Exod. 30:6; Heb. 9: 3–4), which implies the consecration of the high priest because only the one who offers the absolute sacrifice can approach and stand before the place where God encounters man. But what is offered here, symbolized by the incense, is the prayer of the saints. We find then the following meaning in this spiritualization: before God it is the prayer of the saints and martyrs that accomplishes the purification and mediation. But we are also reminded that there is only one Saint, Jesus Christ alone, by whom and in whom all the others become saints. Thus the offering of the incense by the angel relates perfectly the action of man to that of God. But the other act of the angel is throwing the coals from the altar upon the earth: bringing together that which is absolutely sacred, which comes from the Wholly Other, and the human world, provokes disasters (Ps. 97:5). This burning coal is that of purification. The act of the angel recalls irresistibly that of the Seraph taking a coal from the altar of God to purify the lips of Isaiah (Isa. 6). But this purification is at the same time an absolute challenge and because of this launches the announcement (thunder, lightning, earthquakes) of catastrophes. The two apparently contradictory acts of the angel, one toward God and one toward the world, are in reality perfectly related: it is the line between the "beyond" and the creation; it is purification and risk of destruction, the proximity of God and the shaking of the world. But much more profoundly it is the venture of God who merits absolute praise and who comes into the milieu of man. Perhaps it would be possible to compare this scene with that described by Luke (1: 8ff.) where the high priest Zechariah enters into the temple to offer incense while a multitude of people is outside in prayer, at the very moment when the risk of the Incarnation is undertaken —of the one who said, "I have come to cast fire upon the earth." The act of the angel announces that which is going to be the great ordeal of God, the absolute risk of the creation, and the venture of God-with-man; and it must obviously include the two faces, the two aspects, of this prodigious innovation.

The First Woe

Before studying the "plagues" in the perspective that we have indicated, it is necessary to make at least two remarks. The first is that each act of God in Jesus Christ implies an aspect of catastrophe for the men enclosed in the world, in solidarity with the world, separated from God, and in conflict with him. Man is so much the prey of the powers, so closely associated with their work, enjoys himself so thoroughly to their profit, desires so much all that they offer, conceives his life to such a degree separated from God, that every approach of God, every positive work of God, appears to him as an unacceptable disturbance and finally an attack against him. When God comes to deliver him, he does not at all perceive his liberation; he protests against the breaking of those marvelous objects, which are his chains or the doors of his prison: the adored chains. This is clearly the situation of man. And we must take account of the fact that every work of liberation is in fact destructive of the evil environment. And that which assures his liberty is felt by man as a frightful personal offense. "How can God who is good permit . . .?" In uttering this phrase so frequently (either polemically or sadly, according to whether or not one is a believer), man does not envisage for a minute, first of all, that the evil deed is most often the result of the liberty that God allows to man and of the independence and autonomy that man has seized over against God. He is responsible for what is done (and he has wished it), but he protests against God for what is done. In short, he would demand that God mechanize him and take his liberty from him. Next, that evil also takes place by the interplay of the spiritual powers who act in the world and in society, and of which we must speak at length. Finally, that that which does evil to him can very well be the act of God who liberates him. But this liberation causes suffering. I do not know anything better to compare this to than to an operation. The surgeon who takes out a cancer destroys the power of death to the profit of the living body. But he removes something of this body, which had become "flesh of his flesh"; he amputates something which had become the body itself. And the patient who does not know what has been done, from what he has been saved, could perfectly well interpret that as a frightful torture, as an illegitimate extraction, being aware only of the pain that remains after the operation is finished.

It is in this perspective that we must understand most of the "plagues" which fall upon men in the Apocalypse. But in this first series associated with the six trumpets, there is no question of pain, but rather, as we have said, of the shaking of the creation resulting from the decision of the Incarnation.

The second remark is that since Jesus Christ incarnates all humanity ("Behold the Man!" or, again, Paul: "just as sin has entered by a single man, in the same way grace has come by a single man, Christ," Rom. 5:12, 17; 1 Cor. 15:22), all that which happens to him is in reality a catastrophe for the entire human race; and the disasters are a kind of replica, in reciprocity with the suffering of Christ. But also, inversely, all that happens to humanity is in reality that which falls upon Jesus, is concentrated in fact upon his person. Thus we must never read the plagues and judgments of the Apocalypse outside of this perspective of perfect, absolute, unbreakable association between Christ and men—all men, those of the past and of the future, those of all races and religions: man, the sole and unique Adam, come from the hands of the Father with his billions of possibilities, which are the billions of our visages.

The first five trumpets: the Incarnation of God in Jesus Christ is the overturning of the order of the world; it is the absolute putting in question of the creation because the unthinkable thing has happened: God *is blended* with his creation! He is no longer distinct; he has even submitted himself to its law! Unimaginable. And the five trumpets are the royal announcement by the heralds of the perfect majesty: that it approaches, that it is present, more intimately present than could be conceived, since soon it will no longer be possible to distinguish it from that creation, from a body of men. And, in short, the trumpets sound before nothing and the catastrophes unleashed seem to be gratuitous. God has drawn near to the world. But not at all behind his trumpets. In secret, in hiddenness; it is not the devouring fire, nor the thunder that Elijah heard; it is the silence of a sigh which vanishes . . . yes, but it is God even so. And for the celestial powers, and for the entire creation, the overturning begins precisely when the Absolutely Powerful, "who speaks and things are," renounces his power and adopts the way of humility. Then the pillars of the world are much more shaken than if he had come in his fury and in his glory: in the latter case the mountains would collapse, the land would melt, the valleys would be filled up, according to Psalm 97; but this would be according to the nature of things. God who renounces his own power is much more terrifying; the entire order of creation totters. In these verses we find ourselves both in the presence of a recollection of the "plagues of Egypt," which all the commentators have noted (hail, vs. 7; water changes into blood, vs. 8; poisoned waters, vs. 11; darkness, vs. 12; locusts, 9: 3, although these would be of a different kind from the Egyptian locusts), and also, which has been rarely seen, a sort of "de-creation," a putting in question by going back, of the works of the third day (the vegetation and the waters), of the fourth day (the lights), of the fifth day (the fish). It is a true countercreation which is at work (up to the moment when the process of the new creation begins in Jesus). Then a sort of triumph of death commences (vs. 9), a triumph of delirium and intoxication which changes reason and justice into madness (Lamentations of Jer. 3: 15: Amos 5: 7 and 6: 12) (I believe this is the meaning of Wormwood). And there is the end of light: a miracle opposite to the appearance of Christ. This is the miracle of Satan producing darkness at the moment when the Word is made flesh. Finally, in chapter 9: 1–12, there is even the unchaining of the Abyss, that is to say, the return to chaos, the plunge again into nothingness. Abaddon is absolute destruction, the de-creation. It is the triumph of chaos, the return to what was before the Spirit of God installed order in this disorder; it is Sheol that prevails. In all we are here in the presence of the opposite of that which was the creative act of God.

This can be comprehended according to two orientations. On the one hand, that of the Jewish tradition: the Creator is not only the one who is at the origin, but also the one by whose power the forces of destruction and of the Abyss are kept at bay: it is because he has traced a limit to the sea that the latter no longer engulfs everything; it is because he holds tightly the "cover" of the Abyss that the latter no longer bursts forth when God ceases. But on the other hand, it can also be understood according to Christian theology: when God undertakes by his Incarnation to save humanity, when he becomes Immanuel, it is really the equivalent of the recommencement of All, of the new creation, and there must be in some way a starting again from the situation of chaos, a spiritual chaos that amounts to revealing, moreover, the reality of the disaster that his own creation has become for God. Then there happens what is the equivalent of the deluge, or, again, the plagues of Egypt: twice God willed to begin everything over again. He leaves a human root in the deluge and very quickly that entails a new perversion; then he sets a people apart, he sanctifies it to hear his will, his word, among men, by means of an action of salvation; but here again we are engaged in a new process of betrayal. And finally the salvation determined in the Incarnation is a putting in question as total as the deluge or the plagues of Egypt: it is, properly speaking, a total new beginning, even more than those preceding. It is not in any way a matter of annihilating all humanity in order to make materially another world. It is a matter of a kind of spiritual annihilation (this is why, of course, these plagues must be understood as spiritual manifestations, which is, moreover, indicated by the fact of the "torment" of men) in view of a new spiritual creation. God is incarnate in a man; that means that all the former "spiritual" of man, all the religions, the whole sacred universe, all the mystique, are annihilated. That which man believed he had as light, as mastery over the creation, is abolished. His spiritual Whole is blotted out. This is probably also the meaning of Wormwood, and certainly of the locusts. What characterizes these locusts is the face of a man, the hair of a woman, and a crown of gold, the teeth of a lion, a breast and wings of iron. In other words, *mixture* is their dominant trait. But, in addition, the evil that they do they do from behind, like the scorpion. Which means that they act by the power of the lie. It is the terrible character of that which is not terrible, the seductive nature of that which is not seducing; they have the appearance of gold ("what looked like gold"). They represent the mortal and deadly reality which remains secret. A certain number of exegetes see here in fact the power of the lie. And this is not incorrect, but there is more: their chief is *Abaddon* (perdition), which in Greek is translated *Apollyon* (destroyer;

with the word-play often emphasized relating to Apollo, a polemical point against the Greeks). There is then not only the lie and its power, but actually the total risk of destruction. That is pointed out to us by the "mixture" of their attributes. For the Jews of the Old Testament, mixture is the very sign of countercreation. Creation is characterized by separation (God separated the sea and the land, the light and the darkness, the dry and the wet). When there is mixture there is a countercreative act (and all the laws in the Pentateuch forbidding mixtures are thus explained). The locusts are precisely the horror of countercreation unchained (in addition, moreover, the putting in question of how many Chaldean, Egyptian, and Greek divinities and semidivinities that are characterized by mixture —winged bulls, centaurs, sphinx, etc.) Thus the work of the locusts is the spiritual death of man: which is the true, profound torture, anguish, despair, schizophrenia, complete depression, delirium. Then men wish to die, but they do not, because spiritual death is strictly beyond death. But the locusts have a period of five months to act. This number is the sign of a limit; which means that the power of the Abyss remains limited. There is something that cannot be totally destroyed; the annihilation cannot be total. Five months is a year *less* the seven months of grace, as St. Augustine said. The decision of the Incarnation of God represents the seven months, the perfection of grace. The rest is the unchaining of chaos. The total is in fact the expression of the Incarnation, which reveals how profound was the reality of evil. But there is an infinite distance between five and seven.

The Second Woe

The second woe (9:13–11:14) corresponds to the manifestation of the Incarnation in the ministry, death, and resurrection of Jesus Christ. During these developments the forty-two months, or 1,260 days, continually reappear, which corresponds to three and one-half years, a number for which there are many interpretations, beginning with its use in the book of Daniel (8:25 and 12:7) to explain the duration of the persecution organized by Antiochus Epiphanes. But subsequently there has been general acknowledgment that this number designates the eschatological ordeal or the time of the Church upon the earth. I am not certain that this is the meaning. On the contrary, this period seems to correspond to what was often recognized in the primitive Church as being the duration of the ministry of Jesus on earth (there is always uncertainty now between one and three years, in reality a little more than three years). In fact it seems that chapter 10 appears as the proclamation of the gospel upon earth, but a universal gospel (the angel has one foot on land and one on the sea); and then (chapter 11) the death and resurrection are clearly indicated. Nevertheless, there exists an ensemble of complex images to elucidate. And first of all the cavalry (9:16–21). These present nearly the same characteristics as the locusts. Approximately the same interpretation can be given of them, but there are now two major differences: on the one hand, the locusts had tormented without killing (this is spiritual destruction); the cavalry had been able to cause a third of mankind to perish totally (there is always this idea of a limited power, which we find again and again). On the other hand, with the locusts, men had no escape: they themselves sought death; they ran toward suicide. With the cavalry man is placed before a choice to be made; verse 20 clearly tells us this: men do not repent of the works of their hands; they continue to worship demons and idols; they do not repent of murders and sorcery, thefts and sins of all orders. Here we have passed to a totally different stage: men are driven into a corner and must decide. This is, on the one hand, the preaching of repentance (and how can we not think of John the Baptist, just before the ministry of Jesus?), and on the other hand, the appeal to conversion (the rejection of false religions) in order to recognize Jesus Christ. Thus with the cavalry unleashed we have the other face of the locusts: on the one side spiritual annihilation, on the other the appeal to conversion. And the locusts *end* the first "woe" of de-creation, while the cavalry *begin* the second "woe" of Incarnation. This cavalry corresponds then to the fire that Jesus came to cast upon the earth, to the sword that separates man at the interior of himself.

After this the angel appears who holds the scroll (chapter

10). It is not the great book of history sealed with seven seals, but a little book which is open. It is then directly readable by all. Its message has the inverse character of that of the seven thunders. The latter proclaims in a grandiose fashion a mystery that cannot be transmitted or known. The seer must not write it; but having heard, he must keep the secret. That designates the mystery itself of the Word of God, or of God, a mystery which cannot be disclosed and which, moreover, would be of no benefit to men were it to be known. For it must not be forgotten that the Word is revealed only to the extent that it is useful to man. And this distinction between the voice of the thunders and that of the little open scroll reminds us that, contrary to what certain contemporary theologians think, "All of God" is not revealed in the Gospel.

The little open scroll is very clearly this Gospel. "There will be no more delay." Now the great design of God is fulfilled: the Incarnation, which is this fulfillment, is realized. We are indeed in the presence of the Gospel. But the scroll that the witness must make his own, appropriate, identify with himself, as if he were to eat it, is "sweet to the mouth and bitter in the stomach." There are innumerable explanations of this double character; all, however, unhesitatingly refer to the Word of God: sweetness of receiving the Word, bitterness of bearing the prophetic ministry; sweetness of the announcement of salvation, bitterness of the announcement of judgment; sweetness of the announcement of election, bitterness of the announcement of persecution. I believe, rather: sweetness of receiving the testimony (in this Gospel) of the immensity of the love of God, and bitterness of the difficulty of leading the life in which the "little scroll" involves us. For, in fact, the witness must immediately prophesy. This being taken according to the meaning of prophecy in the New Testament; that is to say, announcement and proclamation of Jesus Christ, the designation of who the Christ is and of his mystery. In addition, this little scroll is the exact introduction to that which follows. In fact, immediately after this we are told the episode of the two witnesses; but if what we are going to show, that it relates to Jesus Christ, is acceptable, then this passage is the content itself, sweet to the mouth, bitter to the stomach, of the scroll in question.

To that is joined, as the decisive act which engages the witness, the measuring of the Temple and of the altar with a rod like a surveyor's chain. Here we are very clearly before the resumption of the third chapter of Ezekiel, but the prophetic meaning is not the same. Because we must not forget that for that Christian generation, that of the destruction of the Temple in Jerusalem, the true Temple upon earth is Jesus Christ. Now here it is not a question of the Temple in heaven. Moreover, in the new Jerusalem there will be no Temple. The fact that the prophet, the seer, must measure that which is shown him signifies knowledge, awareness, discernment. Jesus Christ is portrayed as the Temple because he is at the same time, as the Epistle to the Hebrews (not much earlier than the Apocalypse) reminds us, the Priest, Victim, and Saviour. This is already comprehended, included, in the Incarnation; that is to say, all that which is fulfilled in the Temple and upon the altar is now entirely assumed, resumed, in Jesus Christ. But the distinction between the Temple itself and the exterior court means that Jesus as Christ will not yet be visible to the world. In fact the exterior court in the Temple of Solomon was a figuration symbolic of the world; there is identification of Jesus only with the Temple where the faithful know and hear their Lord. The exterior court, the knowledge of Jesus by the nations, is not possible during the Incarnation; and, on the contrary, the time of the Incarnation is even going to coincide with the victory of the nations; the world is going to belong to the autonomy of men, now assured, acquired, precisely by the fact of the decision of God to adopt for the salvation of men the way of nonpower, of incognito, of humility, of the renunciation of his power in order to be nothing more than love.

We enter now into the very heart of the revelation and the first vision is that of the two witnesses. What is it telling us? They have an extraordinary power: by their word they bring fire upon men (11:5), they have mastery over nature (they can stop the rain, change water into blood). (But it says that they have the *power* to do it, and not that they do it.) They are conquered by death; at Jerusalem their bodies are exposed to the gaze of the nations; they are refused burial; the inhabitants rejoice at their death because they have caused many torments among men. After three and a half days they are raised up by the Spirit of God. They rise to heaven to sit before God. Here is the canvas. It is difficult to be more explicit in describing the time of Jesus upon earth (as we have emphasized, the vision must be understood on the basis of this which has been told us; and we must not, for example, become confused by the number "two"). Truly then there is here an exact synthesis of the work of Jesus. The two witnesses undoubtedly represent the two dimensions that relate to Jesus Christ. On the one hand, we must not forget the duality of name: he is Son of Man and also Son of God. And in reality this duality of two personages who are clearly one unique being in the text (because *everything* is identical for the two; there is no difference at all in their destiny, strange as it is) reminds us of what classical theology has called the "duality of nature" in Jesus. But on the other hand, we must not forget either that Jesus is not an isolated, solitary person: he is descended from the elect people and he bears in himself the whole race of David. And he is head of the Church, which is his body. So in him the two witnesses of God meet: Israel and the Church. And finally (we recall that a symbol has inevitably several planes of interpretation), he is situated precisely in the exact center of the Apocalypse, at the juncture between the first part, which is historical (Church and history), and the second part, which is transhistorical, or eventually meta-historical (judgment and new creation). There are then two faces, two visages, of this witness: one turned toward the historical and the other turned toward the transhistorical. Thus Jesus Christ alone (but this duality of names, so traditional that it no longer means anything to us, already indicates it) is in himself the double witness, the double martyr of the Lord God. He is thus tied to those who are the witnesses of the Father; and the two witnesses are also Israel and the Church. If this is true, then it signifies that all that is his is theirs. His Incarnation is at the same time the Incarnation in them. He assumes all of Israel (and also the great "spiritual chiefs" of Israel: Elijah, evoked by the interdict thrown against the rain; Moses, evoked by the water changed into blood), and, on the other hand, the Church is his body. Therefore, they wear his power; they can act with this power itself for the sake of witness. They can light a fire upon earth. But they are consecrated to follow in all things the destiny of their Lord. Israel and the Church cannot hope to be treated better than Jesus, which transforms Jerusalem into the opposite of what it is: into Sodom and Egypt, places of the absolute revolt of man, places of the total refusal of the will of God, places of hatred against God. And the victory of death over Israel and the Church is always the occasion for celebration and liberation for men because they consider themselves oppressed by them. And in fact the fire which comes from their mouth is the total putting in question, the driving into a corner, of men by the preaching of the gospel, which is strictly insupportable. (Of course when I speak of Israel and of the Church in the perspective of this text, I envisage faithful Israel and the Church as body of Christ, not at all the institution and the kingdom of human power, which Israel and the Church establish for their own glory.) That which has happened to Jesus must happen also to Israel and the Church, that is to say, to the two witnesses of the God of Jesus Christ. Because even if Israel does not recognize Jesus Christ, nevertheless she cannot do otherwise than be the witness of the God that Jesus Christ has recognized as his own, has proclaimed and fulfilled. But the two witnesses in everything follow their Lord; that is to say that they pass through persecution and death; and they also pass through resurrection. There is then this resurrection of the body of Christ in its totality; and we emphasize firmly that our individual resurrection exists only as a member of that which is raised, that is to say, the body of Christ. And that which is very remarkable is that, at the end of this vision, what follows the resurrection is not a new chapter of history, but the ascension, the judgment of Jerusalem assimilated to the world and to Babylon, and the final conversion of humanity (11:13). All this being evoked very briefly, as a simple indication of what

will be explained at length in the last two parts of the book.
Such is, it seems to me, the meaning of this vision. And we
must not be surprised if the same symbol (the two witnesses)
must be understood with several dimensions, several significations. Here: Jesus Christ and then "Israel-Church." I believe
that this is the characteristic itself of the symbol: the latter
must absolutely not be interpreted with the lexical equiva-
lences: $X = Y$. The symbol always had many meanings, and
consequently, in its complexity, it adopts elements belonging
to each of the realities to which it refers. It seems to me that
the symbol of the two witnesses is sufficiently identifiable by
the Gospel account, but that it also brings together several
realities: it is this wealth which brings to light for us the profound interrelationship for God of the Son, the People, and
the Church.

The Third Woe

Thus the central revelation begins by referring us to the ministry of Jesus upon earth, to his death and to his resurrection;
and it is from there, subsequently, that we pass to the event of
the Incarnation, but the Incarnation, we would say, taking
place in heaven. It is essentially (and outside of dramas and
combats) presented as the Covenant (11:19). The Temple of
God in heaven is opened and the ark of the covenant appears.
The New Covenant cannot be better described than as the
heart itself of God; and a covenant which cannot be put in
question, since now a true identification of God with man is
realized. It is an eternal covenant, since this ark is no longer
upon earth like that of Moses and David; but it is the covenant
made by the unity in the person of Jesus of the totality of man
with the totality of God. We need not seek diversified meanings here (the ark of Moses being the terrestrial replica of a
celestial ark; or, again, the ark of the covenant will be discovered and manifested anew at the end of time: this is without
importance in comparison with the central mystery of the decision of God). Now this disclosure of the total mystery of the
will of God is marked by a very important proclamation: the

twenty-four elders who worship call the Lord Almighty the one who is and who was. At the moment of the covenant there is actually no longer any question of *the one who comes* or *who will be,* since in this present time the plenitude is realized in heaven and on earth. There is no longer any "to come": because nothing more, nothing other, can appear beyond this covenant. The Lord, "the one who was," fulfills the totality of his design in this instant which is. He is no longer qualified as the "one who comes": he comes in the Incarnation. This formula of adoration then both confirms that it is indeed a matter of Incarnation, and the interpretation of the last times. The same text (11:15–19) tells us that this Incarnation marks the actual moment of the judgment of the world and of the Lordship of Jesus Christ. It is because the Christ has accepted being incarnate in Jesus that the kingdom of the world belongs to him: the kingdom of the world *now* belongs to our Lord and to his Christ, proclaims the seventh angel in sounding his trumpet.

This verse is situated exactly at the intersection of the vision of the two witnesses and the vision of the woman with the dragon. Which means that from the moment when God had chosen the way of nonpower and of death, beginning with the resurrection, then the kingdom of the world truly belonged to Jesus Christ; but also to his Father, who no longer reigned in virtue of his omnipotence, of his qualities as Creator, of his domination (as 11:17 recalls it), which of course always exist, but in virtue of his love and of his sacrifice. The Father has given the Lordship to his Son; but the Son in his obedience has delivered the throne to the Father. And it is indeed quite normal that this proclamation be situated at the end of the venture of preaching, death, and resurrection and at the beginning of the drama of the Incarnation. Because the two are equally involved. But at the same time the hour of judgment is everywhere announced, for this decision of God puts men and nations under obligation to take a position before God who reveals himself, and also to manifest that which they really are. It is no longer possible to consider that God is in heaven and that he stays there, which does not obligate us to anything. God has become unassailably present in our midst. It is no longer possible to revolt against a god who is only Power, anonymous, pure abstract will, etc.; a revolt which would attest the liberty of man, the dignity of man confronting a tyrant, the grandeur of man before the one who wants to dominate him. It is just this God who has become the weakest of men, has renounced acting by constraint, has witnessed to his absolute love: and it is in the face of that that man truly reveals himself, who he is. As long as he revolts against an oppressor, he plays a noble role. But now he responds to love by hate, to non-power by the unleashing of his power, to grace by the triumph of money, to the gift by rape, to the covenant by war—then man actually reveals what he is: and there his judgment resides. For the center of the judgment is revelation. To the revelation of God in Jesus Christ corresponds the revelation of the reality of man against Jesus Christ: such is the *whole* judgment. This is the judgment of the dead (11:18), which is to say, of those who refuse the life which is in God and which is completely assumed in the covenant. It is the destruction of those who destroy, whether this action bears upon creation, or upon other men, or upon the Kingdom of God. It is the destruction which engenders destruction and ends in the destruction of itself. And we have here a second aspect of the judgment: it is finally the product of man's own action. And it is the manifestation of the wrath of God in response to the wrath of man: after the covenant, after the refusal of the covenant, there remains the possibility of wrath. *But,* we emphasize that it is a matter of wrath against the nations. It is certainly not wrath against *some* men. We will have to return to a fuller treatment of the question of knowing upon whom the final judgment falls. Thus the Incarnation is, *in heaven,* at once this Lordship, this covenant, and the judgment, which are absolutely not visible, neither the one nor the other, upon earth. Then it is clearly this secret characteristic of the event Jesus Christ which allows us to say that all which follows refers to the drama of the Incarnation in heaven. It is represented there in its truth, but also in its celestial reality.

And then we enter into the Mystery of the woman, the child, and the dragon.[1]

The woman engages us once more in the plurality of symbolic meanings. She is, very obviously, first of all, *the* woman, corresponding in heaven to Eve: which is confirmed by the fulfillment of the prophecy of Genesis concerning the hatred between Eve and the serpent, the victory of her posterity won over the serpent, and the latter's fall (12:9). But in addition the woman is surely Zion and Israel, who engender the Messiah and the believers. Further, she is very clearly Mary; or rather, the celestial reduplication of Mary, mother of the little child. On the other hand, I do not think that the Church can be added to these many meanings (although it is held by numerous commentators). For it is clearly a matter of the birth of the Messiah as such, the birth of the one who fulfills the prophecies and wins the victory: the Church does not give birth to the child; on the contrary, it is she who derives from him.

But it seems to me that there is a dimension of the symbol which escapes these classic interpretations that I have mentioned. We must not forget that we are here on the cosmic plane,[2] before the involved totality, both of heaven (Michael and his angels) and of hell (the Devil and Satan), and on the plane of the celestial representation of the terrestrial reality, or, further, on the plane of the meta-comprehension of the totality. Finally, we must not forget that the Incarnation is the total union of the *whole* of man with the *whole* of God. In this perspective, the woman appears to me to be the image of the entire creation (of earth and heaven) in some way synthesized to produce the fruit of the most decisively intimate covenant of God with his creation. Then there can no longer be either opposition or rupture. But then the birth of the child is the result of this bringing together of the creation with its Creator which means (if the dialectical schema is adopted, also implied by the action of the two witnesses ending in the crisis of the world) the appearance of a new creation. There is now a new origin, absolutely new, because up to here all that which unfolds *in* the domain of the world cannot be new. That alone is new which is the appearance of a point of departure radically other than all that which had existed up to then. It had been a Creator-creation relation; now an incommensurable relation appears: Father-Son, Husband-Wife, contraries united up to the point of self-loss in a new identity. But if a point of departure is thus posed, inconceivably different and new, that means, on the one hand, that all the old determinations are lifted and abolished. (This is, it seems to me, the meaning of the prophecy that the child will rule all the nations with a rod of iron, 12:5.) On the other hand, the too well-known logical evolutions, implying the power of the serpent, and the conclusion in death, are also reversed: evolution now moves toward life. The creation has given birth to a child god, who is himself the Living One, and consequently it can no longer be destined to death, to being swallowed up. Death is actually, already at this moment, conquered, since the absolute Life (God, the Eternal, the Living) is intimately united with its creation, its creature, even to the extent of losing itself. And we understand even better why the historical development must not be followed: it is necessary to speak first of all of resurrection (11:11) in order then to disclose that at the moment of this birth, at Christmas, the miracle of the victory over death had already taken place.

But this implies that chaos and death lose their power; therefore, the outburst of fury takes place at the moment of the birth. The Dragon, the old serpent, must completely prevent the Incarnation. If the latter comes to pass, then all is lost for them. They will no longer be able to annihilate the creation and destroy man, which they could do in face of the Lord Omnipotent. It is then this decision of the Incarnation which justifies and provokes the appearance of the Dragon (and not at all the memory of those innumerable cosmic combats between the forces of good and evil in the imagination of a redactor conforming somewhat to the average apocalypse; the text uses well-known images, obviously, but it avoids completely these kinds of banalities). Up to now there existed a place, and even several, for the power of death and chaos. It was exactly the interval, the distance, the opposition which obtained between the Creator and the creation. It is *in* this distance that the powers acted. The latter are fully designated in 12:9, and assimilated one to the other. The Dragon, who is at the bottom of the sea and who represents the power of chaos; the Serpent, who is the tempter, the one who proposes the question by which man, each time, discovers that God is other than he, in truth, is; the Serpent, creator of a single reality: doubt, and from this fact he is the father of the lie; the Devil, which is to say the one who divides, who provokes rupture, and not only rupture between man and God, but all the others, the explosions and dissociations, the wars and hatreds, who intrudes as a wedge into all relations, communions, communities, in order to break them up and divide men. The opposite of Love, much more subtle than hate. And the Satan, the accuser, who completes the work of the Devil in launching accusation, either before God to accuse men, or between men. Every accusation is the work of Satan.

If our account shows us an extreme reaction of the powers united in the Dragon, we must not believe that there is a reaction because God acts, ending in a combat full of imagery, high in color, between good and evil, as in numerous myths. (Here, however, very much subdued and reduced in color.) This is not the question at hand. In reality, because of the Incarnation, the perfect union between God and man, the powers are excluded. If this venture succeeds, they will no longer have a place, since from now on the creation is endowed with the very life of God. It possesses the certain knowledge of the truth (there can no longer be any doubt); the union is so perfect that it can leave no place for rupture, and one can no longer accuse the other: it is the triumph of Love in a definitive and absolute Unity. In this unity without fault the powers of destruction no longer have any possibility of action. They are excluded, purely and simply.

In the life of Jesus this exclusion takes place in three events: the birth, the temptation, and the crucifixion. I believe it is that which is envisaged as celestial combat in 12:7–9; that which throws the Dragon out of heaven, the powers out of their place. This is the realization in Jesus of the perfect victory of the love of God in humility, nonpower. To the exact degree that the man Jesus is in perfect and constant accord with the will of the Father, that it is not a matter of servile obedience to the law but of perfect response of love to love, to the degree that Jesus is constantly free to be other than God and nevertheless is constantly the voluntary expression of the will of God, then there is no longer any possible role for these powers. The Dragon is truly excluded; chaos can no longer reign (and this is why we are told clearly that it is in Christ that the world has been *created*). There can no longer be either accusation of men before God or separation of men from God (and this is why Jesus is designated the Saviour). But these powers are not abolished. They have only lost their decisive power, the power to prevail and to establish definitively chaos or rupture. For a rupture on the part of God—meaning that God would reject humanity—would end in his condemning himself and would be a victory of the powers. When there is talk, somewhat thoughtlessly, of the judgment of God, with condemnation and damnation for certain men (and for some theologians, the immense majority of men) it is completely forgotten that this would be not the expression of the justice of God but, rather, the success of the infernal powers. If God condemns, he does what Satan suggests to him. If he delivers man to death, it is exactly what the Dragon demands. If he delivers the creation to destruction, the Devil has finally succeeded in his work of breaking decisively the relation between the Creator and the creation. Thus the "apocalyptic" judgment, which is too often depicted is not at all the realization of the justice of God but of the victory of the infernal powers. And we note in passing that the justice, which, it is declared, demands the judgment of God, is in reality a juridical concept issuing from the interpretation of the Roman law. That has nothing to do with what the Old Testament calls justice, nor with what Jesus shows us as being the justice of the Father (by example, the workers of the eleventh hour or the parable of the talents). Then from the fact of the Incarnation the powers are thrown down upon the earth. For the Incarnation is not the Whole; it is the point of departure, the origin, the new beginning. But it is clearly only a beginning. The consequence, which must take place upon the earth, is to be created, invented; and that consequence implies the victory not only of

God over the powers, but also of man over these powers. We see why they are upon the earth. At the moment of the Incarnation they had lost their eternal power ("you have come to destroy us"). By the decision of God they can no longer prevail. But they still have a considerable force among men. They can cause men to perish (12:11); upon the earth they can accuse and destroy.

Why then this delay? Why then this caution and why is there not an immediate and total victory of God? We are here before two elements of response. First of all, if there were a total victory, this would be once more the expression of the absolute, unlimited power of God. Once more there would be a competition of powers. Now this explosion of power is exactly what the Tempter proposes. He continually provokes God to combat. But if this takes place, God is no longer love. The way decided by God in the Incarnation is the triumph of love; but precisely this love which gives itself, abandons itself, delivers itself up, is not that which kills. They are excluded not because the power of God triumphs. And then they are driven out from there where this love has triumphed. And this "there where" is exactly heaven. So much so that, when an operation of force is necessary, it is not God who brings it about; very curiously (12:16), we see the creation intervene to save the child ("if men are silent, the rocks will cry out"). The Dragon spews forth a torrent of water; it is the satanic reproduction of the flood. God, himself, had seen that the flood was of no use. He had decided that man would never be subjected to it again. But the Dragon by the deluge does not seek to kill men (disobedient and sinners); on the contrary, he wants to destroy the only one in whom obedience and love had triumphed. And he employs the waters because he is the one who lives at the bottom of the oceans; he is the master of the wrath of the seas. But we see that God does not establish a dike nor dry up the waters to protect the child: it is the earth who intervenes; it is she who acts in this plan of God.

But the other aspect of this delay, the text reminds us, is the time of testing for man, for men, for humanity: the time of the desert (12:6 taken up again in vs. 14). The time of the desert is really the time of being put to the test. In other words, the issue here is knowing if man is going to follow Jesus, is going to enter into the plan of God, is going to accept this unity with God. We have said repeatedly that we are here before the new beginning. Yes, but what is going to be the result? The story of Adam is taken up again. There is respect for the liberty of man. God again makes man free, and from this fact man can again refuse completely the love of God. The time of the desert is the time when man is deprived of all his natural resources, the possibilities and protection of civilization, when he is truly "unchained," but with all the risks that that involves. The time of the desert is that when man has strictly no other support, no other assurance than the grace of God. The woman and the child are carried away into the desert. In the work of the Incarnation, Jesus has no human recourse, no power protecting him; he is delivered naked and alone to all the powers. He has only one recourse: the grace of God. But beginning from this moment the time of the desert also begins for men; the new relation with God is then inaugurated but with all which that includes of contingency, of uncertainty, of nondetermination; in a word, of liberty. (And this is why, beginning with Jesus Christ, a ferment of disintegration is introduced in all cultures and all civilizations; civilization changes nature, historically, where the gospel is preached: man enters into this desert.) But this very liberty of man, when God restores it, restores to the powers a place where they can act. And this is why the Dragon stands upon the sand of the sea (12:18), on the boundary between his domain and the new creation which begins, on the border between the indefiniteness of the ocean and the indefiniteness of the new beginning upon the earth: and only there (because for the rest, reconciliation is established). But, upon earth, with still so much efficacy!

The Dragon then engages in combat against the offspring: "those who observe the commandments of God and keep the testimony of Jesus" (12:17), that is, the Church. In this passage we find a remarkable allusion to the departure from Egypt, but with a transposition. First of all, obviously, if the

inundation confronting Jesus is the image of the deluge, if it
is related to the Church (and we must recall that these texts
are precisely ambivalent, because the Church is the body of
Christ), then it is the image and symbol of the waters of the
Red Sea but with inversion: that is to say, the waters that had
drowned the Egyptians are now aimed at annihilating the
Church. We must in addition remember what we have said of
the comparable plagues, the "plagues of Egypt." Then the
passage through the desert is also evoked, and finally the
wings of the great eagle given to the woman to enable her to
flee: this is exactly the description that the revelation of Sinai
gives us on the subject of the flight from Egypt: "You have
seen what I did to the Egyptians, and how I bore you on
eagles' wings and brought you to myself" (Exodus 19:4).
This is not at all fortuitous: the departure from Egypt had
been an endeavor at a covenant of God with his creation, had
been the first attempt for the liberty of man, had been the
election of a people who would be the people of God upon
earth and among men. If it is recalled here, it is certainly to
emphasize that the Incarnation is the resumption of all that,
the accomplishment; this time it succeeds. But this allusion is
one more confirmation that in all this there is clear reference
to the Incarnation.

Beginning then with this disclosure of what the Incarnation
had been in heaven, we reach a new dimension (a new vision):
the appearance of the two beasts, the one that rises from the
sea and the one that rises from the land. These are manifestly
consequences of the Incarnation. But since we are told that the
Dragon has been thrown down upon the earth ("I saw Satan
fall as lightning from heaven"), that he has established himself
upon the shore of the sea, that means that we are in the
presence of powers that act upon earth; then it is an aspect of
history which is revealed here. But the relationship with the
"revelation in heaven" is that, although the events no longer
take place in heaven, the reverse side of what happens on earth
is shown. What we believe to be a simple unfolding of events
conceals in reality a secret power with a personality, a coherence, a purpose. We are not in the domain of the simply

natural, but in that of a profound action of which the event is an accidental spectacle.

One of the two beasts is generally indentified as the Roman imperial power (and we always persist in thinking predominantly of the persecutions), the other as the false prophet. But prophet of what? It is not said, except to speak of propaganda for the imperial cult. Generally the line between the two beasts is not drawn, which nevertheless is clearly established in the text (13: 12, 14, 15). However, how can we not see the difference of plane between the Incarnation and the cosmic drama attached to it and then, brutally, the reference to a circumstance of the Roman empire, certainly important in actuality, but of which we cannot fail to note the transitory character? In reality, in order to situate ourselves on the plane where the author of the Apocalypse has firmly established himself from the beginning, if the first beast is actually incarnate in the Roman state, its symbolism is not exhausted in this simplistic allegory. (For the author, as we have already said, and we will find it again with the seven churches, the circumstantial is only the occasion to denote a more profound, universal, and fundamental reality.) This is an authority which claims sovereign and permanent power, and to whom the second beast refers upon the religious or psychic plane. I will not hesitate to say that the first designates authority, political power in the global, universal sense. The second, propaganda; that is, the establishment of a privileged, exemplary, and magnified relation between the power and man. This may surprise one; and I use here modern terms, dependent upon our culture. But we are going to see that in fact these are the ones which correspond best to the characteristics given by our text.

The first beast has ten horns and seven heads. Of course seven hills and ten emperors can be read, if the reference is to Rome. This is not excluded and we will find it again in the sixteenth chapter. But it is strictly limited. Because finally, all through the Bible and also in all the writings of the Near East, the horn is the symbol of Power, traditional, perfectly comprehensible, and so spontaneously understood. The horn multiplied by ten is power carried to the absolute. Likewise the head is the sign of direction, of commandment, of consciousness in action; which is carried to universality by the number seven. And in this power of commandment resides a blasphemous claim, "upon the heads there is a blasphemous name"; which means that this power of commandment claims to equal or usurp that of God. Finally, in order to insist the more and to accumulate emblems of authority (in the Greek sense) we have the diadems worn upon the horns: this is the insignia of royalty. There cannot be any doubt, then, concerning the meaning of this symbol. But already the fact that there is a plurality (seven, ten) also indicates that it is not *one* particular power which is envisaged. It is, rather, a more general, constant power. It is not Rome; it is what Rome has expressed in its political expansion, in its organization, what Rome has carried to a summit practically never surpassed. This is Political Power in its *abstraction* (an operation that Rome had been the first to effect), the absolute power of the political.[3] Then comes the description of the actions of this power. It is struck by a mortal wound but recovers: this marks the fact that political power is continually put in question, wounded, and under one of its aspects, even destroyed; but that it is reborn time after time, and increases its force and its prestige in and through each crisis. Each time that political power is attacked but regains control people are "astonished" and put still more confidence in it. Military victory or victory of the revolution, which each time institutes a growing and accepted power of the state. In the second place, it exercises a totality of power (13: 7) and since peoples, tribes, languages, nations are concerned, it can be truly said that it is a political power that tends to be total and universal. This is clearly the characteristic, not only of the Roman empire, but of another more abstract power from which nothing escapes. For, once more, we must take the terms seriously: inasmuch as we are told that it is a power over *every* nation the author knows very well that it is not the Roman empire. In Asia Minor he is better placed than anyone to know that the empire does not rule over all: at the frontier the empire is threatened, very especially at this oriental frontier.

It is perfectly well known that many nations escape the authority of the Roman empire. Modern historians detect better and better to what degree the populations of the empire had the feeling of the relativity of that empire. Even if it is taken as an actual example, beyond it is denoted a political power which will be exercised over all people. Not an organization, an empire more vast than Rome, but the Power itself in its political face (today, the state). It holds the sword and brings death. It decides captivity and imprisonment (13:10). But in addition, in regard to the Church and Christians, it holds power and conquers them (13:7) upon both the material and the spiritual planes; for this state is not only force and power but also seduction and the capacity to make itself adored. And that has in view not only the claim of the emperor to worship (the simplistic affirmations that I have encountered in numerous commentaries concerning divinization and the cult of the emperor have to be modified considerably, since it was established very much later than is generally believed); but it is the orientation of men themselves to adore the political power (see my book *The New Demons*). There is the state religion, but there is also the religion of the state, and that which Raymond Aron has called the secular religions. On the one hand, as our text reminds us, the political power enters into competition with God (13:5–6): it blasphemes and attacks God (which is true both of the powers that are called Christian, for example, Louis XIV, and the anti-Christian powers). But on the other hand, it does not itself seduce and demand to be worshiped: the text is very clear; it is men who run toward it in order to worship it. The inhabitants of the earth, that is to say tied to the things of the earth, characterized by their belonging to the earth, find of themselves no higher divinity than the state and put their hope and faith in it. Now this power of the state is given to it by the Dragon: vs. 4, the Dragon had given power to the Beast, and vss. 5 and 7 (it was given to him). Which is to say that the power of the state is not of the natural, naturalistic, sociological order; it comes from the power of chaos, from the destroyer; as admirably organized, regulated as it is, it always expresses chaos. The more the state order reigns, the more the disorder of the Dragon prevails. Such is the message of the Apocalypse on the state. And precisely because it expresses a spiritual power, men, who feel it deeply, worship it.

We are now in the presence of the second beast identified in the classic commentaries either as the false prophet or, from the historical point of view, as the propagandist of the imperial cult. Once more, I believe that the text itself compels us to consider a more vast dimension and to establish a relation between the first and the second without, however, neglecting the actual, historical aspect: we always return to this central idea that the seer of Patmos interprets actual history as a springboard, a sign, a means to express a universal truth. This second beast is presented under the form of a lamb, but speaks as a dragon; this is fundamental: it *imitates* the nonpower (since it possesses two horns, which marks the difference); it is benign at first glance; it offers the good, the kind, the realization of values, submission. But its word is that of the dragon, that is, destruction, nihilism, rupture, blasphemy. And it acts by *its word.* Then it also imitates God in its new way. It acts not so much according to the orders of the first beast, but under its surveillance; that is, with a certain independence, but under its control. Its purpose is to persuade men to worship the state (13:12) in bringing miracles to pass, the great works of Power (do we not speak of the German miracle, or of the Japanese miracle, etc.?) It seduces men by marvels (vss. 13–14), which it is capable of accomplishing: it makes fire fall from heaven to earth. Here we must be silent about the nature of this marvel, for we would have too many temptations to interpret it in terms of modern circumstances (I have read that it is a matter of the demonic inspiration of electricity!). Perhaps it is the claim of the Power to exercise a last judgment upon earth, to make fire fall from heaven upon those whom the Power condemns: in which case we would find a parallel here to the proposal of the disciples to make fire fall from heaven upon the cities that had not received Jesus (Luke 9:51–56), and the latter told them emphatically: "You do not know by what spirit you are moved." It would be then not at all a juridical and external judgment but the desire to judge inwardness, the very ground of the being, and to claim to condemn in an ultimate fashion. This beast in addition persuades men to raise up the image of the other, the image of the state. It animates this image and gives it the word. Once more, the great weapon of the second beast is the word. It puts its words in the mouth of the state; by it the state speaks, makes itself *known, identified, obeyed.* We are then truly before the extraordinary work of the animation of a dead structure, of a sterile organization, of a mechanism of power, which becomes living and vital presence. That which actually fills all these roles exactly is Propaganda. But we clearly specify, not at all a religious propaganda or bearing upon religious themes: it is precisely political propaganda (which sometimes takes a religious form). And it is an inspired analysis of the situation by John, which distinguishes between the organization of power which is the state, and the animation of this structure by the word of propaganda. On the one side, the sword; on the other, the word. On the one side, severity; on the other, conviction. And it is in fact propaganda which produces the claim to know and judge intimate convictions. Obedience does not suffice; there must be love and profound adhesion. And the fire from heaven falls upon those who do not adhere, that is, the judgment concerning an absolutized Good and Evil. But the work of the second beast does not stop there: in addition, it puts a mark upon the right hand and upon the forehead. The mark is the sign of belonging: propaganda makes men *belong* to the political power (which is not only the framework in which they live). The right hand is the symbol of action: men must act in conformity to the order of the state (this is what I have called in my study on propaganda, orthopraxis). The forehead is the symbol of intelligence: men must think in conformity to the thought of the state. It is then clearly the creation of the ideology *of the political,* the adoration not only of the state, but *of the political;* it is the affirmation that the political is All, or further, of the primacy of the political over everything. I believe that there can hardly be any doubt on this subject. What the Apocalypse describes under the form of two beasts is not only *a state,* but rather *the state;* not only a particular political (of right or left, etc.) but the primacy of the political. To return to the second beast, this mark upon the hand or the forehead implies then an adhesion to a regime, to a type of society, a conformity of action and of thought to the model proposed by the state, an integration without reservation in the collective current (represented by the political of the moment) and finally an adaptation.[4] And this power is exercised without distinction upon the "small and great, rich and poor, free men and slaves." It appears then as a commonplace to all. In other words, the community thus created by the mark of the beast is finally the anti-Church. As far as the relation between the power and the society is concerned, we have a very striking indication in 13:17: no man can buy or sell if he does not wear the mark of the beast. This is not exactly the problem of money (although that can also be included here), but it is the mark of belonging to the society: the one who refuses to enter into the collective current, who does not accept the political power of this authority and organization, who does not conform, is banned from the society and is no longer able to exercise any function, even the simplest and most indispensable in order to live, such as buying or selling. Of course, on the basis of this buying and selling, one could wish to consider that the second beast is money. But the multiple traits accumulated in verses 11 to 15 do not correspond to that symbolization; they reveal a power much more psychological and ideological.

There remain two points to be examined; the first is the origin of the two beasts, the one coming up from the land, the other from the sea. This indication is difficult to grasp. It is often said that the allusion to the sea refers to the way followed by the Romans. But that does not clarify at all the terrestrial origin of the second beast. It is possible that the meaning is that the whole earth, all the elements, the two domains (the angel holding the book had one foot upon the land and the other upon the sea), the whole creation here below, is implicated in the movement of the two beasts. But I have the impression that that does not exhaust, by far, the possible meaning. As for what 666 might mean, the number of the beast, it is known that the deciphering of this number, in particular by the gematrical method, has given innumerable and fantastic results, from "Nero-Caesar" to Hitler.[5] But the most correct answer appears to me to be that which is already well known: the opposition between six and seven, the latter being the number of perfection, six being the number of imperfection.[6] But why an accumulation of sixes? It seems to me that it is not at all the number of the human, the imperfect, as is often said, but the number of that which accumulates imperfections, and which by that way attempts finally to reach seven, by multiplying sixes, that is, attempts to reach perfection; in other words, have itself taken for God. But precisely the one who imitates God thus discloses his own imperfection. It is not then an opposition "human-divine," but a movement between God and that which enters into competition with him, that which imitates what Jesus Christ has done, that which is established as God upon the earth. This is the true meaning of 666, and which envisages not only the political power but all that which acts by propaganda in order to inspire adoration.

Finally, on this subject, we find in the text the exhortation: "It is the moment to have discernment" (or again: it is here that wisdom intervenes). But contrary to what could be believed, wisdom or discernment does not have to do with deciphering the number 666 itself: it is a matter of discerning what is happening around us; concretely the exhortation means: look, then, to what does this number apply today? (And consequently I think it is the rejection of the historicizing attitude, trying to shut the Apocalypse up in the first and second century of the Roman empire). Who is *that* one? Who is, today, the imitator of God who is proclaimed Saviour or Father of peoples? What political power uses propaganda to bring about unanimity, to inspire adoration, to produce loyalty without fault? Then even if the personal name of this power does not correspond to the gematrical deciphering of 666, it is certainly the beast at this moment. It is necessary to discern in the world where we find ourselves the successive incarnations that are the inversion of the Incarnation of the Lord.

If now we sum up what we have described we will discover throughout a perfect continuity: the breaking of the seventh seal, which makes possible the reading of history; the sounding of the septenary of trumpets, herald which announces the presence of God in the midst of men. The first six trumpets describe the overthrow of the creation when the Creator decides to be united with it without any distance (8:6 to chapter 9). Then the little book of the Gospel is given to the visionary, who is going to become aware of this decision (chapter 10). The content of this little book, which is "the two witnesses," obviously follows; that is, Jesus Christ bearing witness, dead, raised, glorified (11:1–14). The seventh trumpet, after this Gospel, brings to light the perfect covenant of God (11:15–19), which is the Incarnation of God in a man. The covenant is expressed concretely in the miraculous birth of the child (12:1–6) (which is made explicit *after* the death and the resurrection: which means that the Christmas story is not *historical,* but if the design of God were indeed that of this total union, *Jesus could not have been born differently*). This union of man (representing the whole creation) and God becomes so perfect, so intense, that there is no longer any place for the Devil, who is then thrown down (12:7–17). But an interval remains between the Incarnation and its fulfillment in the created world. During this interval the dispossessed powers seek to annihilate this work of God (chapter 13), and the whole ends with the vision of the immolated, Triumphant Lamb: such is the coherence and perfect logic of this text, at first glance incoherent! Finally it is punctuated by the three woes: the first woe is the fact that the entire creation is put in question, when the Creator himself is put in question in order to enter into the way of nonpower, of Judgment, which falls back upon himself (chapter 9). The second woe is the death of God in Jesus Christ (chapter 11). The third woe is the realization of the design of God at the time of his incarnation in the weakest and poorest of beings (chapter 12).

·3·

THE IMMOLATED LAMB—
THE GLORIOUS LORD[1]

In each of the five parts of the Apocalypse we find a vision of Jesus Christ. But what is remarkable is that the vision varies according to the theme of the section. In the first we have the vision of the omnipotent Lord (1:9–20). In the second, the immolated Lamb (5:6–7). In the third we do not have any particular vision except the two Witnesses and the Child, of which we have spoken. In the fourth it is both the Lamb (14:1) and the Son of Man (14:14). Finally in the fifth it is both the Word of God (19:11–16) and the omnipotent Lord (22:6–21). By this simple enumeration we see several important elements: first of all a confirmation of the symmetrical structure; in the first part and in the fifth Jesus Christ is Lord. In the second and fourth he is the Lamb. This is perfectly clear and shows with what care and exactitude the book has been composed. But there is progression between the parts of the beginning and those of the end. There is a development brought about: in the last two parts the image of Jesus Christ is double: in the fourth he is Lamb and Son of Man *together* (then we observe a synthesis between the second and the third parts). In the fifth he is Word of God and omnipotent Lord *together:*

and we observe here a synthesis between the first and the second sections. Finally we notice the agreement between the visions and the theme of each of these parts. First of all the Christ is seen as the Lord, but this refers to the Church: it is for her and by relation to her and only there that in our time, the time of this "eon," he is the Lord. On the contrary, when it is a question of history, of the world in its entirety and of the totality of men, during the course of this eon, he is the immolated Lamb: there is no other power and no other efficacy than that which results from his death. But when we pass to the two later phases the vision becomes composite. In the perspective of the judgment, he is the Lamb again, since it is upon Jesus that the whole judgment falls; but also the Son of Man in the midst of the angels, the one who is going to reap. Because it is in reality not as absolute Lord and inaccessible God that he judges, but as man: one of the most profound secrets of the Revelation is that finally it is man who judges himself in Jesus Christ. And ultimately when there is the new creation, the celestial Jerusalem, the coming of the Kingdom of God, the Recapitulation, we see him as Word of God who abolishes the Lie, but again as omnipotent Lord in whom, for whom, and by whom are all things. Thus the "visions" of John have a perfect theological precision at the same time as they cover the whole field of what man can comprehend on the subject of Jesus Christ.

Omnipotent Lord of the Church (1:4–20)

The specific vision of Jesus Christ as Lord is inscribed first of all (chapter 1) in a great trinitarian affirmation from verses 4 to 7 (which allows us to affirm that if at this epoch there was still not yet a trinitarian dogmatic theology, nevertheless there was, indisputably, a trinitarian interpretation of the mystery of God in Jesus Christ.) "Grace to you and peace *from him who is and who was and who is to come.*" We can say that God the Father is here characterized as Life, Being: the one who alone fully *is;* and both in a temporal way and beyond time he is the one who enters into relationship with man. He comes, but he embraces all, the totality of time and events. The future is not an emptiness of time, indeterminate, unknown: the future is that which *comes;* it is filled (like our past) with the presence and action of the one who traverses this future *toward us* from the end of time.

Concerning *the Seven Spirits* who are before his throne: the Seven Spirits are the totality of the Spirit and so the equivalent of the Holy Spirit. There is no Spirit except in God. There is only one single Spirit, who acts for God before the throne of his majesty. All that which is Spirit depends upon God; and this Spirit is characterized by plurality, the diversity of his actions, of his interventions, at the same time as by the relation between the Creator and the creation, which implies the number seven.

And concerning *Jesus Christ:* he is characterized as the faithful Witness, which is to say the Martyr, who accepts death in order to render an absolute, irreversible testimony to God, but who at the same time is raised and glorious. He is King of the kings of the earth. That actually announces to us the whole successive unfolding of the Apocalypse.

Then the writer gives an uninterrupted development on the work accomplished by Jesus Christ (1:5–7): he loves us; he has set us free (salvation is entrance into freedom); he makes of us a kingdom: which means that we are not ourselves transformed into mighty beings but we become the ones over whom the Lord reigns; we are a kingdom simply because we are attached to the King. But this is a kingdom of priests. Now this is true because Jesus Christ is perfectly specific. In fact Jesus Christ is himself the Sacrificed Priest, as we have said. Then we are called *to reign as he does,* which is to say not in offering exterior sacrifices but in offering ourselves in sacrifice. All this is well known with Romans 12, and the Epistles of Peter, but it is deplorable to see Christians continually adopt anew an attitude of conquest and domination. Such is, then, the work accomplished by Jesus. But then follows what he will do (1: 7–8). He comes (in the present), which very obviously is known only by faith but which will become evident: those who have put him to death will recognize who he was; he will be revealed to all men for the one he is, which means both Lord and Saviour. And all the peoples of the earth will be plunged into amazement and grief—all the peoples, which reminds us that there is not just one responsible for the death of Jesus: it is not the Jews, or even the Romans: to the exact degree that Jesus has been the faithful Witness, he has died because of the sin of all men, which means that he has died by the hand of all, and at the same time—the two things are indissoluble—for all. Then, in the general revelation, all peoples will mourn, not for fear of the Lord but by remorse for the absolute crime. Each of the two affirmations concerning what Jesus has done and that which he is going to do end with the proclamation "Amen," which means, "It is true." It is then the adhesion of the faith to the objective affirmation, to the proclamation of who God is. And that ends, in verse 8, with the affirmation of the unity of God, since what was said above of God the Father ("I am the Alpha and the Omega, the one who is, who was, and who is to come") is now attributed specifically to Jesus Christ.

The Alpha and Omega is the designation of the beginning and the end: Jesus Christ stood at the beginning of days and he closes history. He holds the whole course of history between his two hands as in a parenthesis, at the interior of which the thread of the historical discourse of men unrolls. And this also is the Witness, of God for man and of the totality of man for God. This prefatory proclamation is the declaration of faith of "I, John," I, man.

And after the word of man on God, concerning God, the Word of God addressed to man is going to be heard. Word of man, "I, John." And the part of the initiative of man in Scripture must not be suppressed. It is man who proclaims his faith; it is he who gives himself as a guarantor of that truth; now it is he who bears witness (1:9), after, and as a response to the total and complete Witness. He has taken the decision to confess the Lord, as a preamble to the Word of this Lord. And without this Word of man, there is no Word of God either. The Word of God falls in the void if there is not an ear to hear it. And the Lord evokes that ear; he awakens this man who sleeps;

he moves him toward that initiative taken by man himself, to speak in order that the Word of God become effective, heard, and even possible. Thus after John has confessed his faith, *which is the confession of certitude in hope,* God speaks. Even in a book so strongly marked by the visual, where visions abound, it is essential to understand that the Word of God *precedes* the vision, and on the other hand explains the visions: in other words, the latter have no value in themselves. The visions are actually situated at the interior, in the framework of the words of God (and this is fundamental in relation to mystic tendencies, to the orientations of silent spirituality, and to the primacy of sight over hearing). What is more, verse 12 is completely clarifying: "Then I turned," said John, "to see the voice that was speaking to me." The true object of the vision and of the contemplation is the word itself; what he sees is the image of the Son of Man. This is not simply a man.[2]

"One like a son of man. . . ." We can suppose that he undoubtedly means the true image of man, or man himself, man in his fullness. Son of Man is he who descends from man but who acquired a perfection that the human father does not have. And this image of man is man made in the image of God. He is truly man, but men cannot be assimilated to him or identified with him because there is an infinite distance between man created by God and his actual reality. There is then similarity but not identity between men and the Son of Man. The insignia that characterize him are easy to comprehend: the robe is the vestment of the priest for the sacrifice of expiation, the girdle of gold is a royal emblem; the whiteness is the mark of the Word of God; the glance as a flame of fire is the sign of the light that penetrates and discloses everything, and penetrates to the bottom of the human heart; bronze is the sign of power and eternity; the sword that comes forth from his mouth is the Word that separates, divides, and judges. Image of Christ raised, in glory, bringing together the signs of authority and of the Word, impossible to recognize by relation to what Jesus had been, and nevertheless the identification is made precisely on the plane of "Behold the man." The omnipotent Lord, the sight of whom is unbearable and provokes the prostration of the witness, has nevertheless indispensable need of a witness; and the first act, the first word is the appeal to the testimony of man: "Write what you see . . ." (1:11). The direct revelation can be addressed to all men only in the new creation. And before that time to those who are chosen to bring it to others. Then this direct revelation can *never* have for its end the pleasure, satisfaction, personal enrichment, perfection of the one to whom it is addressed. The direct revelation has meaning only as an appeal to witness, to engage a man in bearing the attestation of the truth of God in the midst of others. And the latter can receive something from God only by the mediation of other men who have obtained that function exclusively. This all-powerful Lord speaks to his witness and tells him two things (1:17–18): "I died," and "Fear not." "I died": the death of Jesus is the point of departure, the decisive moment (I desire to know only Jesus Christ crucified) of the power of Christ. Much more than the dazzling vision, it is the "I died" that is the true revelation of this power. It is in this death that everything begins, and it is necessary to begin with it. If the Son of Man is now the powerful Lord, it is because he has been the crucified, miserable, abandoned Jesus. Unnecessary to insist upon this theme today completely banal, but which conceals the most profound depths of the Gospel.

"Fear not": first of all, "You have nothing to fear from me. My power is not against you. I am with you. Only see the seven stars. The Lord holds the seven stars in his hand, and your life is among them. You should, on the contrary, fear Satan and death. But Satan and Death no longer have any final, dramatic power. The one who is with you is the First (at the beginning) and the Last (to whom the last word belongs). He is absolutely Living, which means that all life is concentrated in him. And that life is completely victorious. Death, the kingdom of Death, the domain of chaos—all that, now, belongs to me, who holds it. It is not Death who holds me. Consequently you no longer have anything to fear, neither from death nor from the enemy." I believe that finally the whole Apocalypse can be summed up in this word: "Fear not." It is a demonstration (in the etymological sense: "to show, starting from . . .") of the supremacy of Jesus Christ over all that which man could fear.

But this all-powerful Lord stands in the midst of the Church; he holds the Church in his hand. The seven lampstands, in the midst of which he stands, are then the seven churches. We must notice that these churches are all located in Asia, which means, relative to Patmos, to the east, in the east: traditionally, it is from the east that the Son of Man must come again, according to the prophecies and also according to the popular imagination of the moment; it is east from Eden.

In addition we must stress once more the relationship between one and seven. Seven lampstands, seven churches; that means, then, the Church in its totality. But then why not one? It seems to me that this signifies precisely diversity in unity. Seven is truly the number of the whole, of the complete, of the one; but nevertheless not the one identical to itself and immobile: the diversified unity (understood as including God *and* his creation); whether it is local diversities (the parishes, the geographical places, which are actually evoked in the names of the churches to whom the letters are addressed), or the doctrinal diversities (the denominations, which are also noted in the letters). Whichever it might be, we must remember that the Church is composed of various elements and we should not be troubled by this. Each of the separate churches, in this whole, has a part of the truth, a part of virtue, a part of light, and makes a special vocation of it, a unique relationship with the Lord. But all are then represented symbolically by the lampstands (taken up again, of course, by the saying of Jesus about the light that is not put under a bushel). Thus the Church is not the light. But it bears the light, in a way that makes it shine as brightly as possible, in order to clarify as many things as possible and dissipate as much darkness as possible. But there is also a close relation between the lampstand and the light: the latter is only there where there is a lampstand—a Church. There is no manifestation of the divine light outside the Church. And this is certainly the reason why the Apocalypse is opened by the Church, that it is a revelation addressed to the Church, and that the Church is the determining factor in relation even to history. Inasmuch as God has chosen that his light shine in the Church and be borne by the Church, he is faithful; and there is not then any explosion of divine light just anywhere, with just anyone, in just any fashion whatsoever (which points out the frequent error today according to which Christians are convinced that unbelievers, anti-Christians, revolutionaries, and the like, are bearers of the divine light and of the word of God). But if the Church is diversified, if in her concrete truth she is the lampstand (and only that!) of the light, she is also and at the same time in the hand of the Lord, who is not content to be in her midst, but who *holds* her. She is still diversified (seven stars) but unified because he holds all of her in one hand. The right, that of action. The unity of the Church is exclusively the fact that Jesus Christ holds her entirely in his hand. There is no other unity. But that means also that he himself directs the churches (and not a vicar); he communicates his word and his will to the churches who can actually know them. But, moreover, this communication is made by "an angel." (We recall that the angel, messenger of the Lord, bearer of his will and of his word, never exists in himself, by himself; he does not exist except strictly by the message that he bears—at the "moment" when he fulfills the function with which he has been charged.) For certain exegetes (upon the basis of some texts), that would mean the bishop, the spiritual heads of the communities. I believe, rather, that we are in the presence of the designation of the spiritual being itself of the Church in her relation to God. Each church is also mysteriously "represented" by a spiritual power. Such is the first vision of Christ raised, glorified, who appears then as both all-powerful and here Lord of the Church.

Word of God and Lord of the End Time (19:9–16; 22:6–16)

We must consider the corresponding vision, which closes the book, and where we find again the same indications and in particular the affirmation that punctuates the totality of the revelation: "I am the First and the Last, the Beginning and the

End." This vision of the Lord, which relates to the new creation, to the celestial Jerusalem, to the recapitulation, and consequently dominates the last section of the Apocalypse, is double: at the beginning of this section (19:9–16) he appears as the Word of God triumphant; at the end (22:6–16), he is the Lord of the End Time. In other words, the vision of the celestial Jerusalem is situated between the two: it is included between the triumphant Word and the End Time. It is *at the interior* of the Lordship of Jesus Christ. And we are coming to see that just as there is a relation between the glorified Christ and his Church, so there is a relation between the Lord and the New Jerusalem. But not completely the same: the Church is seven, and the Lord is hidden in her midst; the Kingdom is One and it is situated at the interior, in the midst of the Lord who embraces the whole. It is the recapitulation. A formal indication showing that in fact chapters 19 to 22 must be read as a whole, and the *two* visions of Christ the Lord considered as a whole, is the repetition of the scene of John with the angel. Twice John, seized by the immensity of the vision, by the majesty of that which approaches, wishes to prostrate himself before the angel, and twice, the same declaration: "You must not do that! I am a fellow servant with you and your brethren . . . . Worship God!" (19:10 and 22:8–9). Far from being a clumsy doublet, we have, on the contrary, a rigorous indication that it is the *same vision,* but which, being complex, is repeated; that it is also the same personage who is the object of the vision; finally, that it is a reconstituted whole.

Jesus Christ conqueror is then presented under two aspects. Very different; the one is objective, distant, triumphant, animated: the victorious horseman. The other is the Lord near and faithful who guides the wonderful communion of the New Jerusalem. The triumphant horseman is the Word of God. The Word. And several indications encountered in the first vision are found again here: the sharp sword issuing from the mouth, the flaming fire of the eyes, the armies of heaven clothed in white linen; the girdle of gold is replaced by the diadems, but the significance is the same. The sole different point in the description is the robe, which is dipped in blood: which could be an allusion to Jewish images concerning the judgment administered by the Messiah; but it appears to me at least as certain that it is the triumphal robe of the victorious Roman general, the purple of which, according to tradition, signifies the blood of his enemies. But here we must not forget that the only blood is that of the Lamb. Several times in fact we find in our text the formula that the elect have washed, bleached their robes in the blood of the Lamb. The robe dipped in blood is here the attestation of the divine Word, become irrevocably true by the sacrifice of the cross. The robe dipped in blood is not different from the white robe of the first vision: it is not red with the blood of enemies; it is white by the purification obtained through the cross. This Word, personified in the horseman, is then victorious: the sole victory of God is the fact of his Word (the Word incarnate, crucified, and nevertheless also and at the same time, the same as the Creator Word of the first day). He wins no other victory. He has no other weapon. The Word is his only mediation (and Jesus is the only mediator). He manifests no other power, no other judgment. The Word is that of the origin, and his true victory is not the "death of the infidels," the "implacable judgment," but the creation of the New Jerusalem. We are here in the presence of the joyous mystery: just as, at the beginning of days, God said . . . and things were, so the vision of the New Jerusalem begins and can begin only by the Word. There is exact repetition: the Word of God who has been Creator is now Creator anew. But now also we know *who* that Word is—Jesus Christ. He is King of Kings and Lord of Lords not by a military victory but because he is the Word: sole founder, sole originator, sole innovator, capable of an absolutely New, which no King, no Power, no Lordship has ever been able to be. And this horseman is named Faithful and True. Now each of these two terms can include a double significance.

Faithful is first of all the one who is faithful to, which means: this Word is truly faithful to the will of God, actually expresses it. It is the obedience of Jesus in relation to his Father, or again the faith of Jesus, of which the decisive importance is known. He is the one who, even more than Abraham, has lived by faith and it is upon the faith *of* Jesus that ours rests. But he is also the one who provokes faith. The Word of God summons our faith, addresses it, evokes and awakens it. There is here a decision to make in terms of this appeal of the white horseman, and it is the decision of faith.

True: he is at the same time the one who is true; he is the true Word of God. There is not any other. No other than Jesus is the manifestation of the Truth of God. There is no other truth than that of the Gospel: all the rest is the pure fabrication of men with the limits and errors that that entails. But also, and what we are saying leads directly here: he is the Truth itself. I am the Way, the Truth, the Life. The truth is not an idea, is not a theory, is not an emotion, is not science: it is a person, it is the white horseman alone who is not symbolic of an abstraction (as would be the case in gnosis; there is no allegory in the strict sense in the Apocalypse), but who, as we have attempted to show in the preceding chapter, is Jesus Christ. Finally this white horseman bears a name that he alone knows. It is correct to say, which most commentators do, that this secret name refers to his transcendence and divinity—this is true. But precisely, we must emphasize the apparent contradiction in 19:12–13: He bears a name that he alone knows. He is named Word of God: that means that we are strictly unable to penetrate its mystery. Which is to say that, the name being the most profound spiritual reality of a being, we can neither know how it is uttered, whence it proceeds, nor even in what way exactly it is Word of God.[3] We can receive it but never prove it. We can believe and know that it is the truth (faithful and true) but never experience it in its spiritual profundity. It is both revealed (he is called—) and hidden (a name that cannot be known). When he is revealed by his Word, God is never exposed upon a public place; he remains as mysterious as if God had never spoken. But he has spoken; the communication is established between this Thou and this I. We know who the truth is. We can have confidence. And go on from there.

We find now the other face of the Lord of the End Time in 22:6–16. He is clearly always the Word of God, but here as

Recapitulation. And the vision then recalls the first which opens the Apocalypse with chapter 1, since we find again (22: 13) the first and the last, the beginning and the end; while the vision of the Word of God as white horseman evokes the third part where there is also a white horseman of which we will speak again. That which essentially characterizes this last vision is the proclamation that it is the end time. "Behold, I am coming soon"; "the time is near"; there is also the imminence of judgment. Of course, it seems that now we are fairly clear about this end time. Historians say traditionally that the first Christian generation believed that this "end of the world" and the return of Jesus Christ would happen very quickly, before the death of the first disciples ("this generation shall not pass away," etc.). They had taken some words of Jesus literally. Then the end of the world would have been expected at the moment of the taking of Jerusalem, and since nothing happened, that would have produced quick discouragement, a crisis of faith, an uncertitude in the first communities (and, in part, the Apocalypse would have been written in order to respond to this). This whole little drama is a rationalization of what the historians themselves would have felt if they had been in the shoes of the first disciples. I am not at all certain that the exegesis upon which this interpretation rests is objectively scientific. And very particularly it is dependent upon an identification of the end time, the return of Jesus, and the end of the world (in the rational sense of the phrase, in terms of the idea of a time whose duration is finite, or of a creation which will be destroyed according to the image of the Flood). These three elements are not necessarily connected, and it is not obvious that the first Christian generation had confounded them. On the contrary, numerous texts seem to manifest the difference between these three aspects, or at least the relativity of their relationship. If it is true that the First Epistle to the Thessalonians is the oldest writing of the New Testament, the first of the canonical writings, it is just there that we find the affirmation, "But as to the times and seasons," etc. (5:1). Now, precisely, this is a clear warning against the conviction of a rapid return. But the fact that the end of the world and the return are not instantaneous does not at all prevent the real, effective declaration of the end time. This is what we find strongly marked here. On the one side, I am coming *soon;* on the other, the time is near. This last affirmation is relative to the fact that the Kingdom of God is already here. It is in your midst and in you. When we say that we are in the last times, we do not say that the number of days which separate us from the end of the world is brief, but that these times are last *qualitatively* whatever the duration might be. (And the whole of Scripture with us. And this is not a later spiritualizing interpretation; it is truly coherent with the whole thought of the first Christian generation.)

What then is its content? I believe that three aspects can be seen, in agreement with the Apocalypse. First, the judgment of the world, of the evil powers, of the rebellion, of the hatred, *is* carried out. It has been done upon the cross of Jesus Christ; it is a thing already realized, which no longer has need of being done. The decision of the "supreme judge" has been taken; there is no novelty, no repetition to be expected. There is no other judgment because the totality of evil has been revealed, exerted against Jesus; and he has borne, accepted, assumed that totality. There cannot be a *more* to this judgment. How could one imagine an addition to the fact that God has judged God, that God has condemned God, that God has taken upon himself the totality of the evil and error of man? What could there be *after?* In the second place, the Kingdom of Heaven and the resurrection have already begun. There is the whole well-known explanation of the parables: the hidden leaven, the smallest seed, etc. The Kingdom is planted in the midst of the world and it never ceases to grow even if we do not see it. The resurrection has been accomplished in Jesus and works already in each of us (you are already raised with Christ): so much so that a continuous process is inaugurated, of which the logic and power are inflexible. Nothing can annul them or turn them back. There can then be a certain quantitativeness, an increase, an expansion: there is no qualitative or exterior leap to this. How could there be an addition to the fact that the Kingdom of God is here and that death is vanquished? What *other* could there be *after* God himself has begun to be all in all, after the process is engaged that will end necessarily and without deviation, without possibility of evasion (if not without delay), at the complete fulfillment of which precisely the Apocalypse speaks? This is why the Apocalypse can give the feeling of an ineluctable mechanism; but it is very essential to observe that it is this Apocalypse which also describes for us the end of the world and which at the same time declares to us that we are in the end time; that our time, whatever its duration might be, is eschatological, already in A.D. 90 as well as in this day when I write. And third, the conclusion of these first two aspects is that the end time signifies that nothing more actually new can happen in history. Nothing can efface the cross and the empty tomb. Nothing can any longer happen to cause a situation as if these events had not been. And nothing can then efface the work which has been accomplished there, at that moment. Nothing can any longer effect a wiping out and a new beginning. Begin what again? Add what? What could be added to the perfect meeting of God and man, to the union established? If the salvation of man is accomplished in Jesus Christ, what could be added? When the reconciliation between two enemies is effected, in the most complete and perfect fashion, what could be added? The friendship can simply begin to flower and develop. There is then no longer an ineluctability of evil with its apparent aptitude for innovation and liberty, with the discovery every time that evil had won (which makes us revive mechanically psycholoanalysis or Marxism, with their suspicion) but with the disconcerting regularity of which Baudelaire speaks: "The tiresome spectacle of immortal sin . . ., an oasis of horror in a desert of ennui," with death the only novelty: "O Death, old captain . . . at the bottom of the unknown to find anew . . . ."

On the contrary, evil is decisively set aside because God has died and, after that, evil can no longer do anything else. And a new beginning is posed, because Jesus is raised. And after that there can no longer be any decisive innovation. No other beginning can be posed. Neither that of the French Revolution, nor that of socialism: these are false beginnings; the only thing of which man in fact is stripped conclusively is the power from now on to pose a new beginning. Thus the hazardous time, the time of historical suspense, the time of the apparent equality of the forces of good and evil, the time of the invention of an incoherent history, the time of the closure of man upon himself, the time of religion and of the responsibility that man takes upon himself to compensate for the evil that he does, the time of the elaboration of a society, of a Political when the pride of man affirms, "now all is absolutely new"— these times are finished. The corner has been turned. We are upon another way. But nothing tells us the length of this way.

I know well the reaction that such an explanation can produce: "You rob man of his dignity, of the importance of what he does. How can that history still have importance if man cannot add anything; if his works are nullified in advance; if there are no longer any events in that history?" It is true that, at the moment when theologians are striving to give importance again to the work of man, to his action, when man is made a demuirge, co-creator with God, fulfiller of a creation either badly made or virtual, and man is even very simply assimilated to God, who would be only the revealer (or the occasion) of the power that exists in man, of the good that man is, God being no more than the hypothetical possibility that man fulfill himself—then at such a theological moment, our interpretation is scandalous. And nevertheless, I am sorry, but nothing has any more meaning in the gospel if after the cross and the resurrection there is still an uncertainty concerning salvation and life. It is not man who achieved salvation or who recapitulates it in each individual or in the collective life. And if there is no longer any uncertainty; if we are delivered neither to chance nor to the good or bad will of man to pose a true beginning, then we are in the end time. Of course, that takes away nothing from the importance of what man does, but only annuls his pretension, his pride in posing a new beginning (the pride of Cain) and in being able to deviate by himself from his destiny. Except for that, man can act, invent, accumulate his works; it does not at all cancel the seriousness of history. But a penultimate seriousness. It will be a matter always of relative

works. Which does not mean that they ought not to be done.[4]
It is very important, even for God, and we will find it again in
the study of the recapitulation. But it is neither decisive nor
ultimate. There can be quantities of innovations (and we see
them in science) and ventures (we see them in politics), but
neither one nor the other can change the decision made in the
relation of man with God, or rather of the new covenant, or
further: "God with and for man." We can even live out great
numbers of dramas, but these only appear to be dramas; which
does not mean that they are not grievous or serious. But it is
not the ultimate suffering or the last seriousness. Man can
invent what he will, be delivered to whatever aberrations he
desires; he will no longer evade what God has decided in Jesus
Christ; he will no longer evade the love of God.

There is another possibility, which is equally excluded; it is
the possibility of the human aberration (that man cease to be
man). This is the meaning of 22:15, which can appear to be a
banal repetition of former judgments but which, put into relation with "the time is near," with the end time, takes another
meaning: it is no longer *possible* that man become a dog, conduct himself as a beast, be delivered to infernal powers, be
devoted to the vanity of idols, and enter into the nothingness
of the lie. We are in the presence of a "judgment against the
nations" (outside, the dogs, the magicians, the lewd, the murderers, the idolaters, and whoever loves and practices the lie),
but it is the exclusion of the *last* possibility that man cease to
be man, that man become the actual prey of chaos and nothingness: this is simply no longer possible; that is all. Apart
from that there will still be murders and even genocide, aberrant sexual conduct and lies: but we know that all that is from
now on only a superficial infection; there can be neither gan-
grene nor the mutation of the human species into chaos. It is
with this force that we are filled. Jesus is revealed as Lord of
the end time, at the same time as in fact the one in whom all
has been created; then that creation can no longer be divided
nor annihilated. I am coming soon (and that presence will be
the actual revelation of all that we with difficulty apprehend
through a cloud as being the end time); and then in reality

when the moment of the recapitulation comes, when the work of man is added (by grace) to this work of God, when Jesus the risen man is for all at the same time the absolute Lord, when it appears that Jesus is truly (22:16) the offspring of David (which means that the union between Jews and Christians is effected) and the bright morning star, which is to say that the morning announced by the star becomes the reality of Light, then this will be in fact the closing of history and, if one wishes, the "end of the world." But this implies a distance between the moment of the "Last Time" and that end of the world. Exactly as there is a distance between the star which appears and announces the morning, and then the illumination of dawn. But when the star of the morning is there, when it is seen, we know well that the night is ended, that inevitably the course of the day is proceeding and that soon the sun will appear. It is in the same way that the end time begins in the midst of the time where we live out the end of our night and the inauguration of the incommensurably new.

But the proximity of the Lord ("I am coming *soon*"), which must be announced ("Do not keep secret the words of this book"), whether it is a spiritual or a temporal proximity, implies assuredly the double aspect of "consolation-hope" and warning. On the one hand, we are not desperate: all is already won. On the other hand, hurry (not to be converted, or to be improved: that is the perspective of a narrow salvation, of an individual standpoint and of a moralism, which is not the thought of the Apocalypse[5]) to accomplish your work. If it is true that the new beginning has been posed, hasten to make use of it; if it is true that the recapitulation is near, hasten to do the work offered to God, which will enter into that summation of history and without which the *fullness* of time cannot be achieved.

A last remark: in this double image of the same Lord in chapters 19 and 22 we find again in this fourth section the synthesis of that which was divided in the first and second. In fact we have seen the all-powerful Lord as Lord of the Church and now he is Lord of the celestial Jerusalem and of the end time (implying that the Church is the point of inauguration of the Kingdom). And, moreover, in the second section (of history) we meet the Word of God galloping across the world. There is then an actual reunion of the two designations in arriving at the completion of history and at the same time the conclusion of the role of the Church. The final Lord (who is certainly not an omega point, since it is he who *comes*, and not at all everything which converges, which mounts up toward him) is the "synthesis" (so to speak) of the one who has traversed history in modifying it by his presence and the one who reigns without division over the people that he has constituted, as few as they have been.

Immolated Lamb and Son of Man
(5:6–7; 14:1–5, 14)

We come now to the other face, the other aspect of the Lord: he is not only the glorious one whose visage is as the sun, whose voice is like many waters, but at the same time the immolated, slaughtered, crucified Lamb. Here with still two different images: the one is situated at chapter 5 and refers to history. The other is situated *after* the prodigious phenomenon of the Incarnation has been set forth, where he reappears as Lamb for the judgment (Ch. 14). And here again we recall the essential character of these distinctions: the one who is present in history, who unravels the secret of history, who holds it, and allows it to unfold as history is clearly not the All-Powerful Lord: he is the immolated Lamb. In the same way the one who presides at the "Last Judgment," at the separation of the good and the evil, at the condemnation, at the ultimate combat, is not the powerful athlete, muscular and majestic, of the admirable Sistine (but what an error, Michelangelo!); it is not the "chief of the heavenly militia"; it is not the Lord of Lords; it is the Lamb, the crucified, the stripped, the annihilated, the weakest of all men, the one who has neither beauty, nor honor, nor power. And I think that should enlighten us decisively both upon that which history is for the Apocalypse and also upon what the last judgment is.

But first of all a short word upon this choice of symbol: why has the lamb been taken as representative of Jesus Christ? The idea of a cultural image referring to a pastoral civilization is infinitely too simplistic, all the more so as at the time of the Apocalypse this was already no longer the case. The idea is more serious[6] that it is a matter only of a resumption of the paschal lamb, of the death of the lamb in order to recall and celebrate the exodus from Egypt. Assuredly we are here in the presence of one of the signs attesting that the entire Apocalypse must be read in the paschal light. At issue in this case is the granting, the fulfillment, of the promise made during the Passover outside the Church, of the realization of which Passover was the image, the prophecy, and the anticipation. That the immolated Lamb is set in immediate reference to the Old Testament is also attested to us by the accumulation of his titles in chapter 5: the lion of Judah and the offshoot of David. We are then here before the one in whom the diverse representations of the Messiah in the Old Testament come to converge. Which signifies that Jesus is the end of the history of Israel but also that it is in that history that the secret of the history of humanity resides. The book of this history is closed. No one can open it or read it. History is truly the account of folly told by an idiot; it is sound and fury: who can know it and disclose its meaning? It is not necessary that there be an exterior and all-powerful personage who unrolls this history like a cinema reel. The revealer of history is not a cinema operator. He does not show a spectacle nor give in an exterior way a meaning to the reel which unfolds. He does not intervene upon a matter which would remain inert, an object. The one who can disclose the meaning is the one who, on the one hand, has been closely involved in the history that the people of Israel represent as a historic people, and also the one who in person has plunged into history but who also is found at the heart of that history in order to give it a meaning. Now then, precisely, where does history risk finding an axis on the basis of which it can be ordered, which is to say comprehended (in the etymological sense) if not in the unheard-of event of the God who becomes man in the victory of life over death, in

God's willingness to bear the evil of man, which is to say in the slaughtered Lamb which is nevertheless raised up? This implies then that it is at the heart of history that history can be read. But it is a matter of the immolated Lamb, of the paschal Lamb, and that means two things: history is not mastered by a powerful God who does it in his own fashion, according to his own thought and fantasy. History is not an invention, event after event, of the Transcendent. It is not the dream of God. It is not the manipulation of the omnipotent hand of the Creator. Neither is it the mechanical unfolding of a pre-established order. The one who intervenes to unfold this history is the Lamb, weak, without defense, the immolated Lamb, who has plunged into death, who has actually been stripped of everything. The one who has submitted to the mastery of men, has been condemned, put to death by them. He is *under* the power of man. It is this God who alone has power to disclose, reveal, history. And this then means that history is certainly made by men (but also by the powers); and this is confirmed to us by the fact that each time the Lamb opens a seal something *happens:* then contrary to the cinema reel, there is an actual event which takes place. This is not a spectacle which is projected, but an action which is launched, the action of that which constitutes history.

And the second signification is that not only is the whole meaning of history rooted in the paschal Mystery, but the paschal Mystery is that of liberation. The Word, the passage, the crossing, is the celebration of liberation. History can be read only in the light of this liberation. It has no other meaning than the final liberty of man. But we must pay attention: it is a matter of the immolated Lamb, of the work of God in Egypt, of which we are told clearly that the people of Israel have been delivered by the all-powerful arm of the Lord. It is subsequently the acceptance by God even of his death, of his abandonment, in order that man be delivered from evil. In other words it is not at all by the works of man that the latter reaches liberty. He must *be liberated;* he must be *set free.* And consequently it is not in making his history himself that he can lead it toward his liberation. Liberty will be the final product, but by means of the recognition of the sovereignty of the Lamb. The purpose of history is certainly to attain liberty. But a liberty which is never the natural product of events. To leave Egypt in order to reach liberty, it is necessary to depart (to depart from the place where the people of Israel had their history), to pass through the Red Sea (to cross the absolute barrier of enclosure in a historical condition) and to enter into the desert (there where man no longer has any power . . .). It is then a liberty given by God, not made by man, which is going to be the profound signification, at the same time as the objective of history: the combination of historical forces between them, no more than the explanation of events can result in liberty for man. And this is confirmed by the fact that, once more, it is a matter of the Lamb, which is to say nonpower, nonresistance to death. Much more: the slaughtered Lamb, that is, the one who has precisely totally renounced his personal authority (to the profit of the will of his Father) and who has submitted to death, who consequently is in nothing appropriate to attest liberty, since he is plunged into the most total of dependencies, of absences, of necessities, that of death. Here we are in contradiction with the explicit will of history and of men who make history. Triumph of the instinct for preservation at the minimum, of the will to power at the maximum. The work of man in economic, or scientific, or technical, or political history is always the quest for domination, for authority, for success, for expansion, for growth. And this then would be in accord with a devouring and gigantic God; in fact the gods that men have made when they are gods who make history are of this type—Saturn or Jupiter. But we see that the contrary is announced to us. The master of the meaning of history is not the thundering Jehovah dear to Victor Hugo, but the nonpowerful, the stripped. That no man, no historical force, will ever realize. The liberty attested by the paschal Lamb as the meaning of history is not the product of the accumulation of human powers but the intervention *(intervenire)*, the mysterious insertion, of the Nonpower of God. Without doubt, this Lamb is also risen (the Lamb is raised); he is the lion of Judah, he has seven horns (the power of God) and seven eyes (the Spirit of God sent out over the earth). But we must not be deceived: it is as immolated Lamb that these attributes are added to him. This is not an accumulation of uncoordinated images to designate the second person of the Trinity; it is the dead Lamb who *is* the offshoot of David to whom are given the solemn *titles* and expressions of divinity. It is inasmuch as he has accepted the sacrifice that he has been raised above every name (Philippians 2). Consequently, if he reigns over history it is not as crowned King but as the incarnation of love itself, the love which goes so far as to give itself, to abandon itself; and if he has power it can be no other power than that of *this* love. It is this love which has become sovereign. There is no other reign of God over the history of man, and this is why, once more, man is certainly thus independent in order to fabricate his world. But all that he does, the greatest horrors, the greatest injustices, are situated, can only be situated, at the *interior* of the Love of God and lead, whether he knows it or not, toward the miracle of his liberation in God. "You are worthy to reveal the meaning of History because you have been immolated, and you have redeemed men for God by your blood . . ." (5: 9). Such is the song of the animals and elders before the Lamb and such in fact is the meaning of this slaughtered Lamb who is the Lord of history.

Finally in the fourth section we find the Lamb again, but again (as in the fifth) with a composite image (14: 1 and 14). It is, I repeat, the section concerning the judgment. The Lamb (vs. 1) is also and at the same time the Son of Man (vs. 14), which is to say that we now find again a synthesis of that which was divided between the first and the second: the Lord who is as a Son of Man, and the Lamb of which we have been speaking. The Church and history are rejoined in the event of the final judgment. Together, they move toward their fulfillment. The truth of history brutally appears and the Lamb is revealed as being the meaning of it, which implies the destruction of all that which has been the inverse of the Lamb in the course of history (lust for power, etc.). The truth of the Church also appears, but also in the judgment, that is, at its own end: since there is no triumph of the Church, no direct fulfillment of the Church in the Kingdom. The Church no longer exists in the Kingdom of God. The judgment is also the end of the Church and that in the same degree according to which he who was the Son of Man, Lord of that Church, is now, in the judgment, Lord of the new creation. The Church was set apart to be the privileged place where Jesus Christ was *recognized* (discerned and accepted) as Lord. Now and by means of Judgment he will be recognized as the one whom the entire world has as its authority, which is to say there will be *re-cognized* what was not known during the course of history; but the one who is recognized as Lord is the Son of Man. And it is according to this measure that the Church has no longer any reason for being: it was the people of God. *All,* raised, by means of judgment, are now the people of God. That transformation is also what the passage in chapter 14 expresses, from verse 1 where we see the Lamb in the midst of the complete people (the 144,000) who bear his name and the name of his father written on their foreheads, the redeemed of the earth, who follow the Lamb everywhere he goes and who constitute the people of the Church, to verse 14, where the Son of Man reaps the totality of the earth; but the reaping has for its purpose to garner the harvest, "which is now ripe." And here we are in the presence of the Totality (no longer only the Church), which is thus gathered.

The judgment is then dominated by the double visage of Jesus Christ: the crucified Lamb and the glorified Son of Man. It is not the deed of the Omnipotent God, absolute master and judge without law. The law of the judgment is, James tells us, the law of liberty. Liberty here is exactly the distance and play that exists between the Lamb and the Son of Man. Liberty is safeguarded in the judgment itself because it is the Lamb who judges. And also because it is the Son of Man who reaps; now indeed confidence can be had that liberty is assured to man. The Lamb and the Son of Man are not identical. The sacrifice of God and the glory given to man: it is in this reversal that liberty is born: the liberty of the God who is, which is never attested elsewhere than in the fact that it can be the Father who gives himself (and at the limit that *he* can decide to die), and the liberty of man, which begins only when this man finds again in God and by grace the place and stature and visage and image that were destined for him in the creation.

Judgment according to the law of liberty[7] but also judgment of the love of God. Because there is no other judgment than that which is dominated by the love of God. And we find it strongly indicated in the plan of this section: this terrible judgment, of the seven bowls, of the great prostitute of the fall of Babylon, begins exactly at this chapter 14, of which the first image is that of the Lamb. How could it be said more clearly that all that is read afterward, all these abominable things, are under the cover, under the signification, under the embrace of the love of the Lamb. And nowhere else. That all is situated *in* the cross of Jesus Christ, that these texts must not be read in themselves but only by relation to that love which sacrifices itself for those who hate it. And this very positive aspect is confirmed to us by verse 14. The Son of Man appears here surrounded by six angels (three who prophesy the judgment, three who express the actual decision of God to exercise the judgment now). But there is a distinction between this Son of Man who holds a sickle in order to reap and the angel who knows: the Son of Man reaps in order to garner, while after him there is an angel who holds the sickle in order to gather in the grapes (14: 17): but it is a matter of the vintage for the wrath of God. Then it is not Jesus who presides at this wrath; it is not he who throws back into the vat of the wrath of God. He is not charged with the division between the saved and the damned. He is not charged with executing the decision of damnation. But then who? Moreover, we have understood that it is Jesus who will judge men. All men? And finally does not the attribution here to Jesus of his title Son of Man mean precisely that? It is the man completely fulfilled (in Jesus) who judges all men. But he judges them for their salvation. Then who is going to be condemned; who is plunged into the vat of the wrath of God? We will attempt later to comprehend what this judgment can signify in love and for liberty, the judgment which, on Jesus' part, does not envisage damnation. But in closing we must make a last remark: there is clear confirmation that in the text this judgment is exercised by the Son of Man as such: he holds the sickle. But we see (14: 15) that an angel comes out of the temple (from the secret abode of God) and cries with a loud voice to the one who is seated upon the cloud (Jesus after his ascension): "Put in your sickle and reap." We recall what an angel is: the agent of a will of God, without any specific existence, any autonomy, and very particularly the bearer of a word of God. Consequently, in this case there is no initiative: it is not he, as angel, who gives an order to the Son of Man. And if the word that he declares is so certain and strong that the latter obeys and puts in his sickle, it is because we are in the presence of a word of God. In other words the harvest is effected by a word of God, who decides it. And the Son of Man cannot by himself take the initiative to do it. He harvests *when* the Father tells him. This corresponds exactly to the response of Jesus in the Gospel: "But of that day or that hour no one knows . . . not even the Son, but only the Father" (Mark 13:32). Thus for the Apocalypse, even risen, even raised next to God, the Lord still does not know the mystery of the time of judgment; and he awaits the sovereign order. Even in the unity of the Father and the Son, the latter remains in humility and obedience, true Son of Man, trusting and without pretending to usurp being as God, true Lamb who continues to be crucified up to the end of the world.[8]

·4·

THE CHURCH AND HER LORD
Chapters 2 to 4

I will not dwell long upon this first section of the Apocalypse because it is the clearest, the most evident, that upon which the commentators have most easily come to agreement. However, we must notice that it ought not be considered, as is done too often, an introduction or a preamble. On the contrary, we are immediately at the heart of the revelation where Jesus is from the beginning presented as Lord of the Church. Why is it necessary to begin with the Church and not with the world or the general history of all men? From all evidence, for us the Church is a section of society; the history of the Church is included in the general history of men. While that which is conveyed to us here is that the relation of the Church to her Lord, the presence of the Lord for his Church, dominates the whole of human reality. We will observe in fact what we have already indicated for the second section: the Lord is not himself present in the history; that which participates in history is the Church, but the latter would be nothing more than an ideological and sociological component of society if she were not first of all and above all tied, bound, to her Lord. And if Jesus Christ is indeed the Lord of history, it is by his Church in history that this Lordship must appear. Emphasizing, of course, that the Lordship of Jesus Christ over his Church is different from his Lordship over history, as the presentations obviously manifest it: in the Church he is the Son of Man and is revealed in power; in history he is the immolated Lamb (risen, as we have observed in the preceding chapter).

Here then we find seven letters addressed to seven churches. We will not insist upon what can be found in any commentary: for example, that of these churches only one is known to us (that of Ephesus); that they form apparently upon the map a nearly complete circle (and corresponding then to the lampstands that surround the Lord); and we will not attempt to discover the "teachings" that one is always curious to obtain—for example, who are the Nicolaitans or Jezebel? It is probable that the seven letters are related to the concrete situation of the Church in Asia. John has received the order to write "what is" (1:19); but the character of these letters, the number seven, the solemn and general admonition that each contains imply that they hold a teaching given for all time and for every church: for the Church. God addresses to each a message, a special vocation; because all these churches are put in question, some by persecution, others by temptation.

All the letters are constructed in the same fashion with first a specific designation of the Lord of the Church who addresses the letter, a body, and a conclusion, which always contains a summons to combat with a promise of victory and the affirmation of the necessity of the Spirit. The titles concerning Jesus placed at the head of each letter are each (except for the seventh letter) a reminder of one of the attributes of the Son of Man described in chapter 1. Then we find again for Ephesus, the one who holds the seven stars and walks among the lampstands (2:1; 1:12 and 16); for Smyrna, the one who is First and Last, who was dead and who is alive (2:8 = 1:17 and 18); for Pergamum, the one who has the sharp sword (2:12 = 1:16); for Thyatira, the one whose eyes are a flaming fire (2:18 = 1:14 and 15); for Sardis, the one who has the seven stars (2:1 = 1:16, with a slight difference of interpretation which refers to vs. 6); for Philadelphia, the one who holds the key of David, who opens and shuts, who is the holy and true one (3:7 = 1:18, with in addition a reference to 14:11); and finally, for Laodicea, the title does not refer to chapter 1; it is the proclamation that Jesus is the faithful and true witness. Here we have returned to Jesus Christ witness (for example, chapter 12). All this implies then the close, direct relation between the Risen One who has appeared to John and he who is actually Lord in and for his Church. He dictates these letters as Risen One. He is present to the churches (but his presence is perceptible only to the believer). He walks in their midst (2:1): Christ is not in heaven; he is in his churches; he acts upon them and must act by them. He continually judges them, is prepared even to destroy them if that is necessary (2:5) or to punish a certain believer or a certain group (2:16, 22). But he judges uniquely by his word, which separates what is living from what is dead (2:12) and he transmits his own life to the Church (2:17, 18). Finally, he is closely related to the Spirit of God: each letter is written as a word of Jesus Christ at the beginning, coming from the Lord, but always ends with the declaration: "Let him hear what the Spirit says to the churches." All is, *at the same time,* testimony of Jesus Christ and prophecy of the Spirit. The "objective truth" is in Jesus Christ; the personification of the word (with appeal to action and to repentance), the individualized comprehension, comes from the Spirit. Such is the meaning of the apparent contradiction between the beginning (Jesus speaks . . .) and the end (each is called to appropriate this word, to make a decision in the presence of this word).

Thus at the conclusion each letter contains a promise and a warning. The warning reminds that the judgment of God is exercised constantly upon the Church. The history of the Church is the history of judgments executed, *hic et nunc* by God (as upon his people Israel). But God, before judging, warns, puts the Church in the presence of his word, in the light of her situation before him (this is the role of prophets and scholars). And he places man in a combat situation. But for this combat the conclusions of the letters are very clear: the victory has already been won by Jesus Christ; the one who accepts being engaged in this combat is assured of the assistance of the Word of God and he shares in the victory of Jesus. This is the promise precisely made each time, with different symbols, to the one who "wins" the victory. It involves necessarily the whole Church together (*each* bears *total* responsibility). But there is never here a combat or victory of the moral or socio-political order; it is a victory *first of all* spiritual, called to be inscribed *subsequently* in all human forms. It is moreover a victory won on our plane, on our level, but which goes much further: toward eternal life (2:7), communion with God (2:2), victory over death (2:17), lordship and victory over the destructive powers (3:5, 12, 21): then in all these cases there is affirmation of life, the triumph of life.

The first letter, addressed to Ephesus, is apparently centered upon Love. This church seems irreproachable; it is a church of works, capable of perseverance, of enduring persecution, that watches with care over the moral life of her members, and over their doctrine (and rejects those who do not have a correct doctrine), (we are not speaking of the identity of the Nicolaitans). Nevertheless, if to the eyes of men she is impeccable, she is subjected—even she—to the judgment of God: it is not said that she has ceased to practice good works, nor that she has abandoned her sound position. Nevertheless, the contradiction is emphasized between these works and the first, those of the beginning, of the moment of her conversion, of her first appearance as Church. The first works were the fruit of first love, of the joy and enthusiasm of the discovery of love. At issue here is not faith and its content, but love. Which is to say that, perhaps, she has fallen from the spontaneity of the relationship with God, from the attempt to please this Lord in everything, from an attachment, always new, radiant, and renewed, from the power of novelty in work that characterizes love, and from the glow of passion. All this has collapsed. "Your first love you have abandoned." All has become cold, flat. In short, we find a Church become institutional, theological, exact, rigorous, moral,[1] ceasing to live by

the impulsion of a force ever new. Now this is decadence; it is
the illustration of First Corinthians 13. It is love in the Pauline
sense, but also in that of the Epistles of John. The text tells us
that all the excellent works that can be done outside of this
love count for nothing. There is then contradiction between
the "works in themselves" and the exercise of love. "Remember
from what you have fallen." Because love is union itself
with God for the love of God. The works are of value only if
they are the fruit of God's love itself working in us. They have
no other value, no intrinsic value, not even the practice of
justice or of purity. This loss, this forgetfulness of love, is so
grave that God threatens "to remove the lampstand" (which
is logical; since the relationship with the Lord is no longer that
of love, the proximity of the lampstand and the Son of Man no
longer exists). The Lord does not put out the flame but
changes the place of the lampstand; which is to say that the
flame of truth and of love will be given to someone else. From
that time this church will remain a church apparently alive but
in reality empty. To us it would seem that Jesus Christ is
interested in keeping a solid, orthodox church, long at this
place, in her place. Not at all! He is prepared to let her fall
because the only thing that counts is that the Church keep the
love of God. Better to cease having a church than to have a
church of traditions, of good works, of institution without the
love of God. (But this does not mean that each time there is
an institution or theology, the love of God disappears—certainly
not!) Because this love is life (and the life of works also).
The task then is to find again the first works, which is to say
those that emanate directly, spontaneously, from love, those
which were a beautiful ripe fruit, and not a difficult duty. It is
a matter then of no longer putting her own works in the place
of God.

There is finally, it must be emphasized, as for each of these
letters, an agreement between the central message, the titles
at the beginning (here: the star, the light, representing the love
of God) and the conclusion (here: the promise of the tree of
life). If the Church hears this appeal to return to her first love,
she will live.[2]

The letter to the church at Smyrna is characterized by reference to true, authentic poverty before God. Here is a church that has no other virtue, no other value, than its poverty and its condition of persecution.[3] And we must notice subsequently the line that is established between poverty and persecution. In fact the church was probably composed of the poor who had neither protection nor support. This church is, among the seven, one of two not threatened with condemnation, not warned, but encountering only the love and tenderness of the Lord God. She is, we are told, subjected to the calumny and the attacks of the Jews who, from all evidence, are not condemned as Jews but as persecutors. They are Jewish people but they have ceased to be such spiritually. It is the implicit affirmation that, *in this case,* the Jews had ceased to be the elect people and the Christians have become spiritually the true Israel. In fact we must recall that the Jews were numerous at this epoch (perhaps 5 percent of the population of the empire) and were well accepted in the Roman world. (The drama of A.D. 70, the taking of Jerusalem, etc., of which the historians make a perhaps exaggerated case, had had no effect upon the influence of the Jews, on all levels of the empire.) When they put themselves on the side of the Romans against the Christians (which they did in order to separate the peoples judged dangerous), the situation of the church became very difficult. They are then called Synagogue of Satan inasmuch as they become accusers of those who ought to be their friends. This is not a word employed lightly. We are moreover in the presence of a church persecuted by the state. She has before her apparently no future, only testing, suffering, prison (ten days, signifiying a long, indeterminate duration). And Satan (the accuser, here the Jews) must then be distinguished from the Devil (the persecutor because divider, here the state). And nevertheless this poor and miserable church is *declared* rich before God. She is rich *in truth* in a way ignored and unknown by men. And John speaks in the present: "You are rich." Exactly as Jesus in the Beatitudes: blessed are you *(now)* poor. "Blessed because I the Lord, I say that you are blessed. Rich because I the Lord, I say that you are rich. And my word is always the word creative of blessedness and of the true riches." Her consolation and her hope result from the fact that God says precisely to her: "I know. . . ." The persecutions are not then outside the hand of God (and they will be limited, not willed by God: they are the work of man, but the zone of the possibility of persecution by the autonomy and initiative of man is fixed. God respects the will to persecution, which is the expression of the independence of man, but fixes a frontier to it as to the power of chaos at the creation. Up to here, but no further. Here, alas, all the wickedness of man is free to be exercised, because God leaves man to his conquering autonomy, which he had demanded. But in this persecution the church receives two exhortations from God himself: "Do not fear." When God speaks thus it is his own force that he gives. Doubtlessly this church will have to fight against more than flesh and blood; the persecution is not a simple affair of prison and torture: it is the Devil and Satan himself who are at work. But "do not fear": apparently you are alone to endure all this; in reality the Word of God is with you. And in these conditions "Be faithful unto death": this church is faithful, but God exhorts it *(then gives it the power)*. Unto death: this is the very limit of the faithfulness to be acquired. This total faith of which Kierkegaard speaks. The all or nothing of Abraham. To risk her life, and she will find it again . . . such is faithfulness unto death. This is hope lived in the concrete, in reality: if we do not have this measure of faith and hope in faithfulness then the God in which we believe is not the Lord Jesus Christ, is not the Risen One, because the exhortation comes precisely from the one who gives the crown of life; it is he, and he alone, who *makes* us faithful.

Finally we must indicate in a word the relation between the body of the letter, the beginning, and the end. This church is under a threat of death; therefore the one who speaks to her exhorts her, is the one who has passed through death (2:8) to live again. And it is the same for their destiny; these men are going to die in the persecution but will have nothing else to endure except physical death: they are assured of rising again (2:11). Thus the title of Jesus at the beginning as well as the promise made at the end are found chosen exactly in relation to the central theme of the letter, in relation to the real, disclosed situation of the church.

The church at Pergamum. With this church we find ourselves now in the presence of the problem of the truth of the professed doctrine. This church is in a dangerous situation, since it is situated where the throne of Satan is located (Sanctuary of Rome and Augustus? The emperor is proclaimed God here?). It is the capital of Asia Minor, an essential center of Greek and oriental civilization. And Jesus Christ calls it the very throne of Satan. I believe that this is actually the sign of the conflict between Revelation and civilization.[4] Here Jesus is the bearer of the sword. There is no synthesis or reconciliation possible between Revelation and the great works of human civilization.

Certainly this church is good in that it remains attached to the name of Jesus Christ, which is to say that it rejects the imperial cult. And let us not forget that the name is the spiritual sign of the reality. This church refuses to compromise in that which concerns the Lordship of Jesus Christ. Nevertheless the church is judged severely because it tolerates false doctrines. It is unnecessary to dwell upon Balaam: it is enough to recall that Balaam (Numbers 22) is the one who knew the will of God but who taught others how to oppose it. The discussion probably has to do with food sacrificed to idols (Acts 15:20; 1 Cor. 8 and 10). The consumption of this food implies a mystic act of communion with idols and a social act of participation in religious ceremonies. As far as prostitution is concerned: that means either it is a matter of sacred prostitution *(hierodules)* or else there is found here again the image common to the Old Testament according to which to go toward idols is a prostitution. In any case (and again with the Nicolaitans) the accent is then put upon doctrine and the way in which it is practiced. Works do not suffice nor faith (confessed in a formula). An exact doctrine that permits having an exact practice is also necessary. The theological formulation is essential. And we find ourselves confronted by the difficult duty of excluding from the Church those who have a theology of compromise with the world (under its various aspects, all more or less religious). The letter can be summed up: "You have kept my name (the faith) but you tolerate bad doctrines (theology)." As far as the new name is concerned, engraved upon the white stone, it is not the name of the individual, nor the baptismal name, but very clearly the name of the Lord, known individually as truth. And we find the mystery of the transformation of the person: there is upon the stone a new name that no one knows except the one who receives it. And nevertheless we know, obviously, the name of Jesus Christ! But are we certain of knowing who Jesus was? And then it is the name that each risen one receives: it is total communion with Jesus Christ. Then if the name is the expression of the spiritual being, do we know exactly who we will be when our heart of stone is replaced by a heart of flesh? Thus this well-known name (Jesus Christ) is in reality new when it becomes *ours* (when we will have put on Jesus Christ); no one can know who we will be then, except ourselves when the miracle takes place. As far as the hidden manna is concerned, which the conqueror will receive, it is the celestial food that contrasts with the food sacrificed to idols.[5] Finally, we find again the relation between the body of the letter, the address (the one who has the sword is then the one who separates the true from the false), the final promise (the true food, the hidden manna, is the good doctrine), and the stone upon which one builds; doctrinal authenticity is in the person of Jesus Christ.

The letter to the church in Thyatira. The central problem of this letter appears to me to be that of the Spirit. As in the preceding case we find again a church that has many qualities: her works do not cease to grow. She cannot be criticized for her practice of love, for the truth of her faith, for the purity of her doctrine (2:24). What then is the conflict? A woman who is called a prophetess (which is to say inspired by the Holy Spirit). She is called Jezebel, the queen who had done all to extirpate the worship of God, in supporting idolatry. There is here a promise of total possession by the Spirit in "enthusiasm," in the etymological sense. Now we are here in the presence of two categories of "condemned": the disciples of Jezebel (those who commit adultery with her) and her children (those who are defined in contrast to the preceding verse as those who are outside the possibility of repentance, whose spiritual pride forbids returning to Jesus Christ after a certain delay). Certainly here we are before the desire for the knowledge of mysteries (2:24: to sound the depths of Satan), for the gnostic search, Christian esoterism, passionate curiosity for the "problem of Evil," and for spiritual powers. To that Jesus Christ opposes clearly that there is no need of exalted mystic knowledge. It is a matter of retaining uniquely what one has, that is, what has been *given* to us (and we have no need of conquering heaven or hell). In answer to this pretension the prophetess will be thrown upon a bed (symbol of impotence) of distress (recognition of failure) and her children put to death, whereas the Holy Spirit is the Spirit of life and true power. There is then in this church another spirit than that of Jesus Christ, with his two characteristics: knowledge and power. Consequently, what Jesus requires of this church is that she exercise the discernment of spirits, that she expel the false spirits of God, the imitators.

The relation of the message of the letter to the title and the final promise is as follows: the one who speaks has eyes as a flame of fire; it is this very glance which discerns the Spirit (the fire is linked to the Spirit, flames of fire, etc.). He is the one who, at the end, will rule with a rod of iron: which is to say that he will impose discipline in the face of spiritual excesses and exercise complete authority; the Holy Spirit alone gives authority in the Church. Thus the theme of this letter is finally knowing who has authority in the Church: the Holy Spirit, who is the Spirit of Jesus, or another spirit? The last two letters that we have read have some relation to each other. They suppose three similar factors. First, there is a certain division between the members of the Church: the physical assembly of the Church contains members that Jesus Christ does not recognize as his own (partisans of false doctrines, inspired by a false spirit); so it is attested that there is not coincidence between the parish and the body of Christ. In addition, these two letters imply that *each person* has a responsibility for the totality of the Church and also for all the other members of that Church: each is responsible for what happens in his church and for the orientation that it takes. It is not a matter of a few leaders. All are equally called to act in crises such as this. *All* are likewise called to repent for the evil committed only by some. Finally, the last common point is that we find here a very broad concept of works (2:19: works embrace both faith and doctrine), and the fact of giving oneself to a spirit in order to know mysteries.

The letter to the church at Sardis. The central theme is life in Christ. We find here a church which has a good reputation but which before God is dead. However, the whole problem of this letter lies in the contradiction between "you are dead" and "nevertheless there is a remnant" (3:2–3). That probably means: before God, in the light of his truth, in the terrible discernment of his glance, you are really dead. You have no participation in the life in Christ. Your works are not found perfect, for only that is perfect which has put on Christ. Then your works have not been covered with the perfection of Christ. You have forsaken the life hidden with Christ in God. It is not a matter of the "Christian life" (on the contrary, this church leads just such a Christian life, as everybody knows) but of life *in Christ*. Nevertheless, in spite of this assured death it is *still* a church: and the letter is clearly written *to the church,* and even to her angel. And God still addresses himself to her as church and the Lord comes to her. Consequently, that means that in spite of her death there is still a reality of Church which can revive. There is then *in* this church a Remnant (probably some people, as there always is, through the worst crises, a Remnant in Israel) and on the basis of this remnant all can be reconstructed, fortified, built up. But it is evident that this remnant must neither form a sect (separate itself from the church in reproving it) nor harden into a closed core. The problem posed is then: either the remnant alone will be saved —these men, taken individually, each according to whether he is worthy (3:4, but the worthiness comes from faith alone in the Lord Jesus Christ); or the church is going to *recognize* the remnant for what it is, which is to say the sole living presence, the sole vivifying force in this church. She is called then to regroup around this remnant, which, *as collectivity* (not the individuals who compose it, but the group, the communion of the group) is infinitely weak and ready to die (3:2). Because this remnant cannot endure for long by itself as such. It is not *itself* the church. It cannot survive if the church is not reconstituted. It is the ferment, but if there is no dough the leaven is lost. A group faithful to the heart of the church does not survive indefinitely if the latter does not become truly the church. The mass in decomposition ends by killing that which still lives. In this situation God addresses his Word to his church. And it cannot be repeated enough that when God speaks he gives to the one to whom he addresses himself the very creative force of his word. But he does not transform the situation by the wave of a magic wand. He speaks in order to say what the church has the responsibility to do: four decisions, engagements.

Repent (the change of direction. I do not dwell upon repentance, theme of innumerable theological studies and meditations). *Remember.* Here, on the contrary, the importance of memory must be firmly emphasized. We do not have a permanent and immediate relation with God. We have had some personal encounters; we have experienced some interventions of God in our life; we have received the revelation of the truth of his word; and we have to live by memory. The moment of our conversion (for Israel the moment of the election of Abraham or the exodus from Egypt; for the Church, the moment of her constitution as Church) appears humanly only as a memory but it is nevertheless actual and living, *because the one who had acted then* is the Living One, the same today, yesterday, eternally. Our memory is our past, but it is the actual present of God to whom it refers. Israel, remember . . . . The memory of the deeds which enable us to live is essential. "Remember what you have received and heard": this is not a pure subjective experience, an illusion more or less effaced; that which has been received is a message perfectly objectifiable, perfectly taken up again into memory. Thus it is this past which undergirds our present. It is this memory of the past which guarantees the fidelity of our present; and this church must not seek extraordinary things, but return exactly to what she had received from God himself at her origin (this is completely offensive to a generation such as ours imbued with progress and convinced of the excellence of the groping search for one knows not what).

But the third order given by God to this church presents still more difficulty: "Keep, conserve" ("Keep the good deposit of the faith," said Paul to Timothy). And this provokes immediately the derision, the anger, of our modern theologians! Conservator of a museum, guardian of a mummy in his bandages, etc., etc.; to keep the word of the past is to prevent it from being active. But I am sorry, it is more than a question of fashion: it is a whole attitude of life. To keep the Word is not to put it in cans but to *respect* it (not to violate it, to waste it, disperse it), to consider it an objective reality exterior to myself and which measures me (it is not I who measure it; it is not I upon whom it depends; I am actually only its trustee!), to consider it a grandeur independent of me that I can *only* keep as that from which life comes to me (it is not I who give life to the word, a generally absurd pretension of so many of our theologians), and finally *to transmit it* (for if I receive it as a deposit, a deposit is transmitted; I am not its owner, and in addition, that means it is more enduring than I am and that I have only to deliver it to the one who follows in order that he in his turn may live from it). If the Church does not thus *keep* this word, she is sure to die. And this is certainly what happens to our churches today, so sure that they have the responsibility to make this word live (dead, of course, since written, etc., etc.) by modernizing it, actualizing it, furnishing it with a new cultural content, that they burst with this prodigious misunderstanding: we believe that we are charged with making this dead Word live, while it is us who are dead and it is the Word that remains alive. And this refers assuredly both to demythologization and to the theology of culture, or that of revolution, or the application of neolinguistic methods to the text, or certain aspects of hermeneutic.

Finally the last appeal addressed to this church is *vigilance:* "If you will not awake . . .": this vigilance being a manifestation of life. In reality it is a matter of not being lulled into security, neither the security of faith received in times past, nor that of judgments and values of the world. To watch and pray being the sole rigorous commandment for the expectation of the Lord. And we must not forget that for the Apocalypse we are precisely in that end time when vigilance is most essential. Here then are the four ways by which life can return to this church. And we notice two complementary elements: on the one hand, when God judges and even condemns, he at the same time exhorts and appeals to live; on the other hand, the one who is dead receives a word to live, but he himself must make the decision to do that which is commanded him. The content of the letter is confirmed by the address (He is the one who has the seven spirits of God and the seven stars, which evokes the fact that life in Christ is the essential fruit of the Spirit, and that the light is a sign of it) and by the final exhortation: the white garment that is promised is the sign of a celestial transfiguration, of participation in Christ himself, who is also clothed in a white robe, and of the gift of eternal life.[6] Of course, we relate this to the promise that "their name will not be erased from the book of life." Thus the whole theme of the letter is: You are dead, return to life.

The letter to the church at Philadelphia. Here the central theme appears to be Faithfulness to the Word. We are with the second of the seven churches not condemned by the letter addressed to her. She escapes judgment because she has little power. Power according to men as well as the spirit of power which that brings about is truly the absolute enemy of God. God is with those who have little power whether they have chosen this way or whether they are found involuntarily in this situation; and at issue is both material and spiritual power. Inversely, those who have power, of whatever kind, always turn away from God. (How can we fail to think of our own venture today with our power of money, of technique, of science, of quantity?) In her lack of power, this church of Philadelphia is that of faithfulness. She has wished to know nothing other than Jesus Christ, and Jesus Christ crucified. Doubtlessly it is not by chance that faithfulness is tied to lack of power. She has not exchanged the Word for some kind of power; "this is Faithfulness to the Word." "My Word" says the Greek, with the possible meaning "Word concerning Me." And this faithfulness is the essential work of the church more than political or evangelical or moral action, etc. In reality it is Martha and Mary once more. Listening and faithfulness (which implies, of course, also putting into practice). To this faithfulness, to this absence of power, corresponds the triple promised recompense: the first, which is terrestrial, corresponds to the power of conversion ("I will make them come . . ." 3:9). She will receive from God those who will be drawn out by him from the Synagogue of Satan; and he will bring them to recognize where the love of God is. She exercises then a mysterious influence, not by the excess and superabundance of her actions and works, for it is God himself who converts and enlightens those in whose presence this church is found.

Two other promises are spiritual: God opens the doors of the Kingdom and that corresponds exactly to the lack of power of the one who acknowledges herself subjected to this king and who claims nothing more; to the one who is poor and unprovided for but who remains in the Word of God, the door of the Kingdom is indeed open. And finally God promises to *keep* her: there is always the reciprocity to which the whole Gospel testifies: because you have kept my Word, I will keep you. The trial at issue ("I will keep you from the hour of trial which is coming") is the putting to the test which consists in placing all men in the presence of their responsibility and seeing those whose faithfulness persists. It is then our attitude toward the Word of God that decides whether we are or whether we are not kept by God at the moment of the test, the trial. This test is perhaps also, moreover, the judgment itself, because it is said immediately afterward: "I am coming soon." But we must always remember that the Word of God is neither objective nor objectifiable. It is individualized, which is to say that we do not have the right to apply each word improperly to ourselves. This "I am coming soon" is a promise made by Jesus Christ, here, to the faithful. It is evident that the one who is "unfaithful" to the Word does not have the right to appropriate wrongfully this promise, because here it is made, in a way, particularly. But whatever be the situation of this church, nevertheless, a commandment or an exhortation must be addressed to her: "Hold fast what you have." All is not play, even for her; this beloved and admirable church can still lose everything and become involved with power or security. To the word which is kept corresponds the title of the one who speaks: the Holy One (the Word of God who elects and sanctifies), the True One (the Word of Truth), who holds the key of David (the word itself is the key). And the final promise: the one who has little power upon earth becomes a column which supports the very temple of God, then the sign of the power God uses. And he receives a triple name: the secret name of God, which is evidently the unpronounceable Tetragrammaton and which supposes the absolute revelation. The name of the New Jerusalem, which is the new creation in which the faithfulness of man participates. The new name of Jesus, which is to say the Kyrios, the risen Lord, who, because risen, has a new "spiritual being" and who is the very power of life. Because you have not denied my name (3:8), I give you my name.

The letter to the church at Laodicea.[7] Here I believe that finally in this last letter the central theme is hope. Perhaps, as in the other letters, this epistle contains details unique to the city itself. Laodicea was considered very rich (some take as proof that, having been destroyed by an earthquake in A.D. 40, she had refused the help that Rome offered for her reconstruction) ("I am very rich," 3:17). The city contains a celebrated school of medicine (*salve,* 3:18) and thermal springs. It is in this epistle that we find the formula so often cited of the cold, the lukewarm, and the hot. I believe this is very simple: the lukewarm is the one who desires nothing, who does not feel any lack, any absence, who does not understand that there is anything missing, who does not aspire to anything and because of this does not hope for anything. The cold is the one to whom much is lacking and who knows it but who does not ask for anything, who is shut up in the consciousness of his failure. The hot is the one who moves and who acts. But these latter two aspects are ultimately aspects of hope. The lukewarm, who is satisfied with that which he is, is led to do nothing to change, since the actual situation appears satisfactory to him. He then does not see his real situation before God. We must always remember that as God sees man, man is (in the same way, and reciprocally, for the Beatitudes). We do not say that God sees man as he actually is, but more truly, man is such as God sees him. The gaze of God creates the reality of man. This church does not know her truth, does not know herself: this is the evangelical definition of hypocrisy (which is not a conscious lie). And from the moment there is nothing to hope for, there is no longer anything to receive ("I will spew you out"); but the opposite of hypocrisy is hope. The hypocrite does not act out a comedy, but he does not know who he is and because of this always shows only a false appearance that he believes to be his truth; and he deceives in being deceived, but in this game he shuts himself up in a situation that he does not try to leave. The one who sees his reality can only launch out in the incredible effort to leave it; and the sole possible issue at this moment is hope. Now, once more, when God pronounces judgment or makes the diagnosis known, he immediately appeals, counsels, exhorts: "Buy from me gold refined by fire, that you may be rich." Give up, as the price of that which God gives, your present riches. It is that which makes it possible for God to give the remedy for sight (to see yourself such as you are in truth), which is to say deliverance from hypocrisy and commitment to the way of hope: to expect to receive from God purity; life; purified, refined gold; and white garments. If Jesus Christ is so harsh, so rigorous, it is to lead this church to lucidity, to awareness, and thereby to conversion (the change of orientation and meaning). The severity of the Lord is the only means to produce hope. The judgment is that which provokes the salutary reaction: Not, "Lord, it is not possible that you are the one who rejects and condemns." For Jesus Christ loves this church: it is the admirable revelation of this letter, which makes us think of the story of the rich man toward whom Jesus was so severe and who went away very sorrowful; but "Jesus loved him." Even though he declares that he is going to spew her out, he says to her at the same moment: I strike, but it is because I love you. And there is the play of ambivalence: I condemn and I strike you. But at the same time I knock on your door in order that you may open and that I may enter. Although he announces his disgust for the one who is lukewarm and hypocritical, he comes to this door in order to be received. It is not the church at the end of its faithful pilgrimage who ends at the door of Paradise guarded by St. Peter; it is Christ who comes to our door, and when he arrives our door is shut. This is the symbol of the loss of hope: the one who does not hope closes his door (and here again not to hope in the Lord is not to comprehend the meaning of his judgment upon us, his apparent abandonment, his tests). He no longer wishes to have anything to do with this God; while hope is like the waiting lover: indefinitely in the silence and absence she watches to receive the one who, at the unexpected moment, cannot fail to come. But he always comes differently from what one had believed. The one who comes to respond to our needs, who brings that which will be wealth, celebration, fire, light, leading, sight, clothing, for us comes as a beggar who knocks and waits at the door until we are surely willing to open to him. He brings with him the Lord's Supper. And so it is to the most lamentable of the seven churches that Jesus Christ announces his visit and the solemn Meal taken *with her.* In none of the letters does the Lord speak with more tenderness and emotion.

Finally we find again the line running through the general meaning, the title, and the conclusion, for (3:14) Jesus is called the Amen, the Witness, the Beginning of the creation: the Amen is the affirmation that he is true, coming from God as response to the hope of man. The Witness is to tell us again: "You can hope because it is the Lord who himself bears testimony to the love of God." The Beginning: the one who is at the beginning of all things (Col. 1:16) is in himself the meaning of hope, which is the movement of life flowing from this beginning. There is not a logical deduction from the "principle" to the "consequences." There is not here a metaphysical or scientific affirmation: there is not the declaration that the initial "bang" is Christ, nor that the play of chance and necessity is the expression of this "beginning": that which is put in movement by this beginning is Hope, which promises life in spite of nonlife. Finally at verse 21 we are reminded of the ultimate fulfillment of Hope: participation in the reign of Jesus Christ.

·5·

THE REVELATION OF HISTORY
Chapters 5 to 7

We are here before the scroll, rolled up, sealed with seven seals, in the hand of God, written on the interior and exterior, and destined for men. In the hand of God, which means that it refers to his action, and since God is "the one seated upon the throne," it is the expression of his sovereignty. Written on the exterior and the interior, which means first of all that it is complete, finished, that nothing can be added, but also that there is a possible exterior reading (relative, and unimportant) but that the interior reading, the meaning of the text is itself hidden, impossible to obtain without opening the book. It is held out to man. Which means that it is intended for him. This then is not an act of God directed to himself, nor a secret that God wishes to keep; on the contrary, it is a revelation for the one who is Son of God, image of God. The latter addresses himself to his whole creation. The seven seals are probably the seven spirits. In any case they express a radical closure. How can we know what this book is?[1] We proceed by elimination. On the one hand it is certainly not the Bible (which would be

held out to the Church, and which, on the other hand, is not
a closed book; on the contrary, there is no esoteric comprehension of the Bible: this goes counter to all that the biblical
text affirms to us). This is not "the book of creation" (there is
no doublet of Genesis here), nor the book of Destiny where
the life and lot of each would be written: here we encounter
a deep-rooted error. Biblically and through the God of Jesus
Christ there is no destiny. Precisely, the work of the liberator
is to abolish destiny. Further, this is not a book that concerns
Jesus Christ himself: we do not have in this part of the Apocalypse a doublet of the gospels. Finally, this is not the book of
the Church (the question of the Church has been raised in the
preceding part) or the book where the names of the saved are
written: we are told not that we are in the presence of a list of
names, but of a text. And moreover, that would not correspond at all to the events launched by the breaking of the seals.
It can only be the book of that which man is called by his Father
to be, to do, and to become (this is why it is held out to all
men). But there is also an action of man which launches and
provokes an action of God, a work of God. This man is both
the heir of God and engaged in a process by which he becomes
himself, which is to say, a history. This book appears then
as both the book of man and of the history of man. And
this history permits an external reading—superficial, event-
oriented, naturalistic. And then a reading of the secret, of
the meaning of this history; consequently it is the book of the
secrets and of the meaning of human history, both accomplished, assured, but incomprehensible, illegible, which on the
other hand is disclosed as a succession of time, which is in fact
to fill all time. This book contains then the secret of the history
of men, of humanity; but this secret is inevitably the disclosure
of the profound forces of this history and, much more, of the
action of God in the history of men. This is why there is
mention of the throne (the place where God reigns and pronounces his decision) and why it is sealed by the Spirit (the
plan of God for man is realized by the Spirit and it is that which
gives meaning to all history). And finally only the immolated
Lamb can open it, the one who, being perfectly obedient, has

fulfilled the will of the Father without ever transforming history into a destiny.

The Lamb both immolated and triumphant, the one who is both the Lamb and the Lion of Judah, discloses the action of God in history: this action is the judgment upon man and upon the world. But the whole judgment falls back upon Jesus. The disclosure of the action of the Sovereign then becomes possible; without this action there would be a disaster. Therefore the fact that only the Lamb can open the meaning of history is essential for the reading of all the rest: the calamities described to us several times in the book are the "judgments" of God upon history which *would have had to be,* if man had been left to himself, if God had judged this history and man in themselves. But then, rather than disclose and execute these dreadful condemnations, it would be better that the book remain closed. At least men would not know that the catastrophes (which appear to them natural) are in reality the judgments of God. Better that he stay with his interpretation of the evidence: it would be a thousand times worse if he knew. But beginning with the moment when the judgment of God falls back upon God himself, upon his Christ, then the meaning can be read: the creation and man are really spared, disclosure of the judgments becomes possible without being abominable because without issue, without hope. And, in addition, only the immolated Lamb can open the meaning because he has redeemed *for* God the men of every people and every nation. Thus we perceive another direction: it is the disclosure of the universalization of the love of God, and that there is continually a presence of a people of God is part of the secret meaning of history. Thus the sealed book contains the design of God for man and reveals the meaning of what happens, the meaning of history, and that history is not the result of chance, of an ensemble of automatisms, but the result of the interplay between the will of God (which is the love of God and not his imperative power), the will of men, and a certain number of abstract forces. The secret, the meaning of this history, is then both its components and the import, first and last, of that which happens in the world of men. We comprehend then, before a matter of such importance, why the one to whom the book is held out and who cannot open it weeps bitterly: man will never know either the secret or the meaning of his history, of the history of humanity as well as his own history. He will live in the night; he will go on groping without knowing whence he comes, or where he goes, or what he does, or if anything has a value or a meaning, or why that which he does does not correspond to the intention that he had.

There are seven seals. But only six give the components of history; the seventh sounds the trumpets, as we have already seen, which is to say that the first six furnish us with the meaning and the profound matter of history: the seventh is the ultimate secret. The first four provoke, evoke the four horsemen; the fifth, the prayer of the martyrs; the sixth, at the same time, the cataclysms and the appearance of the people of God.

The Four Horsemen

The white horse gives rise to diverse interpretations. For some it will be a matter of the Scythians representing war. But then there is great difficulty explaining the red horse, who is explicitly war. In addition, the only argument in favor of the Scythians is the bow. It would be necessary to explain why the horse is white and to what the crown corresponds. Further, while the three other horsemen provoke calamities (mutual slaughter, death by famine, etc.), if it is war that is here represented, it is very curious that nothing is said of the disasters of war. Also a promise is given by the text: going forth as conqueror. But how, in war, can there be only conquerors? These arguments suffice to show the impossibility of assimilating this horseman to war or to the spirit of conquest. In reality all the elements of the description agree in giving a radically different meaning: white is always the symbol (not of military victory, certainly!) of salvation, life, purity, sanctity; indisputably, in the Apocalypse it is *always* a celestial symbol. He wears the crown, sign of life and of sovereignty, exactly as the Son of Man (chapter 14). This crown is given to him; then he does not conquer, take, seize it (here again we see the impossibility of war). He carries the bow, which is biblically the sign of the covenant. And we next encounter a completely explicit dualism: he goes forth as conqueror (he is *already* a conqueror, the victory has been won for him from the beginning, in eternity) but at the same time *to conquer* (to realize, fulfill, that victory—to make it evident, obvious to all); this is the dialectic between the already and the not yet. Finally, this white horse must be identified with the one we have already met (19:11). How can we believe that within an interval of thirteen chapters the author could describe to us two white horses with their riders and give them two totally different meanings? It is obvious that what is said in chapter 19 applies to the earlier horseman: he is the Word of God. The white horse, who is sent into the world, who departs first, who is the bearer of life and covenant, is the Word of God. But the objection has been made that it is not possible in the same text for Jesus Christ to be represented, on the one hand, as the Lamb of God and, on the other, as the white horseman. I would say that there is, from one aspect, he who is sacrificed/risen, his work accomplished once and for all in a moment of history; from the other, he who is the word, and who continues without ceasing to act in the course of history. There is no contradiction.

But after the white horse come three other horses, each representing three aspects combined but different. Each is at the same time an "immaterial" abstract power, acting nevertheless on a material plane, and also provoking scourges, catastrophes. The first of these is the red horse, blood and fire. He presents two characteristics: first of all he has the power to take away peace; he is then the source of war and combats— national, revolutionary or repressive, and international.[2] Thus we apprehend that when armed conflict breaks out there are all the human, economic, political, naturalistic reasons that we wish; but in addition there is the decision of the red horse, of the spirit of war, of the "spiritual power" hidden in the heart of history. The decision of man and the political factors do not suffice: an *exousia*, a dominion, a power symbolized, personalized here but secret and immaterial, acts also and even determines the rest.

In the second place this red horseman has received the sword. The latter does not signify simply war: this would be an improbable duplication. It is not solely the instrument of combat; it is the traditional sign of power, of authority (cf. Romans 13): this means simply that, in reality, the one who wages war is the political power (ultimately, the state). The two things are tied together. He is given the power and the sword. It is not said who gives them. Probably God. But this horseman uses the sword according to his own will. The sword given for justice is used for war. But then we can also comprehend, reciprocally, that God himself uses war to judge rebellious humanity launched into evil and violence (bear in mind, we repeat once more, that the judgment falls back upon the Lamb). So this horseman is at the same time an *exousia*, the state itself, and the political scourge of war.

Then with the third seal the black horse appears. This is the horseman who measures, rations, sells, and weighs. He has the balance for a symbol, sign of weighing, which means sale; but also of money, for the pieces (clippings) were still frequently weighed out. It is generally said that this horseman represents famine, which is both true and false. Because a denarius is the wage of a worker for a day, and a measure of wheat is the provision of a man for a day, we are then exactly in the presence of the affirmation of the "vital minimum." As for saying that wine and oil are outside his power, this is very difficult to explain. For some, the power of the horseman is limited to a season of the year (wine and oil are not produced at the same time as flour), or else this would be an allusion to the fact that Titus, during the siege of Jerusalem, had ordered the vineyards and olive groves not to be destroyed. For others this carries a spiritual meaning (the wine of the Lord's Supper and the oil of unction: but then why not the bread of the Supper?). I believe that in any case this means that the power of the horseman is limited (that which expresses the limit is of little importance): he cannot dominate all and master all. This horseman then appears to me to represent at the same time the power *(exousia)* of the economy (and especially money), the economic system (economic life and organization, whether it be liberal or controlled), and the economic scourge (scarcity, poverty, famine).

Finally the pale horse comes, livid, sickly, anemic, ridden by Death or Pestilence (the one and the other are identical in the thought of the time). It represents the active power of death and the material means of his action: for example, sickness, wild beasts. It is followed by the Habitation of the Dead, which gathers up their work. Now we are told that the totality of the works of death can destroy a fourth of the earth: so we are still in the presence of a limit (which holds for the last three horses, while the first horseman does not have any limits). It is again the presence of the God of Genesis who sets limits to the powers of chaos and annihilation and who separates the light from the darkness. Of course it is not said at all that these scourges strike specifically the "wicked": all men are subjected to them; it is the sin of all, together and without discrimination, which manifests its consequences, and upon which, in function of which, the destructive power falls. But humanity continues. And it has been announced to us from the beginning that the Lord has the keys to this prison of the dead and of Death.

Finally, then, what do these four horsemen represent? First of all we must say that they are the four chief components of history. The history of men is made up of the intermingling of political power, economic powers, forces of destruction, negation, and death, and also of the Word of God. These same forces are at work always, in all epochs, and in all regimes. It is vain to hope to eliminate one or the other: this would be to abolish history itself. History is a thread woven by these four forces in movement, always renewed, always present, always in action. It is not a stable and constant combination. But history is not a series of accidents, of probabilities, of fortuitous acts, of throws of the dice, of unexpected and surprising events. Nor is it a rational, mathematical, and rigorous combination of a certain number of delimitable and coherent factors. There is not any explicit causality, any system of history. With this description of the four horses we are between the two: between chance and the dialectic, for example. The four horses have always been imagined as launched in a terrible and vagrant course; and this has not been wrong. I believe that it is in fact the meaning of this image of the horse: they run through the whole earth and appear sometimes at one point, sometimes at another, without our being able to grasp a logic in their gallop. So we can have the impression that it is chance. But there is no chance in history.[3] This is one of the fundamental lessons that we receive here. There are forces which act; there is no true chance, only chance for us, chance to our eyes. But it is necessary to take heed: here as in many sciences the recourse to chance (including chance mathematically understood or interpreted) is exactly that which the religions have been so much reproached for doing: putting a name upon what we can neither comprehend nor explain (God or Chance). Mathematical chance does not make the actual knowledge of reality progress by an inch. But if there is no chance it is obvious that the combination of the four unchained forces with their diversity of action registered in an undetermined duration produces such a great number of possible configurations that we can have the impression of chance. On the other hand, on the contrary, there is no rigid causality, no clear connection of event to event. All is finally delivered over to a furious gallop, which provokes and unleashes conflagration and death, which causes war to break out and which then disappears. We try to establish explanations, to divine some determining factors, to comprehend some processes and regularities, and we are not wrong because there are some; but at the very interior of these regularities, of these connections, a major uncertainty is introduced: the gallop of the horsemen surging up and disappearing. They pass by, overturning not only our lives and our comprehension of society and of history. They are the forces without which there would be no history! All history depends upon them and there are only these forces in history. No other intervenes. All events, all the connections can be analyzed and we always return to economic power, to work and commerce, to political power, to war and "justice," to the influence of death, epidemics, and demography: there is nothing else. And since the horsemen are always the same, we can also conclude from this that there is never any progress, nor any degeneration, no deterioration of history and civilizations. We go neither toward the radiant city nor toward increasing catastrophes. The play of forces remains the same. Nevertheless sometimes the red horse is here, sometimes he is not: we find him again elsewhere. Sometimes the black horse appears, sometimes he goes away—that is all.

However, it is necessary here to elucidate a point that causes difficulty for a modern reader. I certainly do not mean that these four horsemen exist in reality, that they take the form of horsemen. But, more important, do they exist as concentrated power in a sort of being that acts with a kind of will? Do we not enter here into demonology with angels, devils, and concretized "powers"? I do not mean to say that war has a kind of entity, is an "essence," like Bellona; neither does economic power nor political power. We admit that everything happens on the human plane. If war breaks out, it is man who unleashes it. Human, nothing except human, too human. And we have the whole gamut of interpretations: the facts of psychology, of character, of temperament, of ambition, of hate, of the spirit of power, of lust for prestige and glory, of greed; facts of sociology, of demographic density, or economic misery or, on the contrary, economic expansion, of escape from daily life, of disequilibrium between groups, of historic weight, of culture and polemic diversion. When we have said all that, and much more, we can affirm that certainly all is of man; but finally we know well that no man ever decides. There is never a man who clearly, consciously, wants war and decides upon it. Nor a group of men. Nor a society. All is of man but in this domain all escapes him. To take refuge in the unconscious, the subconscious, or collective psychology does not resolve anything either. In reality we always find again "the Trojan war will not take place," the most admirable demonstration ever made of this process where men who wish at any price to prevent war become the very factors of that war's declaration (by the play of circumstances, but are they not strictly the masters of circumstance?). I do not say that there is a Mars and Bellona who use men as pawns upon a chess board and manipulate them without the will of these men having any part in the action. But everything happens as if in fact we found ourselves in the presence of a superior determination, an irresistible force, and ultimately a kind of polarization or inciting intention. Everything happens "as if." Whatever the advancement of knowledge might be in economics, in military science, in medicine, there remains an incommensurable, inexplicable part (and I do not say only momentarily inexplicable), a margin in which the intervention of something else is registered, something that we discern very quickly as independent of man. Then, whether it has been personalized in Bellona or in the red horseman, that is understood, without in the least attaching real existence to such a personage. Everything happens as if. . . . There are all the human motivations and a strange kind of transhuman which is disclosed. No man is any longer able to do anything when this Eros or Thanatos seems to be present.[4] Everything happens "as if," and nothing more. But that marks both independence and dependence in relation to man. For here it is a matter of a horseman, a human figure; certainly it is also men who exercise economic and political and military power. Men are the agents as well as the inventors. But there is more than men alone.

These forces in action are of limited number. There are four. And only four. All of history is made up of the intermingling of these powers; they inspire but men act. The scourges are traditionally those of Jewish apocalyptic. Ezekiel tells us of the sword, the famine, and the pestilence (6:11, 39; 7:15–39). Zechariah even gives us the image of horses (but yoked to a chariot, 6:1) and he specifies that they are bearers of the wrath of God. These are in the texts of the Scourges of God, and Second Samuel (24:14) differentiates clearly among the three scourges: two of them (famine and sword) are active by the mediation of men; the other (pestilence, mortality) acts by itself. Now we have a common reading in these texts: the unleashing of these horses, of these "forces of history," is the expression of the judgments of God; they are the divine chastisements of the sin of man. So their action, for two of them, is carried out by man; it is men who wage war, who oppress from every standpoint; but at the same time it is the wrath of God that is actually expressed in history and that thus becomes the creation of history. In these last years it has been affirmed with a little too much enthusiasm that Adam having separated himself from God had thus become "capable of history." The history of humanity begins with the moment Adam takes his independence, his autonomy. Maybe. But he is not the glorious demiurge who creates the event that he desires. Everything continually escapes him and becomes other than he had desired. This history that Adam makes is the place of the unleashing of that which acts "as if" it were the wild horses, as if history were the place of the wrath of God. And we know well the undecided debate with Marx: for example, it is man who makes his history; yes, but the forces of production and the relationships of production for the most part escape his will, his mastery. There are then forces of "Evil," which are unchained and which are by a singular reversal the divine chastisements of the sin of man. The judgments of God are inserted all through history (and not only at the end) but we must emphasize firmly that it is not a matter of individualized chastisement, corresponding to the sin of this one or that one: it is the history of the collectivities that is here in question and each individual is involved.

But by comparison to Jewish apocalyptic and to the naturalistic vision of history this text furnishes some startling novelties. The first is that these four horses are set in motion by the opening of the first four seals, brought about by the Lamb. There is then finally the affirmation that, in the last resort, it is Jesus Christ who is the master of this unchaining. And not the Christ triumphant and judge: the crucified Lamb, precisely the one who has borne the weight of the gallop of the horses, crushed by the justice of men and by the cupidity of men and at the same time by the historic, military, and economic expansion of one of the greatest civilizations. The Lamb is, finally, the one who does not at all create the Scourges, nor even evoke them, but who *discloses* them. And in fact it is clearly in the moment of the crucifixion that there has been disclosed what Power is, and what the Justice and Government of men

are! The Lamb who opens these seals does not perform the
creative act that causes the horses to come to birth. Nor does
he even open up their course, permit them to act. No. We have
said that the opening of the seals made it possible to read the
interior of the book, that is, the meaning of history. The Lamb
discloses, reveals, what our history is, what the forces are com-
posing it, and in his own life and in his own death this revelation had taken place. In this way he is its master. But in the
course of history, no more. Nevertheless he also acts. For this
history is not made only by the three horsemen—black, red,
pale: it is also the place of the Word of God. History is then
made by the intermingling of the three powers and the action
of the Word of God *in* the heart, in the course, in the thread,
in the unfolding, in the gathering up of history. This Word of
God is not an exterior, foreign power, falling from the sky,
representative of the Wholly Other and of the Incommunica-
ble: no, here very clearly it is integrated into the general movement. It is not only the preaching of the Gospel but all that
which contributes to the glory of God (which we will see further on), every act of love which makes God present in the
midst of men, all that which sustains life against death, all that
which makes a light shine and gives joy, all that which is true
power (the crown) against the established violence (the
sword), all that which is abundance (the bow) against famine,
all that which is covenant against divisions, all that which is
true victory against the final defeat, defection, decomposition
of the chlorotic corruption. This Word of God also makes
history with the others. This is why if there is no progress
toward the Kingdom of Heaven, there is also no collapse into
the "Habitation of the Dead," Hades. There is no triumph of
death because it is to this white horseman and to him alone
that finally victory is promised; and, already, he is himself the
Victory. That he is with the others *is* already irreplaceable
victory. And there is a sort of dialectic (constant in the Bible)
among these powers that are combined. And it is also because
all biblical thought (and principally its prophetic aspect and its
apocalyptic aspect) is dialectic that we are assured that the
white horseman is certainly the Word of God: if he were war,

and the red horseman revolution (or civil war) there would be no dialectical movement: all the horses would be upon the same line and there would be no interplay between them. They would not be the forces of history: because, in order that there be history, dialectic process is necessary (and I do not say this to conform to the fashion). But our dialectic, that of the Bible, operates between the historical powers and the metahistorical power that is historicized. It is the only true dialectic possible. The final dialectic. Every other being penultimate and relative. The other horses have visible and commensurable effects; they are manifested in their consequences, while the counterpoint of the white horseman appears only in Jesus Christ; his victory will be comprehensible retrospectively only at the end. But it exists already all the time.[5] It is necessary in addition, in order to complete this picture, to add the image of Zechariah (6:8): the black horse comes toward the north, and he bears the wrath of God. But expressly the order is given to the white horse to accompany him. The scourge is always accompanied by the Word of God, who at the same time brings the expression of the judgment of God *and* his pardon, which makes comprehensible that the scourge is of God but that it is limited by God, and that it proceeds always accompanied by grace, the promise, and the awakening of hope. The two are inseparable.

The Prayer of the Martyrs

The fifth seal is the fifth component of history. We must not believe that because there is a clear group of four horses the following (fifth and sixth seals) are situated elsewhere and upon another plane. We know that interpretation according to which there is a clumsy and stupid superposition of a septenary (the seals) upon disparate things (the horseman, the prayer of the martyrs, the scourges, and the people of God). On the contrary, the septenary is determinative and if in this section the meaning of history is at issue, then that implies that what is disclosed by the fifth seal is an integral part of history. Assuredly, to say that the prayer of the martyrs is a decisive factor is not a common conception, but is it not exactly specific to Christian thought? Can we conceive of history independent of the spiritual action provoked by prayer and testimony? The prayer of the martyrs (witnesses who have maintained their testimony at the price of their lives) is presented to us as accelerating the course of history and leading it to its end, its fulfillment (how long . . . . they were told to be patient). The text (6:9–11) presents a certain number of problems. We can comprehend well enough that those who have been judged by the world are called to judge the world with Jesus Christ because, definitively, the judgment that the world has pronounced against them is the judgment of the world upon itself. And this all the more since, if they have been put to death, it is because of their testimony; the world has not received this attestation of the truth, consequently it refuses the sole possibility of its salvation. This explains the idea of judgment (to make justice) but not at all the demand for vengeance, which can seem scandalous ("to avenge our blood"). Here we must understand that these martyrs do not demand *their* satisfaction. It is not in order to be avenged (moreover there is no idea of personal vengeance); what matters is the triumph of the justice of God, the manifestation of his glory in this "vengeance": knowing that the "evil" must be conquered, they are scandalized that it still continues. And let us remember that this evil is not the transgression of moral commandments but something much more fundamental, which has two faces: that of rupture with God (of which the putting to death *of the Witness* of the Word of God is the proof) and that of the evil that is done to men (of which the very fact *of the putting to death* of these men is the proof). It is the evil with a double visage that must be excluded by judgment and vengeance. Moreover, on our plane equally, when we work, for example, to establish justice on earth, does not that also, and always, imply the condemnation of the "wicked"? When communism claims to establish the finally human society it is necessary first of all to get rid of the capitalists, exploiters, imperialistic powers, etc.

But we encounter another necessary point: vengeance must

be exercised upon the inhabitants of the earth—or perhaps even more exactly upon "those who are established in the earth." And here is the beginning of a theory that we will have to explain progressively.That can—and it is the meaning that comes immediately to mind—denote the men who live upon the terrestrial globe. Therefore we are directed toward images of judgment upon men, hell, chastisement of humanity, etc. The major difficulty of such a position is that, even so, we are in a Jewish milieu where faith in the promise after the deluge firmly persists: I will never again utterly destroy humanity, says the Eternal. But we must also emphasize the importance of the opposition between heaven and earth, not in the physical sense but in their symbolic import. The earth is like "the world" in the Gospel of John, that which is opposed to the "sphere of God," the world of God, the Kingdom of Heaven, etc. The vengeance which is here demanded does not necessarily fall upon men but upon all that which belongs to the earth, all that which is included in the terrestrial, and consequently upon the powers of evil, of opposition to God. In fact the children of God already have their abode and place in heaven (even while still living upon this "terrestrial globe"). We must then, already at this time, attempt to detach the idea from our thought that all that which is said in these judgments concerns human beings. The judgment and the vengeance are at the same time more restricted and more extended than humanity. We will return to this.[6]

The prayer of the martyrs is one of the motor forces of history. Why? We notice that this is not at all related to their quality, their virtue, nor even to their fidelity and faith (which is still "theirs"), nor to some kind of merit. In fact they have not themselves "bleached" their garment: a white robe is *given to them.* Which is to say that they also are justified by grace; they are not just in themselves. Their martyrdom has not saved them; but it is necessary for them as for all other men to be transformed by the grace of God. The white garment which is given to them, we have already been told, was made white by the blood of the Lamb. Consequently, to what does their martyrdom correspond? In reality, they are the exemplary witnesses. And it is as witnesses that they are a historical power. We must comprehend the meaning and the bearing and the importance of this testimony. The simplest aspect is surely that the witness, here, is the bearer of the Word of God. And inasmuch as they have been bearers of that Word before and in the world, up to the point of death itself, reciprocally they can bear their word before God, a word which comes from the milieu of the world and from the history of men. A word that concerns this world in which they have experienced the truth and the lie of this world. And they *alone* can speak that word because of the fidelity of which they have given proof in bearing the Word of God. Absolutely "credible" here, their word becomes "credible" for God in heaven and for eternity. They bear the world with them. They are the prophets in the Kingdom of God. Because they have been faithful in little, a considerable role is attributed to them. And they alone are capable of it because they alone have borne the Word of God. Their testimony has been just in the world; it is still a testimony which is received as true in heaven. But it is clearly the *prayer* of all the witnesses that is a power at the interior of history. And this leads us to ask concerning the nature and the decisive importance of these witnesses. They seem in fact to be the pivot of history, since not only do they demand its acceleration but, further, they are told to be patient until their number is complete. Which obviously does not mean that there is, in the secret of God, a *numerus clausus,* an absolute number of those who are to be martyrs, which would be a simplification not at all in accord with the Apocalypse, but which is, rather, the symbolic, allusive, and concretizing manner of the text in saying: "until the testimony of the Word is completed, accomplished in the world."

The witness is always the one who brings into a situation or debate something which comes from the exterior and which he introduces into the debate in order to make the balance tilt toward a meaning. A tribunal, for example, is a closed setting where a procedure is carried out; the witness is not a participant in the debates: he comes from "outside the tribunal"; he furnishes his knowledge of a fact and he withdraws. In the same way the witness to a juridical act is one who does not belong to the process but comes to answer for something else: he brings his person, his authority, his word, as guarantee. He becomes in a sense the very place of the authority of the act, since that act is not worth anything if it is not attested. And because of this the witness becomes the heart of the affair, the one who leaves an indelible impression, but who precisely is not himself concerned with the affair in question; he brings something (his guaranty) from the exterior of the act, of the procedure, of the parties. It is beginning with this very normal conception, consistent with Greek or Roman juridical thought, that we must comprehend the role and importance of the witness and the testimony in theological thought. In fact, it is only by extension that we speak of someone who is "witness to an accident": this means that he has seen it, that he was there and *consequently* that he can come to tell what he has himself seen and heard, in the development of a process. At the same time he will bring his guaranty and his experience of an "elsewhere" or of a "then." Thus the witness of Jesus Christ is first of all one who, in the closed, necessary movement of an ineluctable development, comparable to a procedure, comes and causes something else which was not foreseen to enter, something which does not belong to that procedure. He causes a dimension or an ensemble of facts and exterior words to enter into the dialectical movement of history. He brings a nonnecessity, an independence over against the movement of history; he furnishes a "play," a disadaptation of the pieces, a halo, a "report" (relating to information), a trembling. He inserts an unexpected into the inevitable development. There are the four horses and their mad gallop, and then there is an accident in the course. It is the appearance, the intervention, of the witness. He causes doubt concerning what logically is going to happen; he brings an unassimilable existential grandeur; he introduces an unforeseen. He is not a force of history but he denotes and signifies another force of which still nothing can be said. He is *only* the witness, but being that he opens the mechanism to that which is exterior to it. The witness refers to that which is outside of the piece.

But he himself is within and therefore he creates the line between the unknown, unexpected, unforeseen, irrecoverable outside and that which is within. If he is faithful he introduces by his very presence this whole unexpected, this whole irrecoverable. The witness is the exact place where the Transcendent and the *hic et nunc* meet (and this is why the first title attributed to Jesus Christ by the Apocalypse (1:5) is precisely the faithful witness).

Consequently the testimony, because it is rooted outside the system of the world, is the form, the place, and the only expression of the freedom of man in history. Confronted by and against the presence and power of the forces at work of which we have seen the complexity and which are independent of man in their relationship to him—men are cattle who are dominated, exploited, starved, and driven into war—where is the specific role of man? How can his freedom appear? Our text responds: uniquely in the testimony rendered to that which is strictly inaccessible to these powers, that which comes from outside the world, that which introduces uncertainty into the glorious certitude of the triumph of the powers. And that is done, can only be done, by the testimony rendered to Jesus Christ. When is man free? *Exclusively* when he bears this testimony, when he assumes the role of witness, and in no other way. The witness does not enter into any action, neither political, nor economic, nor mortal; he points to that which is at the exterior and makes it actual and present. But very obviously that exists only if the witness remains tied to that to which he bears testimony, which is not only a historic past (which as such cannot be changed) but also an eternal present. And this relation can be carried through only by prayer. The witness is then one who speaks in this world while pointing to the Wholly Other and prays to the Wholly Other while pointing to this world and bearing it with him. That is why, we understand, the Apocalypse opposes to the group of horses running through the earth, the group of martyrs, upon whom history depends, upon whom the fact depends that history is not a closed door. The fifth seal is that of the freedom of man.

The Setting Apart of the People of God

The sixth seal is the occasion of a description of two shutters, which can be considered as composite but which includes an internal coherence. Verses 7 to 17 of chapter 6 describe to us a certain number of calamities; then chapter 7:1–11, tells us of the people of God. The line between the two is very exactly established by verse 3: the angel who holds the seal of God (the mark of his property, but since God is the Living and Holy One, it is then by this fact the mark of salvation, of the setting apart) gives the order to the angels, who can unleash the catastrophes, to hold back their action until the people of God are completely assembled. And this is very clearly marked by the contrast between the terrible events of the end of chapter 6 (earthquake, blotting out of the sun, fall of the stars, etc.) and the calm that presides over the gathering of this people: "that no wind might blow on earth or sea or against any tree"; not the slightest breeze which could come to trouble this calm and this peace. The contrast of images is evident. But in the two cases it is a matter of what happens in history, in the present world, and it can be said that there is another dimension of history: the progressive setting apart of the people of God in the course of history, in the milieu of catastrophes, and the unchaining of calamity. The latter are the expression of the rending of the world when the part loved by God is set apart, sanctified, consecrated. When that which is loved by God is withdrawn from the world there now remains only terror and drama and disorders. This operation of gathering is effected then in anguish and fright. It is a true surgical operation. We must not imagine that this happens easily, gently. A man who is chosen, called by God, is a man who is torn out of a world that is going to be deprived of a contribution, of help. Sanctity is always a drama, also for the group in which the saint appears. This discrimination is, properly speaking, sacred history. (But we will have to see further on upon what this discrimination bears. Let us not say too quickly: there are some men saved and some men lost.) But this sacred history is not history isolated from the Jewish people or from the Church;

it is not the history of the mysterious relation between God
and his people: an affair, then, totally independent of a "non-
sacred" history. In reality it is a history of the entire action in
the course, in the milieu, of the history of men, but tending to
create, in the milieu of that history, a particular people, the
people of God. It is not a secret duplication of the life of
humanity; it is, at the very heart of that life, an action which
concerns all men and which brings about the liberation of a
specific human group. For it is certainly a liberation. And we
find again this similarity with Exodus: it is the liberation of the
people of God in the midst of catastrophes that strike nature
and men. And the seal of God at question here surely evokes
the cross of blood upon the lintel of the Israelites on the
evening of watching for the great departure, the separation,
the passage, the liberation, the sanctification.[7] And this separation is a rupture, an explosion: it is not a quite wise arrangement into good objects to be kept, and objects to be thrown
away; it is not a sorting out. It is a rending of nature as a whole.
The "setting apart," the "sanctification," is not a pious embel-
lishment; it is a terrible drama: the rupture of the living totality
which creation was. Israel is set free in the midst of the dramas
of the world; and here also when God withdraws even one
saint from the whole there is a cosmic drama. That is why when
the commentators and exegetes of the Apocalypse bestir
themselves either to observe that there is here a doublet of
what will be said at the end (the final judgment), or to explain
that it is an image of the end time, or a prophecy of what will
take place later, I think that they miss the meaning, which can
be understood only by setting this passage in relation to the
whole (the six seals and the place of chapters 5 to 7 in the rest).
The cosmic drama of which the symbols are delivered to us is
that of the rending to allow passage for the gathering of the
people of God whose constitution is announced exactly at
verse 11: this verse is the rigorous transition from the prayer
of the martyrs to *all* that which is elucidated by the sixth seal:
the constitution of the holy people in the midst of cataclysms.
At issue then is neither a last judgment, nor prophecies of
judgment, nor judgments *hic et nunc* concerning a certain

group at a certain moment: the accent is not upon judgment but simply upon the evidence that when the love of God is concentrated upon this holy people, there remains behind only wrath (and we can refer here to all the images of the Gospel concerning the winnowing fan and the chaff thrown into the fire, etc.). The process of discovery and gathering is constant throughout history but does not end history, does not impede it, or draw out of the world those who are sanctified: they are only set apart, recruited for something else.

The cataclysms presented in chapter 6:12–17 seem to be of two orders: events which appear natural, such as earthquakes, and those which appear supernatural (the blackened sun, the fall of the stars). Of course the supernatural is symbolic; it attests only that at this moment the world is no longer preserved, that the established order in creation no longer exists, and that all is reversed: the sun no longer gives light. Because the spiritual light ("you are the light of the world") is withdrawn from the whole, because it is put aside, there is no longer then any light at all. Because the representatives of the Kingdom of Heaven upon earth, those who are in themselves the Kingdom of Heaven, are set apart, then the sky is rolled up like a scroll; there is no longer any presence of the world of God in the world of man. But even the mountains and islands are shaken. And that evokes irresistibly certain texts of the Old Testament, in particular Psalm 82,[8] which tells us that when man ceases to be man, when he ceases to practice justice, when he is no longer "there" as son of God, then the pillars of the earth are shaken, the mountains totter, all is put in question: the order of the world rests upon the presence, in the course of this world, of those who are the Kingdom for God and his Christ. The material cataclysms surely allude just as much to social, political, economic disasters. That which characterizes this withdrawal is then disorder, incoherence, the destruction of assured foundations, anomie, the disappearance of meaning, which provokes the Terror.

Nevertheless, two remarks must be made here: the first is that the considerable importance given to the presence of the bearers of the Kingdom for the continuance of the world should strictly not give to Christians the least sense of pride or superiority. And for the following reasons: if they are the bearers it is by grace and not by any intrinsic quality. Also: who then, if he is seriously Christian, could contend that he assumes the word of Jesus: you are the salt of the earth, you are the light of the world? All that which we can recognize of ourselves is that, precisely, we are not. Finally: if we allow ourselves to become the least bit proud, to have the least feeling of importance, that alone would suffice to demonstrate that we are not among the saints, among the bearers of the Kingdom.

The second remark: the withdrawal, the separation of these "Christians" to constitute the people of God is not a historically realized reality. This text is fulfilled only in the "final Judgment," but it is here to warn us that every setting apart, effected by God, every constitution of the people of God willed by God, is inevitably associated with the putting in question of the world. And that consequently this is not a happy and peaceful venture, beneficent for creation and society. It is an enterprise as terrible as the historic formation of the people of God. And this is clearly seen in the events themselves of these two thousand years. In a certain measure it can be said that this describes for us an irruption into history of the events of the end (there is, of course, no increase of cataclysms as the end approaches and these events are not at all to be confounded with the judgment itself). But under these conditions we must clearly understand that God alone decides that. In other words no church can close up, fold in upon itself, conceive itself as Noah's Ark in the midst of the fury of the world, can shut itself in against the exterior darkness: it is lampstand and not bushel, which is to say that it shines as brightly as possible *in order to illuminate* the night and not, in a closed milieu, to illuminate itself. The Church herself has not the right to constitute herself the holy people, closed up because then it is she who unleashes the cataclysm upon the world (by her withdrawal); she is responsible for the world before God (who loves the unlovable world), and by this very deed she would cease to be the witness of the Kingdom of Love. Witness: it is not for nothing that the sixth seal comes after the fifth. But the two cannot be separated. The fifth seal is that of the witnesses, which is to say those who have been present in society, in events, who have been dispersed, scattered in time and space, who have brought the word into the milieu of men and who *pray.* The sixth is that of the people of God, who are gathered, concentrated, outside time and space, outside the currents of society, and who *give glory* to God. But the two aspects are inseparable. Those who are within and those who are withdrawn. There is a time to be with, and a time to be separated—this is what the double vision means.

The catastrophes which happen when the people of God are withdrawn, exactly like what happened to Sodom when Lot was withdrawn, fall equally upon the powerful and the slaves, the rich and the poor: there is no human condition that authorizes favor before God. But the text insists much more upon the powerful (the kings, the great, the generals, the rich, the authorities) because they believe themselves to be safe, because they have in hand the means of their security (though there is none), because finally they incarnate the powers. Verse 16 must be emphasized: all the inhabitants of the earth cry out: hide us because the day of wrath has come. In other words we are in the presence of an awareness of the meaning of that which happens. Suddenly the man who does not believe in God, who is not interested in revelation, who is not part of the people of God (but, once more, we will have to study later if there is a division between two categories of men) learn to *read* the events that happen, the disorders of the world and the meaning of history, the material cataclysms and the political confusion. The cataclysm ceases to be natural and becomes significant event, that, without comprehending in the least the Truth of the God who has called his people, one relates to the action of God, but a God who can then be conceived only as a God of wrath and judgment. Thus (and this is a second face of the interpretation of the text, consistent with the first) what the writer of the Apocalypse wishes to show are not the happenings (even eschatological) that take place but the historical events in which men discern that which they think to be a judgment of God; while, though misunderstood, it is evidence suddenly surging up of the reality of the world and of history *as if* God did not preserve it, *as if* the Kingdom were not present in the midst of men. The threat is that the creation disappear; it is the putting in question of the whole creation in its fundamental structures and of the order of history, which happens not by an active decision of God but by the withdrawal, the gathering, the summons, the setting apart, of the people of God. And men are deceived about the meaning of these dramas. They find themselves before what would be reality if God were not continually their protector, if the men who are bearers of the Kingdom were not continually among them imperfectly, mysteriously, incognito—the Witnesses and those who pray. But it can be said that under these conditions the world nevertheless endures because this gathering of the people of God is carried out progressively through the course of history; and it is not the problem of an absolute number of the elect as if there were a number fixed in advance, an original destiny but, on the contrary, the question posed is that of the faithfulness of man. Up to what point, how long, have men been faithful? Will there still be, at a particular moment, Martyrs and Witnesses (cf. Matthew 24:9, 3, 21–22)? As long as there are some upon the earth, the world will continue: there is still something to be reaped for God. But when faithfulness to the Word of God ceases, then the world will be destroyed, the people of God being then completely withdrawn. So the duration of the world, the open possibility of history, still depends exclusively on the presence of faithful witnesses. The "complete number" (6:11) is then the end, the goal that commands positively the unfolding of events. It is a positive and not at all a negative end. It is the end of salvation (its fulfillment, its plenitude) that determines history. None of those who would be able to participate in the glorification of God upon earth in the midst of men must be excluded by a premature destruction.

In chapter 7 we come to the question of the composition of this people. We see very clearly that there are two successive aspects: the 144,000 (vs. 4) and an innumerable multitude. Certain exegetes estimate that the 144,000 represent converted Jews and the others Christians coming out of paganism. That appears to me very weak. Other exegetes have had the curious idea of considering that these are the same, but once *numbered,* "according to the model offered by Israel in the desert" (one does not see why this model is chosen, though the Kingdom of Heaven is not exactly equivalent to the desert), the other time considered "in the celestial and glorious fulfillment"; but there is no rupture between the two visions, which are closely connected. I believe, on the contrary, that it is the total, complete, vision of the entire people of God composed of these two factors. The first gives us three elements as its particular character: there is a limited number (even if there were no figure, this would be indicated by the counterpart, concerning the innumerable, unlimited multitude); but it is twelve times twelve, which is to say a total figure, a totality without any lack. In addition, it is a group that comes first; it can finally not be evaded that there is the designation of the tribes of Israel (and even with the device, become traditional, of the suppression of the unfaithful tribe of Dan, replaced by Manasseh, still an issue of Joseph, as the tribe of Joseph). All this denotes the first people of God, composed as this people has been, with a specific election. And under these conditions how can we fail to see the people of Israel itself? The people of Israel reconciled with their God, not because there are some Jews who have converted to Christianity, but in the very fulfillment that was foreseen by Paul. It is all the people of Israel: the totality indicated by twelve times twelve. All the people of Israel in their whole duration from before Jesus Christ, in their period of rebellion against the Messiah, and in their period of reconciliation. The whole people of Israel in their whole historic and spiritual dimension without any being lost, and whose presence in history is so decisive that it can be said even today that all history is formed around her. But whose absence would be the end. And whose total conversion would be the end. A complete people who had been the first bearer of the election, first witness and chosen people. And that election

had been clearly marked, we remember, by dramas, the con-
vulsions of birth, and the apparent condemnation of the rest
of the world. In this people of Israel, Judah is here named first,
although he is not the eldest; but here the benediction of Jacob
is fulfilled: it is from him that the lion has gone forth whose
victory brings the elect people in its train (7:5). The "whole
Israel" appears then as the first people of God, following
Judah. Complete, but nevertheless, in the midst of men, of
limited number. Then comes the immense and innumerable
people, the Church, in the second rank, coming from all peoples, and for whom no numbering is useful or possible; because there is no visible, concrete, and human sign marking
the election. They come from all nations: the same nations
condemned because of the kings, the generals, the rich, are
sanctified by the elect. There where sin abounds, grace
abounds the more. All men are shut up into disobedience in
order that mercy might be given to all. Thus the very people
of God is constituted with the first and second election. Thus
the process of history unfolds and it is the elect people in its
entirety, Jews and Christians, who form the bridge, the way,
and the passage to the Kingdom of God. And who are already
there. And that which characterizes them all, together, is that
they declare and affirm that salvation is the act of God (which
is to say, at the same time, life, peace, and reconciliation).
They do not then attribute any merit to themselves: "Salvation [total] belongs to our God *and* to the lamb." They
ascribe nothing to their own account. Humanity in this
moment becomes aware of its true salvation, and glorifies
God alone.

The second characteristic is that they receive salvation and
eternal life by the sacrifice of Jesus Christ (7:14). The third is
that there is addressed to them a promise of resurrection and
of entry into the Kingdom at the end of time (7:15–17). Which
clearly means that we are always in history and that the vision
of the people of God is both historic and prophetic. So long
as it is not complete, it lives under this promise. And this
promise is the end of death, the end of rupture (separation),
the end of suffering (remorse). Thus the act of election for the

constitution of the total people, the act made twice to two peoples, but millions of times to the individuals who constitute them, is constitutive of history and enables it to go on in rupture and rending.[9]

·6·

THE JUDGMENT
Chapters 14:6 to 20:15

We enter here into another perplexing sequence of the Apocalypse; most commentators discover innumerable repetitions, doublets, very embarrassing new beginnings.

Nevertheless if we take account of the necessity of repetitions for the connection of sequences, if we take account of the astonishing inlay work intermixing adroitly songs of praise with terrible actions, we are, on the contrary, here in the presence of a development which is perfectly comprehensible.

In a first sequence we have the prophetic announcement of and the preparation for the judgment (14:6–20), with a first very discreet series of six angels. In a second we have the catastrophes, which represent the judgment upon men (15:5 to 16:21). In the third we have the judgment *and* the destruction of the historic forms of incarnation of the powers which have dominated history and humanity (chapters 17–18). And this is, properly speaking, the cause of the drama. Finally, in the last there is the completion; after the great canticle of praise, the great prophetic chorale of the resurrection, there is the damnation of the powers who have acted in heaven, who are the point of departure of the rupture, the introducers of death (19:17, 21 and chapter 20). And this is closely tied to the resurrection: it is what, literally, makes the resurrection possible.

But we encounter first of all three preliminary questions. The first concerns the importance of this "judgment." The present theological and spiritual tendency consists in minimizing it, and even rejecting it. We return to the terrestrial reality of the vocation of man, to his full historic dimension, to his condition as creator with God, as demiurge; we drop all this phantasmagoria of celestial combats (so inspired, are they not, by Near Eastern cultures) of damnations (Ashur and her demons are not far). These ideas of judgment appear completely outmoded; modern man has come of age. For some it is complexes and fantasies that have produced this idea of damnation, while for others it is the state of famine and of the vital animal condition on the plane of subsistence, and for still others it is a mischievous invention of exploiters and the powerful in order to compel the poor and the oppressed to remain quiet. All these explanations are very fine and have no other foundation than the opinion of their authors. If we continue to consider that Jesus Christ is truly the Messiah and that he attests what Scripture tells us, which is to say if we remain Christians, it is impossible to reject this judgment of the creation by God. The whole is strictly coherent. The conception of judgment that we find as much in the prophets as in the psalms, as much in the Gospels as in the Epistles is not a cultural phenomenon: it rests upon that evident conviction that if God is God, both perfect and just, how can the encounter between this God and the world as we know it take place without some sparks being produced and without, at least, revealing in the absolute light what we have been *in truth?* The judgment being never juridical but revelatory, it is not the expression of the servile terror of men, but of their comprehension of the divine reality. Still we must come to an understanding concerning what this judgment could be. This we will attempt to elucidate. And already it appears clearly in our text that it is indispensable to separate judgment and condemnation. Those who are judged are not necessarily condemned. Much more, we must not conceive the judgment as a kind of simplistic separation of the men judged good from others who will be condemned because judged bad, according to the puerile interpretation of the celebrated text of Matthew 25, where it is a matter not at all of the judgment of individuals but of *nations,* as said explicitly in the text. If we enter into this perspective of judgment we cannot avoid the juridical formulation and the touching and medieval images of the balance: the sum of evil done by a man is put on one side and on the other the sum of good, and according to which weighs the most he is damned or saved.

The judgment of which the Scripture tells us has nothing to do with all that! And it is not at all certain, if men pass through the judgment, that it is finally men who are condemned. All this being, in that which concerns man, subjected to that unheard of grace which caused Jesus Christ himself to be condemned in place of men. But having said this, there remains nevertheless a condemnation that is expressed at the last day. We must disclose, then, what it means.

Finally a third preliminary remark: are we in the presence of a final judgment or of a judgment that is exercised every day (a consequent or realized eschatology)? I believe that we cannot eliminate one of the two and make a choice. Undoubtedly, since the Apocalypse describes for us, in section 2, the components of history, and since here we are in the presence of section 4, which makes it pending, the judgment is clearly an end of history that results in a final work of re-creation, of the reinsertion of time in Eternity, of the destruction of death in order that there be Life. But on the other hand, it is just as correct to say that it takes place during the course of history, at each epoch, at each generation. God also intervenes in this history of men, not as the Cause or as the Omnipotent who overturns everything, but as one who has accepted being involved with men, the God with us. And this presence, which is the attestation of grace, nevertheless cannot be other than the presence of judgment also.

In addition, what our text describes for us is, following the

Incarnation, the fall of the Devil to the earth. He is then very definitely unchained, which manifests a sort of radicalization of the conflict. There can no longer be a natural order "in place," a divine providence acting from afar upon the creation: we are, from the fact of the Incarnation, plunged into a last combat, but at each moment of our life and of our history. We live the last judgment continually, and the last trial: we are upon the edge of the crater and contemplate under the fire and ashes the very boiling up of the Ultimate. For the more the powers are unchained, the more the judgment of God is, appears, total and rigorous.

Announcement of the Judgment

Very curiously, from 14: 6 to 16: 21 we meet two series of seven angels, or rather a very discreet series of six angels who surround the Son of Man (14:1, 20), and another series, on the contrary, thundering, explosive, of seven angels who hold and pour out the seven bowls. The first bear the prophetic announcement and the preparation of the judgment. The second pour out the wrath of God upon men, but a wrath which, on the one hand, is not ultimate; on the other, brings about the revelation of what man is before God. There is then no doublet or repetition.

The Announcement: first of all there are three angels. They fly, which is to say that they bear the proclamation everywhere: the announcement from "mid-heaven" must reach all men. This proclamation includes three elements: the Gospel, the Condemnation of Babylon, and the "If" of a choice proposed to men. But the first essential remark is that this triple proclamation (of course inseparable) begins with the Gospel, the good news, which derives from what had been said immediately before, at the beginning of chapter 14: the victory of the Lamb and the salvation of his people. Beginning with *this fact,* the Gospel can be proclaimed, given to all. And the text tells us that it is an *Eternal* good news: which is to say that it was before the creation and that it is brought to realization beyond, that it is not subject to accidents or events, being the good news that God always willed to give to men and which does not change. It is the good news of the possibility for man to return to God, which is the fulfillment of the desire of Adam now accomplished in Jesus Christ (for it must not be forgotten that the Apocalypse is the book of the granting of the prayers and aspirations of man). And this Gospel, which must be proclaimed to *all* those who live upon the earth, entails an attitude on the part of men expressing this new relation with God (14:7): *fear* (but it is not possible to make here a detailed study of the fear of God, which is not at all terror. I will limit myself to recalling the marvelous image that St. Augustine gives of it: the loving wife fears that her husband might go away and embark on a voyage; the unfaithful wife fears that her husband might return). *To give glory* (which means, we remember, to reveal him for that which he is: the creation finds again its true role, which is to reveal the splendor of the creator). And *to worship* (which means to recognize the power of the Creator in accepting being annihilated, if necessary, before him; then in following the very way that Jesus Christ has followed. Worship here is the imitation of Jesus Christ). The Gospel begins the judgment, but the latter then can take place only when the Gospel has been proclaimed, announced, given, delivered, to all nations.

The immediate counterpart is the declaration of the second angel, "fallen, fallen, is Babylon the great," which of course has caused clever exegetes to say that it is not true, since Babylon falls three chapters later (they have never heard tell of mingling of times, flashback, and other cinematic devices), who deduce thereby either a doublet and consequently two sources, or a clumsy cutting up, etc. It is clear that we are here before the declaration of the dispossession of Babylon, the great Power, beginning with the moment when the Gospel is proclaimed, the Gospel, which is the way of Nonpower. The Power is ruined in its foundations, its bases, its roots. And the angel declares that which is before God before being accomplished in the course of the transhistoric. It is the exact reverse of the picture of which the Gospel is the obverse.

But we see that this double presentation immediately entails the declaration of a choice, which is the deed of the third angel. The obligation to decide is placed before man: "If" (14:9) . . . it is the hour (vs. 12), which is to say that it is necessary either to receive the eternal Gospel and be associated with it, including all that that calls for, or to enter into communion with Babylon. We comprehend that bringing this choice to light is the prelude to the judgment. And this is going to be expressed by the summons not to worship the beast and its image (the State, the political power), nor to participate in the activities of the world. Otherwise the Gospel's cup of communion becomes the cup of the wrath of God. And subsequent to the evil choice of man the great chastisement is the definitive absence of repose (vs. 11). It is the development of the curse of Cain who flees endlessly without finding a place of rest; it is the anguish, the ceaseless search, the uncertainty. Would this mean that human history continues after the judgment, underground, without significance, without issue, in the infinite drama? In which case Dante would be right to describe hell as he has done. But we will see that there is another way. Up to here there is only a *possible* threat, and this absence of repose takes place (vs. 10) in the presence of the angels and the Lamb. That does not at all mean that the angels and the Lamb are the complacent spectators of the suffering of the damned (to keep for the moment the traditional vocabulary and images). What is described here for us has an inverse meaning. It is not the Lamb and the Elect in the presence of whom, etc., but: the damned suffer in the presence of the Lamb. Which means expressly that it is the becoming aware, the knowledge of who Jesus Christ is, that is the essential point of the suffering of these "rejects." It is that which appears to them the definitive rupture and the impossibility of rejoining what they now see, having always refused to recognize it. The judgment at this moment is then: to be what one has actually wished to be, but seeing in the light of God what it was. As for the duration of this separation and these torments, they are declared to be "for eons of eons," which is not infinity or eternity. They last "through a long succession of eons," and it is not a question of a duration limited by a passage of time but by the proclamation: "I make *all* things new," and "there will be no more curse" (chapter 22); then God by grace puts an end to this impossible situation. Opposite this first alternative of the option (to worship the beast, 14:9–11)there is the other (vss. 12–13): "Persevere," continue through the vicissitudes of history. The "Saints" are characterized here not by good moral conduct nor by theological virtue, but by this endurance; for it is the moment of the increase of temptation (Matthew 24), of the crisis of this drama. Firmness, hope, capacity to resist seduction, discernment of spirits, closure to the demonic work of allurement and separation, resolute keeping of the commandments and of the content of revelation—such is endurance. And the angel can say, in this trial of the Saints: "Blessed are the dead who die in the Lord" (14:13), because at least they have finally escaped the harshness of these last times. They know repose.

Such is the proclamation of the first three angels, which is the perfect inauguration of the judgment. Then comes,[1] in the framework of the two triads of angels, the Son of Man, of whom we have already spoken, and who prepares to harvest the people of his Father. With him are three other angels: the first, we have said, transmits the order of God to proceed with the harvest. The second holds a sickle (as does the Son of Man), and the third gives him the order to reap the vineyard. The latter is the vintage of the wrath of God, and that which is then harvested is destined for the fury (when the vintage is put in the winepress there flows from it what is comparable to blood) and that fury is extended to absolutely the whole creation, which is indicated by the figure 1,600 stadia: 4×4 (the figure of the creation multiplied by itself) and multiplied by 100, which denotes an immensity without limit. What then is the significance of this totality? There has often been seen here a first judgment, or rather, a doublet of the judgment clumsily reutilized. In reality this text appears to me very clear. Its objective is to tell us (after the presentation of choice before men) in a heading, an introduction to the series of judgments, *who* exercises this judgment: the judgment for the salvation and the recapitulation of humanity is carried out by the Son of Man, Jesus, upon the order of his Father. On the other hand, the judgment for wrath is not by Jesus; it is some angel who also acts according to the order of God the Omnipotent. These verses *are not* the judgment, which is made perfectly comprehensible in the preamble, but simply, clearly, the designation of the one who exercises it. The angel who speaks to Jesus and gives the order of salvation leaves from the *Temple;* the one who gives the order of the vintage leaves from the *altar* (then of the sacrifice: but that could also indicate that what will be then slaughtered is not perhaps *men* but expiatory victims offered upon the altar). And this double element comes to confirm the idea that there is clearly a differentiation of roles in the judgment. Two remarks must be added here: the vintage is trampled in a vat outside the city (14:20). To my mind this makes the first allusion to the Holy City, Jerusalem, the New Jerusalem which will descend from heaven: it is the first allusion. There is the frequent and very complex system of "first allusions" in the Apocalypse: each time that which will come later is in some way "picked up" as if accidentally by a first indication, which announces in the course of a passage that which implies a reference to what follows; it is a system of linkage somewhat comparable to the connections of which we have spoken. And this holy city is totally undamaged by the shed blood. The whole creation is covered with it, but not the New Jerusalem.

The second remark concerns a question that has led commentators far astray. It is evident that the harvest and the vintage both evoke for a Christian the Holy Communion. Evident, too evident. The Communion here is surely only one subsidiary aspect (which can be retained). But this can include some interesting elements: first, the text presents the double visage of the communion: that of the relation to the Lord, but at the same time that of the possible threat that we find with Paul (the one who does not discern the body and the blood of the Lord eats and drinks his condemnation). The important fact here is that the world has really killed Jesus Christ, had crucified him after the Supper; and it follows then that the communion in the cup is a communion to wrath: the Eucharist has become judgment. But also in this Eucharist is humanity in its entirety, which is gathered by God and for God. And it is also this idea of gathering that we meet in the harvest and the vintage. The communion that is instituted is a given; men are really united one to the other, and the Eucharist in the Church is always an image of the last meal and the last gathering. Finally, the text is also a reminder of the death of Jesus Christ, which had taken place outside the city, like the vat where the vintage is trod. And we see that we find here again the great affirmation that Jesus is surely the one who has borne the condemnation. The death of Jesus was actually the absolute condemnation of all humanity. For what can humanity do worse than kill not only the innocent, and not only God himself, but even the innocent, just, and loving God? The blood of Jesus Christ, which flows upon the cross, is the absolute of the blood of men; it is without limit, it covers the totality of creation. But at the same time it is the whole wrath of God that falls at that unique point; it is the blood of all men that is the blood of Jesus Christ. It is he who is upon the altar; there will not be any other human blood shed. There will not be any other victim upon the altar. And this is also why if it is the Son of Man who garners the harvest of salvation, it cannot be he who gathers the grapes and treads the wine. Because *he is* the trampled grape, the wine poured out, the dead for all the dead, the condemned for all the condemned. And by this detour we return then to the principal theme of this pericope: who finally presides and decides the judgment? Thus we see once more that the plurality of planes of interpretation of the symbols, even their ambivalence, both present and eternal, concerns the Church and the End Time, but functioning always in their plurality of meaning by relation to a central axis, which is determined.

Judgment upon Humanity

We arrive now, after the proclamation and the designation of the judge, at the first phase which is properly speaking that of judgment (chapter 15:6 to 16:21) before passing to that of condemnation. It is the phase characterized by the seven bowls, which represent in fact the bowls of the wrath of God. Thus a new septenary. But what happens then is very badly interpreted when this septenary is entitled "the last plagues." That signifies nothing: it is as if the Apocalypse were a book of images without progression and without any other value than to describe for us the catastrophes falling upon men, decided by a somewhat foolish God who distributes the series of plagues. But there is nothing of all that here. The point of departure is evident and simple: the seven angels leave from the Temple, and there will be also a voice from the Temple which will give them the order to pour out the bowls and no one will be able to enter into the Temple as long as the plagues are not ended. This already calls for a remark: the Temple is not the place of wrath! It is the place of the revelation and the attestation of the love of God. It is not the place of destruction, of death, of rejection: it is the place that furnishes the foundation to the creation; it is its center; it is tied to the affirmation of life; it is the place of reconciliation. How could this *positive* image, repeated four times at the beginning of the septenary, inaugurate a negative and destructive action? There is complete contradiction. In fact this sequence tells us of disasters, of suffering, of terrors: but nowhere is it said that men are put to death and annihilated or damned. A second fundamental remark: all these texts relate *to men*. There is the constant insistence: men are struck by a malignant ulcer (16:2); men are scorched, or men bite their tongues (vss. 9–10); hail falls upon men (vs. 21). Then all the plagues express wrath and the arrival of judgment falling upon these men. On the contrary, in the sequence that follows (chapters 17 and 18), there is no longer even once a question of men. The word so frequently repeated here is not found once. By contrast we find here, on the one hand, the powerful, the rich, the kings; on the other hand, "those who belong to the earth" (and finally still one other thing that we will see later, but which does not concern man). There is actually a systematic contrast: what are subjected to suffering and pass through the *judgment* are in fact *men*. What are rejected, destroyed, annihilated are not men.

And it would be too simple to see a contrast between the poor and the rich (alone damned): we will have to see that the kings and the powerful insofar as they are men *also* (which today is too often forgotten) are not more damned than the others (at least according to the Apocalypse).

We sum up: the catastrophes then represent the judgment upon all humanity. Therefore that which is disclosed is the power of God. We have seen how it had been put between parentheses all through the Apocalypse (contrary to the impression that can be had), how God is veiled behind the Lamb. But this power of God nevertheless exists (although it is not by any means the most essential "attribute" of the biblical God); and sometimes it appears, but never completely—fortunately for us!—only, as 15: 8 says, through the smoke (the Temple was filled with smoke *because* of the glory of God and his power): a veiled power in order that, precisely, it does not bring about the death of humanity. As for the fact that no one can enter the Temple until the end of the plagues, it is in fact only after the totality of the judgment, after all and each will have passed through the fire, that the universalization of the Temple will be possible, in other words, the new creation. Once more, we notice now that the plagues that are described recall astonishingly and more than ever, the "plagues of Egypt," as in chapters 8 and 9, which is to say during the separation of the "Saints," of the people of God, from the rest of humanity.

It is unnecessary to say, on the one hand, that the seer does not at all claim to describe thereby, photographically, what will be, nor, on the other hand, is it necessary to study plague by plague "what it is" (what does he mean when he speaks of "hailstones"? etc.): rather, we must recall that the Apocalypse does not proceed by enigmas but by symbols. He does not propose to use either riddles or charades. It matters little if the sore is cancer or leprosy, if the scorching that is greater than the sun is the atomic bomb, and if the frogs are venomous or if they represent modern music. This kind of research has no meaning. By contrast, we must repeat that the evident allusion to the plagues of Egypt is essential (there are here six plagues

out of ten that are identical to those that had struck Egypt): the
meaning is the same; it is the "putting against the wall" before
the liberation, the harsh appeal to listen, spoken by God in
order that man be converted, and the refusal to be converted,
which provokes the annihilation of that which chains, shackles,
enslaves, alienates, and reifies the elect people: but now the
elect people is all of humanity. Therefore the issue has
changed: in Egypt God threatened Pharaoh and his people in
order to win the liberation of Israel. In this first time of judgment God drives humanity into a corner in order that the latter
might herself be set free from that which alienates (since the
people of God is humanity). And both times there is failure;
which is to say that the call of God addressed to man by means
of threats and plagues, by misery and suffering, in order that
man act of himself and freely, make his decision in the presence of the decision of God, understand that it is surely a
matter of a decision of God and enter by himself into this
design, make himself the final decision—then for Pharaoh the
free and autonomous decision to let the Hebrew people depart
—this decision is not made and the call of God is not heard.
On the contrary, in the two cases the effect is the reverse.
Pharaoh hardens his heart and is confirmed in his own decision, in his will to be the master of slaves. Humanity, all men,
refuse to perceive grace, a gospel, in the suffering that they
endure, to hear an appeal: on the contrary, they decide that
God is bad, that God is unjust, that God is a tyrant, that God
wishes finally evil for men (and there is, for example, the
famous story of the contradiction between the wicked God of
the Old Testament opposed to the good God of Jesus, or,
again, the theology of the death of God because God holds
man in slavery or in his minority, etc.). Man judges God on the
basis of these trials of which he refuses to comprehend the
meaning. The text constantly insists upon this: man is struck
by hailstones, he blasphemes; man is scorched by the heat of
the sun, he blasphemes. He totally refuses to see that the
liberator acts thus in order to liberate him (and so by means
of suffering). He imputes the evil that befalls him to the wickedness of this liberator. He does not change the direction of

his life. Thus man himself is placed in judgment because he pretends to judge God. Not only is he not freed from his alienation but he pretends himself to be the judge of God. And it is this very thing that judges him. It is not the plagues themselves that are the judgment; it is the fact that man sounds the most profound abyss of evil, of perdition, of remoteness from God, of dehumanization, of slavery, when he now declares himself judge over against God. "Master, I knew you to be a hard man, reaping where you did not sow, and gathering where you did not winnow." Man blasphemes, shows thereby that he has heard absolutely nothing, received nothing, experienced nothing of the work of God, the love of God. He fills to overflowing that which happened at the moment of Genesis. The rupture between man and God appears even more fundamental than with Adam. And of course God is going to be that which man says that he is. As in the parable of the talents! But when man thus blasphemes he does not injure God himself, who remains God; which the text clearly says when it emphasizes: they blaspheme God *who has power,* or again, the God *of Heaven.* On the contrary, when he blasphemes he manifests how far he is from God, which is to say that he proclaims his own perdition, his definitive death. But note: this means that man is not condemned; he condemns himself. And still more, it means not at all that man is lost, but that he declares himself lost, which is a wholly different thing.

As far as the plagues are concerned, the first four strike men themselves and are chosen according to the law of reciprocity, which is emphasized in the text. Thus men are afflicted with a malignant sore, which is the counterpart, or the response to, the mark of the beast. All have upon them this mark, which grants permission to live according to the ways of the society and to make a pseudo-communion; this mark is transformed into another mark, or rather, its reality is disclosed and revealed as cancer, leprosy, etc. Just as the water becomes blood because men have, throughout the course of their history and without fail, shed the blood of apostles, prophets, witnesses, saints of God; in the same way it could be said that because they have stolen fire from the sky, the sun then becomes the source of a terrible energy that destroys men; or again because they have transformed the sun into God, then that will be the very point of their suffering.

The law of reciprocity is frequent in this genre of writing, but, moreover, full of meaning and does not present any particular difficulties except that we must clearly take account of the fact that the judgment of God takes place in the direction established by man himself. In some way, God lets the act of man develop: it is in this sense, and *in this sense only,* that "our acts judge us" or again that "each will be judged according to his works." We must not, as we have already said, consider this an adroit weighing of good and bad works effected by a God who is prepared to give blame or benediction. It is not that. But God lets the work of man bear its own fruits: and that *is* the judgment. Man suffers the consequences of that which he has done. The mark of the beast becomes a consumption destructive of flesh and soul. But it always was, and man has chosen his own way. It suffices that the works of man be disclosed in their profound reality, which is to say, that we know that this mark we bear—with what delight—is the mark of the beast in order for it to brand us and consume our life. It suffices that the spilled blood be revealed as that of saints and martyrs for it to become the source of the poisoning of our race. The only intervention of God here, in everything, is the revelation, the disclosure, of what the profound reality of the work of man has been: then man is requited according to his work and according to his due by the simple development of his specific work; there is no need of anything more. Such is the judgment according to our works.[2]

Now we see that beginning with the fifth bowl a change takes place. It is clearly always a matter of the judgment of men, but no longer of men alone; which is to say that each time man is taken in his relation with something else. And perhaps this is only taking responsibility for the apotheosis of the work of man? Thus with the fifth we see the throne of the beast appear; with the sixth, the dragon, the beast, and the false prophet; with the seventh, the great city of Babylon. The plagues always attack men; for example, the enormous hailstones when the city is destroyed, but there is a sort of apparition of more than man in this event. These are manifestly the powers, analyzed before, which now come into play. But it is still the moment of the judgment of men. But what men? The exemplary text here is that of the fifth bowl: it is poured out upon the throne of the beast, whose kingdom is plunged into darkness and men then bite their tongues in anguish and howl in suffering. A clever exegete, who understands nothing of the text, declares that we truly do not see why man would cry out in anguish because the kingdom of the beast is plunged into darkness. Then, he concludes skillfully, there is here a mixture of two verses, and since the second phrase speaks of sores, he disconnects it from the text in order to attach it to verse 2 where it is also a question of sores. What genius! But does it not suffice very simply to refer to the meaning of "the Beast": if it is, as we will see, the political power, today the State, what does this plunge into darkness mean except that this power becomes blind, no longer knows what it does, acts at random, uses its power without discernment, is incapable of leading and administering the human group, the society? If it is thus, do we not believe that in fact man begins to howl in fear and anguish? If the ordering power becomes blind, if the bearer of historical omnipotence strikes at random (we know it well, it is enough to consider history), then we are certainly in the presence of a frightful plague; and the slaughter of wars, revolutions, and extermination camps remind us of this continually! But although the political power has become blind, man does not repent of his work: on the contrary, he desires still more of it. Which is to say that he continues to make politics and to put his confidence in this marvelous power. Therefore what is stressed here, as in the sixth and seventh bowls, is the association between men and the powers. With the sixth it is the gathering of kings, the union of all the powers of man added to the demonic powers in order to enter into direct combat against God, with the monopoly of spiritual powers (three demonic spirits, a triad, or trinity which corresponds to the seven spirits of God, and working of miracles, of wonders, in order to seduce men and enlist them in the action against God

—the miracles of Science? too easy? but perhaps not foolish?).
With the seventh, it is the association of men with the divinity
of the City,[3] with Babylon the great, ultimate power of the
revolt against God. The three sequences, then, make a new
dimension appear and announce what is to follow, namely, the
judgment, *and this time the destruction* of the powers which alienate man and destroy him. We are once more in the presence
of the system of first allusions, or, again, of connection: chapters 17 and 18 (judgment of kings, of Babylon, etc.) are here
fitted into the established relation between these forces and
man.

But then what is the particular judgment evoked here? What
judgment upon man? What is properly speaking the suffering
of man, the trial? I believe that inasmuch as this series expressly envisages the plagues upon man, inasmuch as the communion (the assembling) between men and the powers is in-
sisted upon, and the annihilation of the powers here
announced (the great city is already broken), the true drama
of this series is that we observe the very harsh action of God
in breaking man apart from the powers with which he has
established his covenant, with which he has associated himself.
It is the break between man and the angels, the *exousiai,* the
beasts, etc. It is the moment when the sharp two-edged sword
capable of separating bone and marrow passes through the
world of men; it is the moment when the cancer that consumes
man is operated upon, leaving him with a gaping wound, an
absence in his eyes irreparable. It is the moment when the
communion that man had established is ruptured, when the
power that he had finally acquired is seized from him, when
the world that he had constructed for himself is destroyed (there
is surely the darkening of the political power, the assembly of
the Powers for a defeat, and the disintegration of the city,
which man had desired to make his exclusive domain). Then
we comprehend the lamentations and the suffering, the sur-
gery and reduction to impotence, abdication of the pretended
sovereignty of man (which was his degradation), experienced
demonstration that his autonomy that he claimed to be his
liberty was in reality his alienation. Here is the last judgment.
Here is the meaning of the last three bowls.[4]

Destruction of Human Works

And now we pass to the period of destruction and condemnation in chapters 17 and 18. But we observe that all this refers to the Great Prostitute, to Babylon, the great city. Of course this reacts also upon all those who are associated with her, or rather, upon all that in man which is associated with her. But we are going to interpret this point more closely. Of course, we find here again the plurality of meaning in symbols. At times a certain symbol is here explicitly designated: the seven heads of the beast are seven mountains but also seven kings (17:9); but at times the author gratuitously complicates the situation when he writes that the beast belongs to the seven but that it is nevertheless an eighth king. It is very evident that one of the aspects (but by no means the only one!) of this symbolism relates to the fact that the Apocalypse is a historical document, written in a given historical moment, envisaging an actual history, that it is also a political document concerned with the political organs and political powers of its time, but that it extends the field considerably; it takes this historical and political circumstance as the point of departure for a totally new interpretation; it inserts this historico-political dimension into the traditional apocalyptic structure; it charges the event with a meaning that it did not naturally have; and finally it transforms, precisely, the utilized concrete given into symbol. (In that it is radically different from gnosis: the latter never has ideas or concepts that are symbolized. Also in that it is attached to Jewish thought: real history serves as the base, the support, the point of reference for the symbolic expression.) However that may be, here the historical given is particularly clear. We cannot expatiate upon this. But Babylon and the great prostitute is Rome. She sits on the shore of the sea, upon seven hills; she has known seven kings. This, moreover, presents a little problem from the historical point of view; finally, we do not know exactly where we are. The first seven Roman Caesars (improperly called emperors: the empire actually began much later) are Augustus, Tiberias, Caligula, Claudius, Nero, Gallia, and Othon. And this is very embarrassing for the exegetes who absolutely insist upon dating the Apocalypse according to the number of "emperors." In fact the last are situated in A.D. 69. And there is no correspondence between the seven "emperors" and the persecutions of Domitian, who in reality is the eleventh. Still more, on condition of not counting as the Romans of the epoch did, who made the new regime begin not with Augustus but with Caesar, in which case the seventh prince is Gallia and Domitian the twelfth. But on the contrary, if we focus on verse 10, declaring that the *sixth is reigning* (the seventh has not yet come, and will endure only a little time, which was true for Gallia), that brings us back to Nero. In which case the Apocalypse would have been published about 65, which very few historians admit. In reality this research on historical identification—so-called historical—is as uncertain as the old allegorical speculations of which so much fun is made today.

As for the ten horns that are also ten kings, why not then go as far as the seventeenth or eighteenth Caesar? Why treat the seven kings of verse 9 and the ten kings of verse 12 differently? Finally, a last difficulty, the text speaks without interruption of *basileus*, "king." Never did the princes bear this title at this epoch. On the contrary, they had resisted when some wished to give it to them. In other words, these historical researches appear to me essentially inexact, and it is not an enumeration of the "emperors" of Rome nor a dating that we must seek here.[5] The problem at bottom is that of symbol. We interpret in a completely superficial fashion that Babylon is the symbol for Rome; then the seven heads that are seven kings are the symbols for Roman emperors. But here we simply confound the symbol and the coding. Because, for many exegetes, if the writer employs such an obscure language (not so obscure—all the elements for deciphering are given us) it is to hide the revolutionary character of this text from the eyes of the "police." But at this moment it is a matter of a coding in order to issue a secret message, not at all a matter of symbol. When we have "deciphered" that Babylon is Rome we have not explained the symbol in the least; we have simply situated the text historically, given its historical reference, which is a wholly different thing. I would say the process is the reverse: Babylon is not the symbol of Rome; it is Rome, a historical reality, which is transformed into the symbol of a more profound and polymorphous reality of which Babylon has traditionally been the expression. Rome is not first of all Rome; when this has been said, nothing has been said. Rome is an actualized symbol, the historical presence of a permanent, complex, and multiple phenomenon. That the seven heads are the seven mountains where the woman resides is here the coding: the woman is Rome. But that she is also the seven kings is symbol: the king is assuredly the constant image of the political power. Seven is the perfection of this power (and surely Rome represents the perfection of the political power). There is still imperfection (the conquest and organization of the power are not completed: the sixth reigns), but the seventh, which assures the perfection of the power, will certainly come. Only, having arrived at the summit of its perfection, even so this political power will not endure. *The beast is itself the power, the* exousia, *the Spirit of power:* in this sense it is both an eighth king and, nevertheless, part of the seven (which, to those seven, represents all power). And two more symbolic messages are addressed to us; the woman is seated upon the beast (then she rests in her historic actuality upon the political power! *She is a historic actualization of the Power*) but the beast detests the woman, which is to say that Rome finally will be destroyed in the very place where she has triumphed; she sits upon the political power and it is the political power that will destroy her. With the numbers seven and ten to designate the kings (ten being the unlimited) we find again the same problem as the preceding: it is *the* political power, perfect and unlimited, but it is not unitary; it is distributed, divided, portioned out: it is exercised by a certain number of kings, emperors, etc. There is then the double vision: this political power which has a constant reality and the exercise of this power in different forms and with diverse durations through the course of history. For the moment it is Rome who is seated above and who maintains the entire totality.

The second essential indication is that *the woman is the great city.* Rome is then not only the actual, historic representation of the political power, but also the city. The city in the absolute, like Babylon; and there is a double judgment upon her: as political power and as city, concentration of the culture and the work of man. But there is still a problem, which can be taken up before coming to the judgment itself: Rome with its "Satanic" power is represented under the form of a woman, while we are told in chapter 12 that it is the Mother of the new creation, the point of Incarnation, who is represented as a woman. Then the two texts belong to two different sources because it is not possible that the same symbol (I would say the same image) represent two things so radically different. But, once more, this appears to me very flimsy as an argument,[6] since there is explicit utilization of the same image to signify its ambivalence. In fact the Woman in heaven is the image of the mother; on earth she is the prostitute. Exactly as throughout the Bible she is at the same time Eve and Mary! She is the Mother of the new creation and the concentration of everything terrestrial. That does not appear to me abnormal in relation to the biblical data, but, on the contrary, completely conformed to the representation of the woman in the Bible (cf., for example, Hosea). And it is not for nothing, but intentional that the author tells us in both cases that the woman is "in the wilderness." She represents the exact opposite of the work that God carries out in the Incarnation.

We find then three principal themes on the subject of this Woman: she is first of all *the great prostitute* (Rome, to be sure, for the given historical moment; but not she alone: in reality the summation of all that which is prostitution, as Babylon in her time, who became the symbol of it). Prostitution that is not of the moral and sexual order. It is the being in communication (by sacred prostitution) with the religious and spiritual powers, with the satanic sources, and esoterism (but this also implies the immoralities, which are completely secondary). It is certainly also the sign of infidelity, this dispersion of figurative sexuality being the image of the impossibility of a true *covenant,* of a fidelity between being and being, of a trust and a faith, we would say today of an authentic communication. It is, further, the sign of the insertion of "love" into the domain of money, of exchange, of power: it is not for nothing that we are told, first, of the character of prostitution in order then to pass to power and then to money. Prostitution is the diabolic parody of love. So the opposite of God. It is at the same time that which binds this "love" to money and to power: and this ends in being the opposite of the work of the God of Jesus Christ (the woman prostitute is the exact opposite of the woman mother of the child). This is prostitution, not at all a moral, sexual affair, more or less "traditional and bourgeois." All the characteristics described to us are true of both the Woman and the Beast. That the latter is covered with blasphemous names does not signify, as has been said too often, participation in the imperial cult (which in fact existed in the oriental part of the empire, but which at the time the Apocalypse was written was not nearly as important as it later became); these are, rather, the designations of powers who pretend to reproduce the truth of God by reversing it: we must not forget that the first meaning of blasphemy is to defame. There is defamation of God in the affirmations of the powers. We must never forget this when we declare that God is this or that in order to be able to deny him more easily: it is then that we blaspheme. This is related to the characteristics of both the Woman and the Beast: power, wealth, persecution of the truth (17:6), and of course also immorality. As we have said above, we must not overestimate the latter, making this immorality the cause of the condemnation of the Great Prostitute, but it must not be totally ignored either: it is true that the destruction of morality, of ethics (not necessarily *Christian*) is a significant factor of the power. The latter is always the destroyer of values.

This woman is named Babylon. And we must not forget that this means, first of all, *Babel:* "the door of the gods," which is to say the place where "the gods who are not gods," the pretenders, the inverse, the seducers, penetrate into the human world and drive toward the perversion of man, to divert him, to prevent him from hearing the appeal addressed by the only Father, by the God who is Love. But Babylon is also the place of the historic capitivity of Israel: that is, the place of the captivity of the people of God, of the witnesses; and beginning with this it has become the symbol of the captivity of the revelation, then of the Word of God, which will signify the myth of Babel: the destruction of the unity of the word; and henceforth it is the world of the negation of the Word of God. This woman holds a golden cup: exactly as the seven angels. She does what God does. She claims to establish a communion, as God does. And this is surely what happens. But if the cup of God is communion with the blood of redemption by his Son; if the cup of the angels of God is communion with wrath, judgment, and condemnation; the cup of Babylon can be only the cup of communion with the perversion, the corruption, of the Woman. Each gives communion with that which he himself is.

We come then to the second face of this power which is judged: Rome *as political power.* She has the same accessory representatives and designations as the Beast, which came from the sea and which was the State, the complete political power (17:7–18). Rome is mounted upon the political power: she is borne by this *exousia.* And her hills or her kings, her political chiefs, are identified with the marks of power qualified to the absolute. For the text tells us that these temporary historical incarnations (for example, the ten kings) have only one single purpose: "to give over their power and authority to the beast" (vs. 13). This is very important: the political *exousia* is the base, the source of the concrete powers, but the latter in the very exercise of their force imagine, invent new actions, new forms, new means, which implement and augment the political power itself. These constitutional forms are nothing by themselves; they exist by "the Beast," but they have from the beginning of their existence an autonomy creative of a renewed expression of the fundamental power. It is this action that is the very place of the political. The ten kings who have not yet received the throne, but who put their power at the service of the Beast, are certainly, historically, Rome's rival powers; they will be the "successors" of Rome (much more than vassal kings). They are that which Rome had been before her triumph, by relation to the Beast. And they will destroy the

Woman, by that terrible logic of the political that is necessarily destructive of every form that has come to its completion. And it cannot be otherwise, since the Beast, image and representative of the Dragon, is a force that always leads finally to annihilation. There is an autodestruction of political forces at the interior of history. That which makes them live, that which gives them authority, that upon which they are based, is the very spirit that finally repudiates them, because it is the annihilator. This is a mechanism in which God has played the role of "logician"; verse 17 is extraordinary: "for God has put it into their hearts to carry out his purpose by being of one mind and giving over their royal power to the beast, until the words of God shall be fulfilled." Thus God accepts the action of the revolt of the Beast and of the political power. He simply provokes these powers to be logically, faithfully at the service of this Beast who is the Destroyer of itself. In awaiting this realization, Rome is, verse 18 reminds us, the actual incarnation of the power and the queen of the kings of the earth.

Nevertheless we insist upon a very important fact: Rome is not a state, but *the City*. This is essential and shows to what degree the seer of the Apocalypse is, even so, alert to the political reality of his time. The historians of institutions know that this was the great problem that Rome had to solve. Up to this time two types of political structure were known: the empires, with an organization of empire and a capital (or rather a King-God), and the cities, which functioned upon another model but which could not be extended beyond a very small territory. Rome at the beginning is a city, a city with a political vocation, with a democratic and popular political structure *(res populica)* and consequently with little capacity for self-extension. But her efficacy had provoked that expansion. She had become mistress of an immense territory, *but which was not an empire.* It had no unitary structure, no preformed centralization, no divine personage at the origin. Rome for two hundred years will seek to adapt her structures of urban administration (magistrates, senate, assemblies of the people) to a gigantic organization without becoming an empire similar to those of Persia or Egypt. The old administrators of Rome become the political men of the Mediterranean world; and it is in this search and this mutation that the discovery of the concept of the state is effected. So in chapters 17 and 18 we see the two faces of Rome: the political center, the political power (which is not the capital but the state) and the other: the city. Whence the *double* condemnation; as political power (17:7–18) and as rich and powerful city, the great City (chapter 18).[7]

In the text we see the great City represented as the concentration of all Roman culture (which it is!), of all the power of men, of all the forms of civilization. Rome represents the world of man, created by him, expressing to the exclusion of every other tendency his will, his intelligence, his purpose—human, exclusively human. As was Babylon. That which characterizes her is political power (18:3); commercial activity (the merchants of the earth are enriched by the extravagance of her luxury, and during her fall the merchants weep because no one any longer buys their merchandise); luxury, refinement, beauty, all that which we can actually call culture, civilization (vss. 3, 14–15), art (the playing of the harpists and musicians, the flute and trumpet players); and production (artistic or industrial; no artisan will be found any longer, the sound of the millstone will no longer be heard). In other words she concentrates in herself all human activity, and, even more, she is the point of intersection of the two historic forces that had been shown to us at first: that of political power and of economic activity. She is, finally, the place of the happiness of man under all its forms, happiness material and intellectual, happiness of luxury and even of human love. And her condemnation indicates this: the light of the lamp will no longer shine in you; the voice of the young bridegroom and his companion will no longer be heard. Place of human fulfillment.

But on the other hand, she is the abode of demons, the place of depravity, of human glory and pride (vss. 2–3). Further, she is the place of slavery and alienation. Here I will insist upon the translation of verse 13; after the long and beautiful description of merchandise of every sort (vss. 12–13) brought by the merchants to the city, after the horses and chariots, and according to a skillfully ascending progression, we come to:

soma kai psyche anthropōn, that the classic and literal translation
renders by: "bodies and souls of men," but which others render by: "slaves and captives." I must say that that does not
appear to me at all satisfactory. Of course, this translation rests
upon the interpretation that when we speak of "souls" we
mean simply man. But then why the repetition: bodies and
souls? I do not think this is a simple poetic formula to mean
banally men, nothing more. It has the sense of two words
being used. And we must clearly translate by two terms,
whence the translation "slaves and captives," which does not
mean anything. We must keep bodies and souls. And what
meaning can that have? That the "bodies of men" mean slaves
there can be no doubt, since the slave still at this time is
defined as *res:* he is a thing, he does not have a soul. The idea
that the slave can have a soul will appear a little later. But then
we must consider that commerce in the souls of men means
something else. I believe, without any doubt, that this refers
to the interior possession of man. The free man who has a soul
is also an object of commerce of the great city. He is also
possessed, as a slave, but interiorly. It is his soul that is the
object of traffic. He is *alienated* to the great city. This is actually
the only coherent meaning. And this alienation of man, the
dispossession of himself, is here bound in a completely clear
fashion to economic activity, to commerce and enrichment: it
is wealth that produces not only exterior slavery but also alienation to the economy and subjection by this interior way.

And this leads to the discovery of the sorcery of the city to
seduce and alienate (18:23). To be sure, this sorcery may be
simply magic and witchcraft, which in fact are found abundantly in Rome; but it must not be forgotten that that is once
more put in direct relation to commerce and wealth: the latter
is the sorcery that, above all, possesses men. And finally the
city is that which kills. She kills the prophets, which signifies
not only the death of men, but the will to hear nothing—even
more, to destroy the Word of God and Revelation. She is the
one who kills the saints, those who by their very lives represent
the will of God upon earth. She excludes all that which is not
herself, all that which does not enter directly into her activity,

all that which does not reinforce her; she kills all that which comes for the sake of God. Exactly as it is described to us in the parable of the vine-dressers, finally to become by herself and for herself proprietor of the world. Such is the city.

And we perceive her complexity: on the one hand, the identification between the city and the total human culture, the most elevated, the most finished; and on the other hand, the double face of this civilization: her splendor, her success, her wealth, her luxury, and her spiritual reality. Of course, the exegete and historian will protest and say, correctly: "It is a matter of Rome, only of Rome; this is an abusive extension." I would respond, first, that if, obviously, Rome is here envisaged, we must not forget *who* she was precisely at this epoch, called gloriously the URBS, with capital letters: the City in herself. I would then recall the symbolic character of the Apocalypse; and I have shown above that in this whole section Rome is a symbol of something else. I would say furthermore that the design of the entire Apocalypse (this vision of the Church, of history, of the Incarnation) cannot be suddenly reduced to the question of whether Rome will endure or be condemned. We know also at what point with the prophets the historic event is the sign of something else signified, and the prophecy denotes another dimension to its subject. We have exactly the same movement. From the strictly political discussion (power or nonpower of Rome in herself), we pass constantly to a larger dimension, concerning the totality of humanity, the structure of society. There we have the arguments of scientific exegesis, which demand interpretation outside the framework of purely historical data.

To that I wish to add a question. Are we very sure, when we desire at any price to reduce the text exclusively to its insertion into a given time and place, to restore it to its past historical framework, and when we refuse as imaginary, metaphysical, fantastic, every interpretation which exceeds that delimitation, are we very sure that we are not attempting thereby to protect ourselves against the text? This word concerning imperial Rome of the first century, the emperors and merchants of the epoch, no longer concerns me. Then I can manipulate it without danger. That which it says was perhaps threatening and explosive for the time when it was spoken, but today . . . . A means pure and simple for getting rid of an embarrassing interpretation under a scientific pretense. Consequently all this leads me to affirm that what is said here of Rome definitely envisages the City, all cities, those of the past and those of the present. Our metropolises and megapolises. And who then would dare say that the description given here of Rome does not correspond perfectly, trait for trait, to the historic city? Even from the point of view of a scientific method of functional sociology we cannot evade saying that chapter 18 is the City.

Let us now consider the judgment and the condemnation. They are triple, bearing upon each of the elements that we have distinguished. We will not return to the condemnation of *the woman, the great prostitute,* seated upon the beast and representing *the political power* incarnate temporarily in Rome: Rome will be destroyed by the other political powers; she will become solitary and naked; the kings will eat her flesh and burn her in the fire (18:16). Nothing can be added to this. But now comes the judgment of *the city,* cultural power and sum of civilization: what appears to me most striking is that all through this text once more a distinction is made between men and Babylon. Even those who have prostituted themselves with her are not included in her condemnation and fall: the kings will weep and lament *over her* (vs. 9) (then they are outside, they see the spectacle); the text explicitly says that they stand at a distance. The drama that overtakes the city does not overtake them. The merchants go into mourning (vs. 11) and they also lament at a distance (vs. 15). Then the communion established by the enchantments and sorceries of the city is broken. She no longer possesses men. The latter weep and lament because some, the kings, have lost their power; others, the merchants, have lost the source of their wealth: they are, with her, deprived of that which made them the Great, the Powerful, the Rich. But they themselves, as men, are outside the blow. The seafaring men stand at a distance (vs. 17) and contemplate the spectacle of the conflagration of the city of

cities. They mourn over her but are not put to death with her
(vs. 19). They are dumfounded at this judgment (that the glory
of the civilization hid from them), at its rapidity (an hour
suffices). But they are not themselves included in this judgment. Thus Babylon is destroyed, but she, and she alone, as
power, as instigator of evil, but not the men who prostitute
themselves with her or have been seduced by her: we find
ourselves then in the presence of the condemnation, the destruction of the *historic forms,* of the "incarnations" (and Rome
is essential as a historic symbol) adopted at a particular moment or at any moment by the fundamental powers, the powers issuing from the Dragon, the two beasts, the power of the
Antichrist. But these historic forms are never a man; they are
an organization, a society, a nation, a structure, an abstract
specification such as money, the state, the city, technique, etc.;
and we will see later that this is confirmed by the judgment and
condemnation of the *nations.* But all this is what has produced
the *grandeur* of man. Now the latter is reduced to being only
himself.

The condemnation consists then in paying her double in her
own money: doing to her doubly what she has done. And on
the other hand, it is the demonstration of the vanity of her
word (vs. 7). She has said: "A queen I sit, I am no widow,
mourning I shall never see," because of that the plagues will
come upon her: death, mourning, famine. This was the word
of the power opposed to the Word of God. The judgment is
the simple requital of that which man does under this impulsion, and the quelling of his usurpations: this double movement causes the disappearance of both the alienation of man
and the power that alienated him. But there is, on the other
hand, a people of God, who are mixed with this population and
who live in this city, and who know this glorious success (vss.
4 and following): the people are called to depart from the city,
as quickly as possible, from this world of powers (cf. Isaiah
48:20–52; Jeremiah 50:8–51:45). The same experience as that
of Lot. It is necessary to abandon this culture of the spirit of
power to her destiny of destruction, not to partake of her
communion. The difference between these people of God who

are in the city and the other men who prostitute themselves with her is that the people of God are warned in advance; they must make their preparations in advance and withdraw (to be in the world but not of the world), while the others at the moment of the event depart in catastrophe, stand at a distance, are dumfounded at what happens, and comprehend nothing. The former are joyful at what happens (vs. 20) (finally the powers of death and alienation are destroyed!); the others are in mourning because they see disappear all that in which they have believed, that which they have created, which they have loved, that with which they have communed. Such is the true (but only) distinction between men. There are no "saved" and "damned," "elect" and "rejected," at least in these texts. And finally the "Saints and Witnesses," the people of God, participate in the work of judgment: they are even the agents of this judgment and condemnation. The prayer of the martyrs encountered above is answered; but we see what its meaning is: not vengeance against other men, but destruction of the powers that alienate *all* men and whose malignant character is revealed in the massacre of the saints! The Word of God at this moment says to them: "Repay, . . . give her a like measure of torment." The judgment of the powers is tied to the Saints' departure from this catastrophe, and to their decision. But God alone can *exterminate* the powers (vs. 21).

A last point must detain us: once more it is a question of the cup (vs. 6). In the cup where she has mixed her wines, mix for her a double draught. Again an act of the Saints and the Martyrs. We must examine this symbol: the seven cups of the wrath of God. The cup of the abomination of Babylon. The cup of requital. We have often said that the cup is a symbol of communion. Babylon has made men commune with her power. But then do not the seven cups (bowls) of wrath also signify communion: the communion of men with the wrath of God? Is there not *still* the hidden symbol of a communion of men with God even in the process of wrath and judgment? And that can have two dimensions. First, to be subjected to the wrath of God, to be under his judgment, his Word of reprimand and threat, is to commune with God. Because of the

Incarnation, every presence of God implies communion. This is not rupture, rejection, silence, turning away. That alone would be the rupture of communion with the Father. But the other aspect is the participation offered to man to concur in the judgment (as we see it here), to enter into the penultimate decision of God, to be seated upon the very throne of the judge. (But who is seated here except the Son of Man, and with him, in him, those who form his body, the men who were faithful?) As Paul reminds us (1 Cor. 6:3), the elect upon their thrones judge even the angels, the powers. The cup of wrath and judgment, which is at the same time the cup of communion, means then that man participates even in this act of God, the act before the last.

Finally, there remains the fact that the text makes a brief allusion to the destruction of the beast itself (17:8). We have observed here the condemnation of the *historic incarnations* of the Beasts and of the Dragon. But this evidently also reaches the Power that is behind them; it is not without effect upon that Power's reality. It is nothing if it no longer finds anything in which to be incarnate, in which to express itself. Its destruction is still not realized (we will read of it in chapters 19 and 20), but *already it is no longer,* when all its expressions are destroyed. Everything happens as if these powers were already dead. The judgment of death is already pronounced by God, whether we see it, know it, or not. The text is clear: it was; it is no longer. It is going to rise from the abyss (which is to say, leave its place, disclose itself for what it is, without its temporary identifications; it is going to present itself for the last combat) and vanish to perdition. Then that which characterizes it is that it is *without future.* It goes inevitably to its destruction. God is the one who is, was, and *who comes;* the Beast was, but is no longer. The absolute political power, in spite of its claim to make history, no longer has any history: no future is any longer possible for it. The Beast is not ever so little creative of true history. At any rate, that which is here condemned, destroyed, is the power, the forms and means of the power, and among them those which are essential: politics and money. If we examine the text closely, it is that, all that, which is envisaged, without any distinction between a good and a bad political power, a democracy and a dictatorship, between a good and a bad use of money: be that as it may, it is never anything other than power. Power expressed by exploitation, domination, enslavement; and we emphasize that it is not solely in regard to man that these are condemned, but also in regard to nature. The image of the city is essential to this subject. For we must take account of the fact that the thorough exploitation, the destruction of the natural milieu, its replacement by a totally artificial milieu, the putting to use of "natural resources" without restraint and without limit, is an aspect of the power as completely condemned as the exploitation of man. And this exploitation (that we know, and which is expressly pointed out in the text dealing with *certain* aspects of the condemned wealth) has nothing to do, strictly nothing to do, with the texts of Genesis and Psalm 8, always invoked to justify the techniques of exploitation of the world. And those who suffer from this destruction of the means of power are in fact the powerful, the kings, the rich, the merchants, the seafaring men (those astronauts of the epoch!): they themselves are not destroyed, but they lament to see their work, their means, their labor, their grandeur, disappear. This is not completely without importance. For from this moment the true judgment upon them is finally having to say: "All this being abolished, I have then lived for nothing. Of all my works, of all my efforts, nothing remains." That is the judgment upon the kings and the rich.

Damnation of the Powers

We come now to the last chapter of the judgment and condemnation. After the destruction of the historic forms comes the damnation of the powers themselves, of which 17:8 is the first intimation. Once more the mechanism of "first allusions" and "connections": the first allusion to what will follow is slipped into the description of the condemnation of the historic incarnations, the point of connection beginning from which the following development, 19:17–21 and chapter 20, will unfold.

But here we must emphasize a difference: the historic incarnations of the powers (state, city, money, etc.) have been destroyed. They have not been damned. They were the *works,* and the *works of man.* As "construction," "structure," organization, they have been destroyed: which corresponds exactly to that work. No damnation, because they have not pretended to abolish God. Now, on the contrary, we pass to the plane of the Powers themselves; and here for the first time that which can be interpreted as a damnation appears. Now it is the Spirit of Power and the diverse forms of that spirit that are attacked. But here we are going to have two more stages: there is the destruction of the beasts (19:20), then the destruction of the Dragon, Satan, etc. (20:10); finally, "the last enemy to be destroyed" (and to find that formula again explicitly illustrated here shows that it was surely a common belief in the primitive Church); it is the destruction of death and the abode of the dead.

There is then a conjuncture in the whole series of judgments and condemnations as we have seen them: first, man who is judged and who passes through his great putting in question; then the work of the power of man, which is a complexity, a mixture, a point of encounter between man and the powers, being at the same time his work (the political power in its historicity, money, the city); then the powers that have inspired that work, that are incarnate in it (the beasts); then that which has given power and authority to the beasts, has created them (the Dragon); finally, that which has been the great agent of history and which is the nonmeaning of that history and of life—Death, in whose name the Dragon could reign, or more exactly the very one who is the origin of the Dragon, and his sole designation. Consequently there is a rigorous connection in the order of judgments and condemnations that are here depicted for us. But we must surely guard against an error easy to commit. When I have written: "there is first of all; . . . then; . . . finally . . . ," my discourse, which follows the order of the discourse of John, develops in time. Sequences *succeed* other sequences. And that then gives the impression of a reflection of an actual temporal series. I will begin with that which *in reality* begins, and I will end with that which *in reality* ends.

Though it is not so. It is a didactic discourse. Exactly as the discourse of the Apocalypse with its minute construction is didactic. Moreover, every myth is in part didactic and pedagogical. But its purpose is to be an adaptation to the possibilities of the reader's comprehension. And these possibilities of comprehension are situated in time, so the discourse must develop as if it were the description of a temporal series. In reality we know nothing of that. Above all we must not read this as a cinematography of successive events. All that does not so unfold in reality, nor in truth according to the logical order that I have set forth: as it is described for us in the Apocalypse. Obviously we must not believe that in the year 2087 there will be the first series of plagues, then in 2095 the judgment of the historic incarnation (Rome had been destroyed in 465, but reconstituted; and the empire had been put to death, but others had taken its place, etc.). And finally there will be a thousand years of history without the presence of Satan, etc. There is no temporal succession of that kind because it is a matter of the design of God, of the action of God, which is reckoned in eternity, so that its historical actualizations are surprising for us. As we have often said, with the Apocalypse we are in the historical (but which most often serves, for example, only as a springboard and that which furnishes symbols) and at the same time in the meta or the transhistorical, and also in "eternity"—insofar as this word can signify something for us. In any case that which it certainly signifies is that the historical succession to which we are accustomed has no place here. It is not a perpetual present, nor an addition to the future, nor to the past. Then we must not interpret any of these texts in a temporal schema; so in particular the "thousand years" when Satan is chained cannot be interpreted as a period of human history. Already, in this text, the immediate junction (20:2–3): "and bound him for a thousand years and threw him into the pit" shows that this is situated in the place—Nonplace—where the relations between God and Satan unfold—the "heaven" if we wish, not our time, which knows only the consequences of them.

That said, we can take up the development of the discourse:

we encounter, first, an essential distinction between men and
the two Beasts (19:17–21). On the one hand, there is a kind
of natural putting to death of men, who remain upon the earth
as dead; on the other, there is the annihilation of the Beast and
of the False Prophet (who is the second beast). Both are
thrown into the lake of fire and brimstone, which expresses
their pure and simple damnation. Their historic role is ended;
their power is destroyed (after their *means* of power have been
destroyed, and without these means they are nothing). They
are actually abolished. It is not the same for all those men who
have served them, who have worn their mark—kings and rul-
ers, powerful and rich, but also slave and free, small and great:
all those who have had the mark of the beast. These die, and
it is the end of the seven bowls of judgment; but I would say
a temporal, historic death and *carnal.* Moreover, the text emphatically insists upon carnal: it repeats the word six times in
four verses where the birds are summoned to eat the flesh of
these men (19:18), which they do (vs. 21). *Sarx* is certainly
meant in the New Testament sense, not "body," nor "matter
of the living being": it is not corporality which is destroyed,
but the *sarx* in the sense of "that which is carnal" of the Gospels and Paul, which is to say, that in man which is separated
from God, hostile to God, which is bound to the world and is
of no avail (it is the Spirit that gives life, the flesh is of no avail),
etc. And we insist once more that is not the body. But of course
it is not the Being itself. Thus in these verses we observe the
destruction of the "negative" flesh: it is that which is uprooted
from man, that which is stripped from him, which is now rejected; it is not man himself. Nowhere has it ever been said that
man is only flesh, that there is in man nothing other than this
sarx. In other words, he is again subjected to a stripping: after
the destruction of his works of power, there is taken away from
him, from his inwardness, from his being, all that which is
"flesh," revolt and refusal of God, attachment to the things of
the earth, to the here-below, to the "World." That is uprooted
from him, by a surgical operation. But that is not *death,* in the
negative sense, in the sense of the triumph of death; it is not
entry into the abode of the dead. On the contrary, I would say

it is the purification preliminary to entrance into the kingdom of the living. The judgment of men ends not in their rejection but in this rupture in themselves, in this extraction of the malignant excrescence of the flesh. And, curiously, those who are charged with the operation are the birds. It seems to me that this denotes the weakest and most timid (there is in fact no question of crows, vultures, or eagles, but of birds in general). That which flies away at the least gesture of man is that which now is charged by God with the stripping of man. It is a terrible image of derision.

We now reach one of the passages most curiously explosive of this spirit: the thousand-year enchainment of Satan. In chapter 20 there are two difficulties; one, that of the "delay" of the judgment in two stages: Satan first of all unchained, then set free and destroyed. Why this delay? The other, the historicity of the delay. The "period of a thousand years without Satan." But in both cases there is the problem of the temporality of that which is indicated here. Is it actually a period of history that is envisaged by these thousand years? Is there actually a temporal succession in the two times of the destruction of Satan (Dragon, Devil, etc.)? Inasmuch as we have attempted to show the coherence of our text from one end to the other, and inasmuch as we have constantly encountered its symbolic character, it is self-evident that we do not here depart from the symbolic in order suddenly to enter into a temporal and historic description. But of course we must recall each time that the Apocalypse is not "anhistoric," it is not "synchronous" only (no more than it is apolitical). For it, history is constantly the first matter, the occasion, the example, the motif of the symbol. In other words, I would be perfectly agreeable in considering that the "slowness of the Parousia"[8] has played an evident role and can be the point of departure of the "delay." Satan is not destroyed at one time, as Babylon and the two Beasts had been; but this delay cannot be historic; that is, it is not a period of history. As we have shown above, if we wish to find succession we enter into endless contradictions: for example, Rome is "already" destroyed and only "after" that is Satan enchained. What then is the symbolic meaning of this delay?[9] I would say that the historic incarnations of the spirit of power are the accidents, the events, which can change without the universe of the creation itself being altered. The two spirits of power, also: they are secondary; as we have seen, they are *emanations* of the Dragon. They can disappear, the world remains, whatever be their importance, their influence. While the "ancient serpent," the one who (without being the last) was at the beginning, and Satan, who sits before God (Job), and the *Diabolos,* whose work is the exact replica of that of God in the act of creation (God *separates* the waters from the waters, Genesis 1:6–7; God separates the dry from the wet, Genesis 1:8–9;[10] now the *Diabolos* is the separator)—these powers are not of the same nature as the others. They seem (in our small human perspective) to be primeval, from the creation, and perhaps in the very act of creation. The creation has had a separation. Of the created from the Creator, and then of the elements. And the disobedience of Adam is the last act of separation. Here we observe the reintegration, of which we have seen the Incarnation to have been the first decisive, radical act: "the reversal of the inclination." Everything goes from separation into separation, from division into division, everything was under the sign of rupture and division. Now it is Love and Reconciliation which *make* the essential spiritual reversal of the whole movement of creation. But beginning with this reunion of the Incarnation the rest must follow; and there is the universality of the reconciliation, then the integration with the recapitulation. It is this which is implied by the elimination of Satan, of the serpent, of the Devil. But this also implies a "remaking" of the creation. The very first tendencies of the creation are reversed: then we comprehend that that cannot be done with the same rapidity, the same brutality. We have seen how the process of new beginning was begun with the Incarnation and the upheaval that represented in the creation. But now we reach the moment of total reversal. And the elimination of the *Diabolos* and of Satan, like that of the power of the abyss, can be carried out only with the participation of that in the whole creation, which God has chosen to be the bearer of his immediate presence in his creation; namely, man. All is going to be reversed, all is going to be begun again; but there is necessarily a bridge, a line between the old and the new. It is impossible to say that this line is taken up in the unique, individualized person of Jesus. Jesus Christ is not without men (since he had come for the reconciliation of men with his Father). Consequently, it is men who have to serve as the bridge. As long as they are rigorously determined by the Beasts and engaged in the process of division of the *Diabolos,* in the process of accusation of Satan (and of auto-justification, which is another form of rupture: I accuse the other to justify myself), there is no possibility of man being this bridge, this line, this relation. If the Beasts can be destroyed without changing the creation, we have said that God can destroy Satan and the Devil only by the absolutely new creation. But this then would be total change pure and simple, new without common measure with the old, event without history—an arbitrary act of God that annuls and begins again. But it is not this that is begun in the Incarnation. All the more so since there would then be no reconciliation, no recapitulation: for the future would be abolished. Therefore, there must be a new expression, not determined by Satan and the Devil, a new possibility for man. This possibility is the entire accomplish-̄ment of his work. But of *his* work, by him. Not that of Satan and the Devil. This work is not the Good either; this does not guarantee that man becomes *good.* It is simply the *work of man* which, as we will see, makes precisely the bridge between the old and the new. This work is situated at the place of encounter, of conflict, of juxtaposition, of contradiction, of agreement, of synthesis, and of dialectic between the liberty assured by God (the liberator, the enchainment of the Dragon, etc., for a thousand years) and the independence demanded by man (the occasion of his rupture with God, and always reaffirmed as independence over against God). This work includes, tightly mixed, that which man had desired in the independence of his pride. It is the decisive importance of this work of man that is expressed by the enchainment of Satan. He, himself and alone, must be disentangled. And it is the accomplishment of the work of man (not this or that, but the whole) which characterizes the "intermediate period." It is neither the completion of the number of the elect nor the conversion of the people of Israel that is the "cause" of the delay. It is simply that man must finish the work which he has to do and which is essential for the new creation, in good and in bad.

Thus the two classic interpretations of the period of a thousand years (millennial historic and spiritual intermediary) are at the same time true and false. The former is true in that this period is actually inscribed at the interior of history; it is in a certain sense a "fulfillment of history in history," as for the theologians who think that this period of a thousand years is a concrete event of history.[11] The "intermediary" theory is true in that we are not before a historical period determined by dates, and it is a matter of historical event that Satan is bound by the death of Jesus Christ. But the postmillennial theory is also false in that we are not at all in the presence of an epoch fixed in advance as far as duration is concerned (the 1000 years appears to me related to the biblical meaning of the figures 10, 100, 1000: a long duration, no more), nor of mysterious celestial events, nor the period of the revelation of the glory of God in history. The "spiritual" theory is also false because at issue is a change in the significance of the action of man and not a delay or an access in actuality to "the paradisiac life." It is certainly an "eventuality" inscribed in the historic. It has its point of inauguration, of rootedness, in the Incarnation, and consequently it is not the possibility of tasting Paradise now. It is the time of the work of man outside the control of Satan; it can then possibly, hypothetically, virtually be characterized by *love* and *reconciliation.* For example, I would also say surely the great modern historic efforts to express fraternity, solidarity, with the poor and weak, the movement toward a pure and idealistic socialism, and nonviolence are expressions of this work of man outside the presence of Satan. For of course by "work" we must understand the most diverse realizations and not only the result of man's labors. The work of man finally is his life, his society; it is man himself. And the fact that Satan is enchained signifies consequently that now the excuse of man and his justification are abolished. "It is not me, . . ." The enchainment of Satan is the closure of the action of referring responsibility, which begins with Genesis: the man saying, "It is not me, it is the woman," the woman saying, "It is not me, it is the serpent." And finally: "It is you, God, since you have put the serpent here." All that has become impossible. And the end of the thousand years is the end of the epoch of the work of man. This work which, to sum up, by the Incarnation *can* be characterized as that of liberty, love, and responsibility. When all is finished, then Satan is released. And what happens then? In an extraordinary fashion he again takes up his role as accuser (it is the preamble to the final judgment): he gathers together the work of man. He is going to seduce the nations. He will gather them for combat. Their number is as the sand of the sea. "He gathers," exactly like the Lord in his new creation. But he gathers to provoke the last judgment. He is the accuser: but in place of being "before God" to provoke the judgment of God against this one or that one, he is always the accuser of God himself to force the judgment and to use the work of man in putting it radically in question. Because that which are called here "the nations" are not only peoples in the neutral and insignificant sense; they are actually human societies. It is not a matter of individual judgment; these are not persons who are thrown into combat. No more than in Matthew 25; it is not a matter of a judgment of men but of nations. This term *ethnē* cannot simply mean here that which is non-Jewish, or that which is not the elect people (the *goyim*). The meaning is much more precise. It means organized human peoples: tribes, societies. We know that sometimes the body of an organized army is designated by this word; in the Roman world it meant the provinces.

And it derives from *ethos,* which means custom and institution. I would not hesitate to say that what is definitely envisaged here are societies with the dimension of work accomplished by man, and *also* the essential dimension of social phenomena different from a simple addition of individuals. This is gathered together, at the end of the human invention, and thrown into battle. Satan gathers finally that which must be annihilated in the work of man. Therefore the condemnation (annihilation) does not at all result, *here and now,* from a decision of God who *separates* (he is no longer the separator) the good works from the bad; but it is the result of the action of the *Diabolos* (who remains the divider): he gathers in and among and through the total work of men, in their generations, their diversities, their cultures, that which will be abolished. He sorts out, he chooses that which can be the expression of the revolt of man against the God of love, all the works of power and death that man has of course also accumulated, and hurls them against the one whom he desires to destroy. This is why the word "nation" is used: in this sense it becomes again the biblical word, which is confirmed by the image of the assault against the holy people and the Beloved City. The nations are those who wish to destroy Israel and the Church and Jerusalem, the body of Christ. We must then carefully keep the multiplicity of meaning of this symbol: the two "levels" of the term "nation." The result of this gathering and of this assault is that, the last role of the divider being accomplished, he is in his turn annihilated (actually thrown into nothingness). And we must insist again upon the fact that in 20:10 it is once more the Devil and Satan who are thrown into the fire and the lake of brimstone: there is no question of men.

And we reach the last chapter: the end of death itself. But since death was as limitation not harmful to life, as sign of our finitude in the creation of Eden, since it was then an integral part of creation; since on the other hand it had been, from the fact of our revolt, from the experience of Adam becoming God, filled with pain, fear, anguish, chastisement, it cannot be abolished without at the same time creation itself being abolished. We have seen the beginning of decreation by a new creation already in the moment of the Incarnation. We come here to its end with the proclamation that the earth and the sky disappear without leaving any trace. This is not at all a "way of speaking" or a "beautiful eschatological image": we are in the presence of a very constructive theological affirmation. In other words that which is announced is not the restitution of

what existed at the beginning; it is not the reestablishment of
Eden: the original creation of which death was a part, in order
to eliminate that which the latter had become, the last and
abominable enemy, the ally, the agent, of the abyss, of chaos,
of confusion, of Nothingness, of the Negation of Life—the
original creation then is now effaced by a radically new creation. But in order to attest the destruction of death, that it is
surely, as Aubigne said, "the dead death," those vanquished
by death must be recalled; all must be raised in the image of
Jesus. And when all are raised, then death and the abode of the
dead are abolished.[12] Now there remain only Life, the Living
One, the Risen Lord, the eternally YHWH, the risen Man. All
men are raised.

And now the double problem appears: the Book of Life, the
judgment according to works. I believe, on this second point,
that we have already little by little perceived that it is not at all
a matter of an affair of morality, nor of works in the narrowly
Christian sense. The work of man is the total product of his
life itself. The biblical teaching appears to me very clear. We
have seen, on the other hand, that all that which had to be
condemned has been condemned in the destruction of the
nations. That in the life of man there is in reality the work of
power, of death, of aggression, etc., which is abolished. But
man himself? We are told that each is *judged* according to his
works, and we have already encountered, in the overturning of
the bowls, the judgment driving man into a corner. It is not
said that men are *condemned* because of their works. Their
works can be condemned: we have also seen that dissociation
in the opposition between the overturning of the bowls which
concerns men, and the condemnation of man's works of power
with the Woman and Babylon. We see here not condemnations because the works are bad but a wholly different distinction: the inscription or noninscription in the Book of Life.
There are the books of the actions of man, of the realizations
brought about precisely during the thousand years when Satan
was bound, of those works which had to be the expression of
the liberation of man and which are the responsibility of man.
And then there is *the* Book of Life. In this passage there is an

intermingling of two themes: on the one hand, that of the resurrection with the end of death; on the other, the theme of the Book of Life. Only those who are not written in the Book of Life (and not those who have produced bad works) are thrown into the second death.[13] There is no correlation between the judgment of works and the gift of eternal life or rejection into death. The sole criterion is: one who was not found written in the Book of Life. "Was not"; then it was written before the judgment of works! And then the crucial question is posed, but without answer: is it possible that some men have not been written in the Book of Life? Is it possible that love rejects? Is it possible that the Living One destroys anything other than destruction?[14] That the one who renews all things perpetuates the ancient status of death? That the one who has come to save all men has not completed his task and has saved only some? Is it possible that the Eternal abandon the temporal? That the one who is All leave outside himself an indistinct group of "Outside of Life"? That the Father expel his sons ("a man had two sons")? That the Omnipotent—for he is also the Omnipotent—finally be limited in his power by the rebellious work of men, which, we have seen, is annihilated? That the justice of God be expressed not in his wrath, which is very normal and well expressed in judgment and plagues, but in an eternal wrath? A wrath continuing forever? Have we not seen the impossibility of considering that the New Creation, that admirable symphony of love, could exist *beside* the world of wrath? Is God still double-faced: a visage of love turned toward his celestial Jerusalem and a visage of wrath turned toward this "hell"? Are then the peace and joy of God complete, since he continues as a God of wrath and of fulmination? Could Paradise be what Romain Gary has so marvelously described in *Tulipe,* when he said that the trouble is not the concentration camp but "the very peaceable, very happy little village *beside* the camp"—the little village alongside, where people were undisturbed while millions died atrociously in the camp? The evangelical image of the justice of God is not that. It is not that of the magistrate who dispatches condemnations. The evangelical image of the justice

of God is the parables of the worker at the eleventh hour, and
the lost sheep, and the pearl of great price (he has given all that
he has, this God, in order to obtain what was in his eyes the
pearl of great price—man; then is he going to break this pearl
in pieces in order to throw some away?), and the prodigal son
and the unfaithful steward—such is the justice of God. Neither
retributive nor distributive. It is the justice of Love itself, who
cannot see the one he judges except through his love, and who
is always able to find in that fallen miserable being—rebel,
blasphemer, slave, powerful, without shame, hating, devourer
—the last tiny particle, invisible to any other than his love, and
which he is going to gather up and save. Not all that this man
has done in his life, not all the evil that he has been, but
himself, this ultimate breath that God has loved. It is not
theologically possible that there be damned men. That would
mean, in a word, that there is an external limit to the love of
God. Only the Nothingness is annihilated. And in the second
death there are not men, there are not lives; there are the evil
works of man, there are Satan and the Devil, there are the
incarnations (invented by man!) of these powers, there is
death. Nothing more.[15]

·7·

THE NEW CREATION[1]
Chapters 21 to 22: 1-5

Even a rapid reading of this text permits us to see that in this new creation absolutely nothing recalls the traditional images of Paradise or of Green Pastures. The image of Paradise, which is probably constituted on the basis of gnosis, mixed with the Germanic Valhalla, then subjected to the influence of Islam, is actually the opposite of that which Scripture tells us. This description of human rejoicing in a universe of nature is not, as we shall see, a small theological error. This is fundamental. We can discern three essential elements: the New of God, the City, the Warning.

The first evidence is that the new creation, which is absolutely new, comes only through judgment and destruction: first, a radical crisis is necessary, annihilation that falls upon all: nature, humanity, history, and the powers. This death is inevitable in order that something truly new appear; this judgment *(kritein)* is indispensable for the separation of the wheat and the tares. There is then no continuity. The city of God is not at the end of human progress, at the end of history by a sort of accumulation of the works of man; at this end there is found only Babylon. Our works then are not a linear and cumulative preparation for the celestial Jerusalem.[2]

In the Apocalypse there is no idea of a fulfillment by historical progress. The old things that are effaced (the first heaven, the first earth, have disappeared) are characterized here only by Death, Suffering, Separation. All the rest that was the grandeur of man has never been exempt. All that which was happiness, good, beauty is transitory and passing. All was under the sign of suffering and separation: which was the sign not of pessimism, but of discernment of the most profound reality. Which, for example, the psychoanalysts discover today in saying that the depth of man is anguish. But a question can be raised here: it is surprising that heaven (in the biblical, not natural, sense) is also marked by this "old": heaven, "abode of God," his environment, the other world. How can tears and grief be found here? Yes! Death is in fact present here as separation. Since the separation of man from his God. Since the death of Jesus, the Lamb crucified to the end of the world. We have already seen at what point the Apocalypse takes seriously the Incarnation and the death of God in Jesus Christ. That which inhabits heaven, which is nearest to God, is no longer the joy of angels; it is the desolation of rupture; it is the sorrow felt by God over man; it is the suffering of the Father, who awaits the return of the prodigal son. In Scripture we see so rarely joy in heaven: it is proclaimed at the moment of Christmas; it is revealed "when a sinner repents": that is nearly all!

All these are the old things: they can only be old, without future (in fact death and anguish are without future); they are already obsolete. It is not that which forms our future. And in fact the universality of death and suffering tells us also that there is nothing new. This is the conclusion of Ecclesiastes, but also of Baudelaire ("The New, the New, the world no longer has it"), who, moreover, strangely asks this New of Death itself: "O Death, old captain, it is time to lift the anchor." Before this fact, and through a total rupture, Scripture proclaims on the contrary that God himself is New ("And God himself altogether as young as he is eternal"). Not only is he

Creator, but he brings forth new things. Each time that there is an actually New in the world, God has acted. But this always implies rupture with the old. The new wine *cannot be* contained in the old wineskins. The old cannot be kept, nor reutilized, nor added to the new. The eternity of God is not an immobility; it is a perpetual beginning, a novelty always being born, an absence of custom, of necessity, of destiny; an absence of repetition. The idea of the circular mandala or of the swastika is exactly the opposite of the revelation of the God of Jesus Christ (there is fundamentally no possible relation between this revelation and Buddhism or Hinduism). The relation with God is no longer a relation known in advance, which could be established and clearly defined. God establishes with each man a new relation. Grace establishes new moments in each life. God posits beginnings in history that man cannot foresee (thus the Covenant or the Incarnation). And eternity is a spring gushing with nonpredetermined instants, always fresh, new, surprising. It is the unexpected, the unforeseen. The great play (that of children!) is to live that. It is that which our text calls Life. The Reconciliation finally realized with the one who is constantly New. Implying a love that does not wear out, does not fall into habit, always as full, as stirring, as surprising as on the first day.

It is that which is contained in the proclamation: "I make all things new." God is himself the absolutely New, with whom total communion is established (that which has been lived in Jesus is now the situation of all). And this then implies the measureless triumph of life (there is no longer any conflict between the forces of life and the impulsions of death) and the abolition of all that which accompanies death (suffering and separation). But it is God alone who does all that. "I make." He is the Alpha and the Omega: the beginning and the end; but we comprehend already that there is no identity between this beginning and this end. It is only between the two that our whole history takes place and unfolds. The one who speaks thus is the Word, which is to say the creative Word. And it is truly in fact a new *creation,* a gift of God. No effort of man can achieve it. Man will create neither a new life nor a total New.

And it is in this very thing that the Apocalypse is not first a political document; the powers of chaos must disappear and even that which was their image: here, for example, the sea (21:1). This mention is curious (the sea is no more), simply because, though it was not the power of chaos, it had been its image: even that must disappear from the new creation. That which *descends* from God's presence, the Holy City, is the place and possibility of a new humanity. It does not rise up from the work of man accumulating achievements one after the other, but descends from the right hand of the Father. If the people are new, it is because they are *His* people. It is He and He alone who consoles (vs. 4). Which means that even if man succeeds in conquering physical death, spiritual death is not within his scope. On the contrary, we are warned that the more man gains the world, the more he loses his "soul" (his *being*).

The text piles up the declarations of his action: "I will give the water of life without price. . . . I am the beginning and the end." And he proclaims that it is he alone who does all. "It is done." All is accomplished. But let us not forget that it is upon the cross that all has been accomplished; nowhere else, without any human participation except that of Herod, Pilate, Judas, and the soldiers. Such is rigorously and absolutely the work of God.

I certainly know what can be objected to that: it is a "demobilizing" text (and teaching): if God does all, man has only to sit and wait. Very curiously, this was already the criticism addressed to the Reformers. And nevertheless who has accumulated more action and good works and technical or commercial or evangelistic activity than the Protestants (and in fact they often would have done better to do nothing)? I would say, for one thing, that that argument would not impress me even if it were true: if it were the genuine revelation of God, it would matter little to me whether it were demobilizing or not. What matters is trying to be faithful and not obeying some momentary slogan. But it does not seem to me that this is the meaning of the text. First, it speaks to us of Life and Death, of a radical contradiction between the living and the dead. Consequently, it is situated at a certain absolute. It does not say at all that in the course of our life everything is equivalent to everything else; but it warns that all that we do is relative, and never ends in an absolute. We must act for justice and peace and liberty, but it is relative. We will never create the absolutely just, peaceful, and fraternal society: to believe that is a modern idolatry. But to do nothing because it is relative? Do we not eat every day? And nevertheless that is truly relative!

There is a human life to lead, which is without final issue, which is not creative of a true New, but which is not without value before God. We will examine it further. At the beginning of the Apocalypse, judgment falls upon the lukewarm, which is to say, precisely, those who do nothing. But between acting and believing that one thereby establishes the celestial Jerusalem upon earth there is a tremendous difference! In addition, the text puts two warnings directly before us concerning the necessity of action: after having said that *All* is done, it adds: "to the thirsty . . . ." And there is contrast between the one who is thirsty (and who receives life) and all those who are not thirsty (and who are referred to in 21:8), that is, those who have found their satisfaction in an attitude or in a human achievement. It is not a problem of moral conduct that is posed in this verse, but that of spiritual need, of the need of love. It is a matter of all those who have not loved God or hoped for his love. (And the love of God, we must remember, is expressed concretely in the love of neighbor and all the works of justice, etc.). And in the same passage we find: "he who conquers" (vs. 7). There is then actually a combat to be fought. Surely we must not be deceived: for the Apocalypse it is not first a political or scientific or social combat. It is the combat of faith. Certainly not the combat of the pride of man who pretends to make *his* history, *his* science, *his* society. But the combat of the faith is never waged in the abstract: it is not a combat in the soul, nor even a combat of ideas; it is the combat incarnate not only in the testimony but in the total human expression, including the political and all the rest. We will also be between two dangers: to do nothing and "to believe in what one does," to put faith in these works.

We are then obliged to say still another word about judgment. Nothing of that which has been the perversion of man can enter into the New of God. This is obvious. But verse 8 declares that "the cowardly [then the lukewarm, those who do not act], the faithless, the polluted, . . . murderers, fornicators, sorcerers, idolaters, and all liars [are doomed to] the second death." Does that not contradict what we have written above on the subject of judgment falling only upon the powers and not upon men? I wish to emphasize only two things: the first is that we are here in the presence not of the pronounced condemnation but of the *warning* of the possibility, the possibility of such an end. "Pay attention": this is the meaning. But this word is valid only for those to whom it is addressed. It is not the objective declaration of a universal truth in itself. In other words, you, Christians, to whom the word is addressed, pay attention. And this concerns only you, since you alone know what the New of God is, his promise, and the price that has represented to God. In fact, the judgment is not pronounced upon moral works but upon the absence of faith, idolatry, magic, etc., which is to say, a perversion of the revelation of God.[3] The other observation, but which does not derive directly from this verse, is that I am convinced (this cannot go beyond conviction) that it is a matter here of the condemnation of works but not of the being. In other words, that every evil work of man is rooted out of him, that it is destroyed, that it cannot enter into the celestial Jerusalem; but that man himself, without any of these human realizations, is "saved as through fire" (1 Corinthians). This is only the counterpart of the considerable importance accorded by God to the works of man for the constitution of the celestial Jerusalem.

Beginning with verse 9 of chapter 21, what is first very important is that the one who is going to show the seer the betrothed, the bride of the Lamb,[4] is one of the seven angels who hold the seven bowls full of the seven plagues. This denotes the absence of a temporal sequence (the seven bowls are always full); *we* read in temporal sequence a text that implies exactly that. But the vision itself does not imply that at all. There is no *before* and *after*. The bowls are emptied and afterward a vision of the heavenly Jerusalem. No. As upon a reredos all is seen together. Which permits sight but not the discourse. But the discourse implies precisely this utilization of inserts, of points of return, of flashback, etc. (That the superficial and scientific exegetes take for negligence. It is sufficient to reflect upon the difference between the discourse and the vision.) Now it is the very same angel who unleashes the plagues who shows the heavenly Jerusalem; which means —it could not be clearer—that these plagues are not condemnation, damnation, putting to death, the rejection of humanity or even of a part of humanity, but only the other face, the other side, the reverse of this Jerusalem that is made for all men, given by God to all men. The continuity of the presence of this angel is perfectly significant of the continuity, and even the inseparability, of pain and glory.[5]

Then it is the "heavenly Jerusalem" as new creation. From the point of view of historical criticism it can be asserted that two Old Testament themes are found symbolized here: the idealization of an eschatological Jerusalem (Isaiah 60, 62, and 65:18–25) of which the historic Jerusalem (of Isaiah's time) is only a prophecy, and, on the other hand, the existence of a celestial prototype of the signs of the presence of God among men[6] (for example, Exodus 25). These two themes are taken up and blended in the Apocalypse: in other words, we pass from the prophecy (for even the attestation of the celestial model is a prophecy) to the apocalyptic fulfillment of this prophecy. This can be said, and is without doubt correct and clarifies certain ways of representing the revelation in this epoch; but it explains nothing: what does the fact that it is Jerusalem, that it is celestial, and that it is the fulfillment *signify?* For certain theologians that has no particular meaning. It is a matter of Heaven, of the Kingdom of God, of Paradise, of Eternal Life, of Celestial Happiness, etc., mixing everything together without attaching a particular value to anything. It therefore could be said simply that if, here, there is question of Jerusalem, this is only to obey a certain apocalyptic mode of the moment, perhaps to attach this "idea" to a current image, to Jerusalem, and also to affirm the realization of prophecies. For others it is a matter solely of affirming both the continuity in relation to Israel and also the superiority of Christianity over against the Jews: the whole Jewish patrimony is taken up and reassumed; Jerusalem is taken away from the Jews to become Christian and that which the Jews have known up to then is only an image of what must be totally fulfilled.[7]

Finally for others (for example, the author of the note in the *Traduction Oecuménique de la Bible*), it is "a representation of the Church seen in the glorious and ideal reality of the Parousia. It can be called Jerusalem inasmuch as it is the place of the gathering of the consecrated people." All this is not false, but seems to me of little weight, having a banal tenor of meaning and, in relation to so many other biblical texts, perfectly redundant. This is so for these diverse explanations because the major fact is left aside: that Jerusalem is a city. However, before examining this more closely, we emphasize, consistent with what we have already seen, that this city comes from heaven. It is not at all a human realization: it is the opposite of Babel whose tower mounted up from earth toward heaven. (And we actually have here a radical contrast of the religious or promethean movement, which rises up from earth to heaven to the movement of biblical revelation that descends from heaven to earth, which is an absolute *gift* of God, the radical New of God.) It *comes toward* the earth (exactly according to the same model as the eschaton coming toward our actuality). It is implanted in the domain of men, but *comes from heaven*, where it has been founded, formed, built, but not without taking account of the totality of the work of man, which we will see further on. In any case, the city here as human metropolis denotes a community founded by God and the place of his abode.

What does the fact that it is a city essentially mean? We are in the presence of a series of meanings. The first is that we observe a total contrast between the first creation and the second. In the first, God had created a garden for man. Man lives in "nature."[8] In the second, he is installed in a city.[9]

Thus we do not observe a return to the origin. It is not the preservation of God's primitive plan. The biblical God is not the abstract God who, having had an idea at the beginning, maintains it over against everything and again makes a garden because it was his plan at the beginning.[10] Here we are in contradiction to all the other religions: for all those, without exception, which have a view of the future, of a paradise, of an "afterlife," there is uniquely a return to a lost primitive age of gold. Here the situation is radically reversed. What does this signify? Very simply that God does not annul history and the work of man but, on the contrary, assumes it. The city is the great work of man. We have seen that. It is well described as the sum of his culture and his inventions; it is his creation. It is the very sign of his history, since it is in the city that the various layers of history and culture are preserved. Well, God takes up the whole history of men and synthesizes it in the absolute city. The symbol of Jerusalem is the strongest sign we can have that the biblical God is a God who accompanies man in his history. He does not pursue his independent design, he pursues his design in and with the history of men. And that which men have freely, voluntarily, created they are going to find again in Jerusalem. We will reflect upon this further. Thus we have this remarkable double affirmation: on the one hand, the celestial Jerusalem is a creation of the absolutely new of God, without common measure with anything else; but on the other hand, it is the perfect synthesis, made by God, of all history, of the total life of humanity, of all man's works, all his creations, all his ventures: it is the recapitulation.

Consequently, the history of humanity is not in vain, annulled by a stroke of the pen, as if nothing of our efforts, our suffering, our hopes, had ever existed: on the contrary, *all* is gathered up. Then man is saved *with his works.* Paradise is not a formless cloud, a rose and blue fog and "nonplace"; it is a good city, a solid place, where the whole creation of man is re-created. Thus in the judgment, God destroys history but without anything being lost; and he synthesizes that same history. He judges the works, purified, borne to the absolute of grandeur and perfection. Perfect, and nevertheless the same! As man *himself* rises.

However, we must be aware of a second motif, equally essential. Throughout Scripture (and here again I refer to what I have shown elsewhere) the city is the instrument of the revolt of man against God. On the one hand, it is the world of man, which he has desired to set up as a counter-creation with the distinct will to exclude God; on the other hand, it is the point of crystalization of the pride and power of man. The city is the negation of the omnipotence of God; it is the closed door of man's walling himself up against any relation with the Creator. Biblically, it is the place of the curse, pitiless, the place of war and oppression, of wealth and slavery. And the judgment responds to that; Babylon is judged as incarnation of the powers; it is also a city. Such is the decision of God. And this double image: judgment of the city Babylon—re-creation of the city Jerusalem shows at what point the symbol of the city is central here. This new creation signifies, then, that God *reverses* what had been the instrument of revolt in order to make of it the work of reconciliation. Such is the meaning of the judgment. It is not an abolition, and then God makes something else. No! It is a destruction of meaning and a re-creation of meaning. That which was the obstinate image of the negation of man against God is denied in itself and becomes the opening of the identity "God with us." Man had desired to make a work of evil and revolt, of rupture with God. But God makes this project end in its opposite. But not by the manifestation of his greater power: there is here no competition of powers. God does not seek in the apocalyptic events to prove that he is the stronger. That would be absurd, mediocre, and perfectly inadequate for the God of Jesus Christ! But he invests this work of man with his love. For what greater attestation of love than to take from the enemy the weapon of war in order to make of it the very means of absolute, limitless, reconciliation! He gives to the city the potential of love. But in doing this he carries the work of man to its perfection. Jerusalem is the perfect city as no human city has ever been able to be. But in addition it answers that which had been the fundamental intention of man. Because if, from one side, man in building the city made of it a work against God, from the other, men had intended to make of it the place of their perfect communication, their communion, their assembly; finally, this is exactly what God does with the heavenly Jerusalem. Man had never succeeded; he had always experienced failure, and the actual urban monstrosity is striking testimony to this. Thus that which had been the historical failure of man becomes the triumphant success; there is finally communion, there is finally assembly (and not only of one generation, but of all). Thus God grants in the heavenly Jerusalem that which had been the purpose of man, that which had been his patient search through all civilizations, that which had been his hope and his expectation. God does not fabricate an abstract place, outside of any relation with man: he is not paternalistic. God answers the intention that man had had in building Babel: "to make a name," and God gives him a new name. To create the place of human community, and God creates total communion. The city was a place of the dissolution of specificities, of the meeting and mixture of all ideas, values, races, social categories: it receives its complete fulfillment. For in this New Jerusalem all races, peoples, nations, tribes meet. But while the tendency was always toward unity by the disappearance of diversities, now unity appears (in God) in the communion of existing diversities, and human plurality is maintained. We have already encountered several times this relation of the harmony of the one and the multiple in the Apocalypse. The New Jerusalem resembles Babylon. Without the corruption of Babylon. Without the will to Power. And this new city then represents the totality of Meaning: "The authentic city does not seek its meaning outside of itself. . . . It does not serve anything or anyone. It is the realization of man. Its relation to God is not a relation of service but of filial and conjugal love. What God expects of it is that it exist. In the same way as a father does not demand that his son serve him but that he exist" (J. Comblin). The city implies also that the encounter with God does not take place by a movement of man who rises up outside himself, a flight of the soul outside the body: on the contrary, God assumes the work of men and descends, makes himself present in the total work of man. There is no mounting up toward heaven. The Apocalypse of John is consequently an antignosticism. And in this city men

will see God face to face. The formula is perhaps of pagan
origin (see Baudissin), but it implies a gigantic leap: No one
in the Old Testament had seen God face to face. God does not
show himself in the Temple. He was present in the void. There
is no theophany. And only his Name was known. It was always
a matter of the *Word.* Never Sight. Now sight has rejoined the
word. As the real, the truth. God is present to the totality of
man; and this face to face has nothing to do with a liturgy of
paganism because of the distance traversed since the origin of
the revelation. It can be said that here God has in fact put his
omnipotence at the service of the human project. And in order
to effect this he uses what man has himself made: in fact we
hear twice: "the kings of the earth bring their glory" (which is
to say that which has manifested them, their major work) and
then "they shall bring into it the glory and the honor of the
nations."[11] Thus the very ones who had been at the center of
the judgment: the kings and the nations, who are destroyed as
powers, are taken up in this Jerusalem, and all that which had
been the cultural, scientific, technical, aesthetic, intellectual
work, all the music and sculpture, all the poetry and mathemat-
ics, all philosophy and knowledge of all orders, all enter into
this Jerusalem, used by God to build up this final perfect work;
but let us always remember that it is a creation in movement,
as we have seen above: in other words, it is not a museum but
an integration into a living whole and a re-creation for development. Because everything here is *living* and not closed and
preserved. What man had wished to be *his* creation, intro-
verted, is now recreated for eternity, in action and liberty.

After this fundamental comprehension we must elucidate
summarily some of the codes of this description.[12] It is not a
matter completely of symbols, but it cannot be said that these
are stereotypes without significance or that they are nothing
other than very general and banal images in order to say that
Jerusalem is perfect or that everything here is light. The description is much more precise and each detail has its content.
That its brightness is like crystalline jasper (21:11), that its
ramparts are of jasper (vs. 18), and its first foundation made

of jasper (vs. 19) is not at all surprising: traditionally, jasper, of diverse colors (and among the jaspers opal can be cited) is the stone of God. Simply, the glory of God is the brightness of this city; and God is its rampart and first foundation. The twelve gates, which bear the names of the twelve tribes of Israel, surely do not designate the Church. We are once more before that mania of Christians to reduce everything to the Church. Here the Church is no more, since God is all in all. On the other hand, the symbolism of Israel is maintained; through Israel there is entry into the city of God. But the foundations upon which the ramparts sit bear the names of the twelve apostles. Thus we have the exact juncture of the *foundation* of Jerusalem and *access* by means of Israel. In both cases there is the first presence of those who had borne the testimony of the Word of God in the world.

This city is square, and even cubical. Some have wished to maintain that it is not a cube but in the image of a ziggurat. Nothing permits us to say this.[13] The text is ambiguous, but the cube is the image of solidity, of immovability, of fulfillment (and not of ascension toward heaven like the ziggurat). The measures are twelve multiplied by twelve, which then means perfection in the perfect union of God and creation. The ideal fulfillment. As for "by a man's measure, that is, an angel's" (vs. 17), which has been a matter of so much concern to the commentators, I believe that it is above all the indication that all this, including these measures, have a *spiritual meaning* and that we must not seek a measurement according to human survey. We come then to the famous twelve stones, which serve as the foundation of the city itself. These stones, of which the translation is, moreover, partially doubtful, are approximately those that we find upon the breastplate of the high priest. They are obviously symbolic. But it is necessary to proceed to an analysis of the traditional representations. We can read the breastplate schematically, beginning with the row on the bottom and reading from right to left: penitence, fear, the broken man— then, the price paid by God, beatitude in God, charity. The third row: power, the writing of the Words of God, union with God. Finally: truth, the love of God, man as God desires him.

We see the coherence perfectly and how, therefore, the twelve stones, representing the twelve foundations of the city, are a symbolic résumé of the whole revelation. But I would not insist that this is the only possible reading. Nevertheless, in order to understand what it is all about, we must not be limited to a vague consideration (there are some stones of all colors, etc.,), and comprehend that the "language" of the stones was then extremely current. But it is difficult to have "magical" texts or texts of the Cabala give the stones' traditional meaning, and above all a unique meaning. It is then only a hypothesis that I advance here.[14] It is noteworthy, and by contrast very clear, that in this city there is no longer a Temple (vs. 22) and that there is no longer any need of a sun to illuminate it. Which surely means that there is no longer need of a particular place to express or enclose a sacred presence, nor to proceed to an adoration of God. Communication with the Lord God is immediate. The Temple is the Lord God himself. Without any mediation: whence, the Lamb is perfectly assimilated to the Omnipotent Lord in this final image: the Lamb is no longer mediator; he is himself the Temple and the Lord.[15]

The Temple is no more. And that is consistent with the word of Jesus concerning the destruction of the Temple. This affirmation manifests once more the difference between this "city bestowed" and most final promises made in the other religions. Since the Temple is no more, then, as many authors have emphasized also, there is no more priesthood, nor cult, nor religion, nor sacrifices, nor distinction between the profane and the sacred. It cannot even be said that, since God is all in all, then all is sacred. For the sacred exists only in relation to a profane, and reciprocally. No: the sacred is no more either. We are in another universe (in the medieval sense: *universum*) which has another structure, and no longer fits our religious categories. And we no longer find mediators (priests, for example): mediation is no more; all is immediate. Man is immediate to man, in the same way as God is also immediate to him.[16]

And in the same way as there is no longer Religion, since the Power has been abolished, there is no political form in the

heavenly Jerusalem. There is no authority. It exists by a spontaneity of all toward all; there is not even submission to the
common good because there is no longer submission. There
is no "collective being"; on the contrary, each is perfectly
individualized. There is no external or ontological coherence;
this is not a hive or an "organism." There is no directing
authority.[17] There is only and exclusively Love. Because each
is with each and with all in a perfect relation of love, all constraint and all "cause" of cohesion are abolished. This is so
because there is no longer any "cause." And that is all. And
there is no repetition because love is permanent, constant
invention, and there is no limit to freedom, because love is
freedom and freedom cannot exist without love.[18] And if the
sun has disappeared, the light nevertheless remains (as in
Genesis, we see the light appear first, and the sun much later);
the light of God himself, the light of the Holy Spirit (in order
not to say spiritual light, a term that can provoke much misunderstanding) replaces the light that emanates from a material source. Energy is no longer what it is here; it is directly the
divine energy. Energy continually creative, the light is the
incessant flux of renewal, of the always new. In the same way
life is now represented as a river, but here again there is a
reversal of our condition. To say that life flows like a river
(everything flows) is a banality. But this is exactly what the
Apocalypse does not say: this is a river of living water, a river
of life, which gushes up from the throne of God and of the
Lamb (once more no distinction is made). This is not life that
flows (and disappears) like a river. This is a continual giving
of life effected by the river, which starts from the throne: it is
a springing up of life itself. Life comes directly (here also
mediation is abolished) from God to his creation and to each
creature. There is a continual current of life, the very clear
symbol of the immediate relation of "God with men." All this
evokes a certain number of traditional images: the river seems
identical to the one we find in Genesis (2: 10). However, there
are only two branches of the river and not four (number of the
creation). We also find again the tree of life, which stands in
the midst of the city (and no longer in a corner of the garden).

And now man is no longer forbidden to take its fruit: On the contrary, the fruit is made for man, and we will have to see the meaning of this. Another image which is kept is that the city is perhaps, according to Ezekiel, situated on a mountain. In other words the New Jerusalem is not the whole world. There is a world beyond it; it is the place of God with man. It is the place of man, but man is not all. It is at the summit of creation, of the new creation; but it is not itself the totality. Inasmuch as it is the Ark, where its Temple is the Lord God and the Lamb, it is the place of total reconciliation of the creation with the Creator; but it is situated in relation to the creation as the Temple in relation to Jerusalem. The river, which flows continually and which comes from this Temple, brings life itself to the rest of creation, to the innumerable galaxies. And the mystery found at the summit and at the heart is the unity of God with man, who is finally the true image of God and the true key to creation: then in him all is reconciled and all is from now on truly alive.

A last problem remains to be examined: that of the healing by the leaves of the tree of life. That this tree of life is itself the replica of the tree of Genesis does not provoke any difficulty; that it produces twelve harvests a year, a sign of infinite abundance and perpetuity, is also not difficult. But there is the question of the healing of the nations. What can that mean since, on the one hand, evil is no longer done, and on the other, death is dead? It seems to me that this consecrates again the transformation of the situation of Eden. We have said that in Eden man as creature certainly knew finitude. His life even before the Fall was limited in time, and this differentiated him from his Creator. But from this time forward death had been charged with an aggressive, annihilating potential, with an image of anguish; it is the mark not of the creature but of the Fall, of loss, absence, rupture, condemnation. And as such it can no longer exist. It is no longer possible for death to be restored as the simple end of the finite. Demonized, demoniacal, the power of negation in the face of God, it cannot be "de-demonized." Therefore, the healing in question is the

healing of finitude. Man is never, here no more than in Genesis, equal to God, identical to God. "God-with-man" does not
mean that man is divinized. This dreadful error of a certain
number of theologies (the Christification of man; God has
been made man in order that man might become God, etc.),
is radically refuted by these few verses. Man, even in the resurrection, even in glorification, remains creature, and though
God is with him, there remains an infinite distance between the
Creator and the risen man. Integrated fully into the body of
Christ, he has not become Christ. He can see God face to face;
he even bears the name of God upon his forehead; he reigns
with the Lord God. But there is a face to face (man does not
look upon himself); he *is* illumined (by an exterior light); *Another* has put his name upon his forehead; he does not reign
alone, he reigns with. And the mark of this infinite distance is
precisely finitude. But it is no longer possible within the limits
of death. Death has disappeared, and this theme is here expressly confirmed by the verse that follows immediately the
healing by the "leaves" of the tree of life: "There shall no
more be anything accursed." Therefore, we are in the presence of a creature who as such must come to an end but who
in receiving the very life of God cannot be ended by death:
then the healing brought by the leaves of the tree of life is the
exact compensation, always beginning again, for finitude. Man
does not have life in himself, by himself; he is not the Life; he
is not a spirit creating and provoking life: he receives the life
of the Living One. God alone is the Living One, the Eternal,
the "I am," the Being, the Giver of Life, or whatever name we
wish to give him to signify this. God alone; there is the whole
distance. But this human being, always marked by finitude,
does not die, no longer dies. His life also is now eternity
(contrary to what it was in Genesis: and there certainly has
been "progress," and not retrogression; by the double venture of the history of man and the accompaniment of man by
God there has been a transformation of man himself in relation to his first condition as creature). But an eternity constantly received, given, accorded. Finitude is always the mark.
If, though impossible, the gift of life ceased, man would actu-

ally come to an end. But the gift of life never ceases; there are twelve harvests of fruit each year. Constantly wounded, constantly threatened by this finitude which is in him, he is constantly revived, constantly healed, eternally. But this is not a status of inferiority imposed upon him, but the situation created by the relation of love and by the triumph of grace. For all is still grace. And this man lives for eternity from grace, in the grace given to him; he lives from the "free gift." And the relation of love implies reciprocally that this human creature is so totally indispensable to God that God would suffer an irreparable loss if man were lost (God also could no longer be himself, since he would no longer be love and his love would have absolutely failed); God would no longer have any respondent and any truth for there would no longer be the "Thou" for the "I."[19]

·8·

PRAISE AND DOXOLOGY

The five sections of the Apocalypse are framed and specified by passages that can be called liturgical, in which we see a certain form of adoration toward God, and songs of glory or prayers are expressed. The first section (devoted to the Church) begins with the attestation of John and his theological proclamation concerning the one who has sent him (1:5–6); it ends with the great vision of adoration toward God the Father, the Creator (4:1–11). The second part (devoted to history) begins with the song of praise addressed to the immolated Lamb (5:8–14), which is a duplication with some significant differences of the one addressed to God the Father. And it is ended by the song of the Church before the throne of God (7:11–17), which attests the end of history. The third section, very different from the two others, which we have studied as the keystone of the whole, does not present this liturgical frame; the doxological text is found exactly in the middle (12:10–12); after the disclosure of the mystery of the Incarnation and before the appearance of the Dragon and the Beasts: the culminating point of the work of God is attained. The fourth part (on the judgment) is situated between the song of the "Conquerors" before God announcing the Tent of Witness (15:1–5) and the song of the great multitude

(19:1–8) after the judgment of Babylon (but before that of the beasts, the dragon, and death). Only the fifth section is not situated in a framework of this order: there is no break between the destruction of death and the resurrection that inaugurates the new creation. This is why the song of the great multitude has two parts: one that closes the fourth section, the other that opens the fifth. And the latter section is ended by a new testimony of the seer, which corresponds to his initial declaration.[1]

But these texts are not indifferent; they are not simple formulas somewhat empty and poetic (in the weak sense); nor are they simple documents that we could exploit to know this or that liturgical form.[2] These texts which, as we have seen, regularly punctuate the whole development of the Apocalypse are also rich in meaning, in their contents and in their differences. We can already make a preliminary observation: for the first two sections, those who offer glory and who address themselves to God are mysterious "celestial" beings—the twenty-four elders, the four animals, the angels, and, accessorily, once (5:13), every creature. Therefore, in the presence of the revelation of the Mystery of Christ with the Church, and of History, it is the celestial beings who express themselves. For the third part we remain in the Incognito of God: the doxology is not spoken by anyone perceptible to us: "And I heard a loud voice in heaven, saying . . ." (12:10). This is at the deepest mystery of the Incarnation itself. There cannot be a concrete vision of the one who speaks about this mystery. God in God. But for the two sections that follow, very remarkably, it is no longer the celestial creatures who sing the glory and praise of God (although they are always present! 19:4): now there are men, the historic conquerors of the Beast, that is (since they sing the song of Moses), those who have led the people of God to their liberation, and then the innumerable multitude, the totality of humanity, saved, liberated, risen. So now the praise and joy are no longer in the situation of rupture between men and God and, it could be said, of the solitude of God in his heaven, but in the total reconciliation, which is joyous even when it is a matter of judgment. And this immense multitude (all men, from the origins) resembles in its song "the roar of loud thunder": which is full of meaning, when we realize that the thunder is very specifically reference to the voice of God. Thus the distribution of these doxologies is carried out perfectly according to the content of each section.

The Revelation on the Church (1:5–6; 4:1–11)

The first text is very brief. It is an inauguration of the whole movement to follow, the simple declaration of John addressed to the churches as witness and doxology. But it is essential. "To him who loves us and has freed [or delivered, or washed] us from our sins by his blood, and made us a kingdom, priests to his God and Father, to him be glory and dominion for ever and ever. Amen." The declaration on the subject of Jesus Christ is not surprising. It describes what theologically the primitive Church (and not only Paul, as certain historians are bent upon saying, Paul betraying Jesus by fabricating an *evangelium de Christo* replacing the *evangelium Christi*) had affirmed: he loves us, he delivers us by accepting death in our place (the judgment, the condemnation, he has paid the price, etc.) And consequently by this work we are (already) transformed into a Kingdom (in the midst of the history of the world there is a Kingdom of heaven which is now present) and into priests for God: in the midst of this fallen creation there is a point of regeneration; in the rupture there is a point of reconciliation; and in the distance from God there is a point of adoration: this people who are a people of priests and sacrificers (not, then *a* priest, but a people of priests). Here then we are in the presence of the work of Jesus Christ, which is declared as such and as accomplished before there is mention of the Church.

But we must be aware of two words that generally slide from our lips as banalities without holding our attention: glory and dominion (*doxa* and *kratos*). To him, to Jesus Christ, glory and dominion. We have already written elsewhere, but it must be continually repeated, that glory, biblically, is not an empty word, nor a reference to what we call historical, political, or military glory (renown, social ascendancy, influence upon events, adulation by flatterers, etc.); glory is the deed itself of revelation. To glorify is to reveal the one glorified. Thus Jesus never glorifies himself. He glorifies his Father. He reveals him. God glorifies his Son: He reveals who he is. And the two are closely bound together (Father, glorify your Son, in order that your Son may glorify you). Man can glorify God in manifesting by his life, by his being, who this God is that he adores. But essentially the one by whom we know who God is, the one who manifests him, who has actually given to man not an exterior image but the unique truth of God (namely, that God loves so much that he gives himself in his Son), is Jesus Christ; and this is why, from the opening of the Revelation, he is designated in this way: to him is the glory (not that he is glorified; it is not said, to him is the glorification), meaning: he alone is the authentic image and revelation of the unfathomable secret of God. And the second title given him by the witness is "dominion." But we must distinguish between power and dominion *(dynamis* and *kratos):* power is the force to do something; it is, possibly, the unleashing of an energy, violence, thunder, tempest, the ocean swelling. He is the All-Powerful because he can do anything and nothing can stop or restrain him. Dominion is not only the victory, the triumph over an enemy, but I would say also the order reigning by a sort of law, by a regularity: it is government (whence the combinations demo-cracy, auto-cracy, etc.). And both this triumph and this reign are from the beginning attributed to Jesus Christ. Not the creative power dominating without challenge from the origin, but the victory and the ordered peace. Such is the doxology proclaimed by the witness who *has seen* and by the man representing the Church before God, the doxology that subsequently will dominate the whole revelation.

The text that terminates the revelation on the Church is much more complex; it is composed of two very distinct parts: first the vision, then the doxologies. John is seized by the Spirit, who brings him into the "heaven." A throne and a being. Nothing can be said about them, except light, the rainbow with emerald reflections, the various and unfathomable aspects of jasper; probably opal with the surprising double aspect of this most mysterious of all stones, which offers an incessant change of colors and also a kind of double reflection. It is seen, but what is seen is not the surface; the light dwells at the interior of the stone with a sort of partition, the surface itself of the stone, between the one who views it and this interior play—nothing else. And this reference to light and to *stones* manifests the insurmountable distance, the incommunicability. There is someone, but without more common measure than the opal itself, and the emerald. The symbolic entourage of this "someone" is the twenty-four elders, the four animals, and the seven torches. For the latter there are no great problems: the text itself tells us that these are the seven spirits of God, then the Spirit of God in his plenitude, reminding us that this Spirit is the communication of God. Therefore he is *before* the throne. He is not exactly the abstract sparkling light. He is God himself communicating the Word of God. In any case, God is neither named nor described. There is no anthropomorphism. According to Jewish tradition, the Throne is only an object upon which rests the glory *(Kabod)*. God reigns alone.[3]

The twenty-four elders and the four animals have made much ink flow. In any case we understand already, from the first step, that God is not isolated in infinity, like the God of the philosophers. He is surrounded, but not first of all by the celestial army of angels: it seems that this is the sign of his creation. There are, of course, innumerable interpretations of these twenty-four elders. They are terrestrial creatures who have found their place in heaven, the twelve prophets and the twelve apostles, or, rather, angels (clothed in white, they reflect the glory of God). They have crowns and thrones: signs of authority, representing the dominion of God? It seems not, since they are in a relation to God that could be called "external." For others, the three principal attributes that identify them (white garments, thrones, crowns) are precisely those which in the course of the book are promised to Christians, particularly in all the letters. They would then represent the celestial assembly, the people of God participating in his glory, celebrating a liturgy of adoration and thanksgiving. Which is not very probable, given that the Church will in fact be represented further on in a wholly different way, and the people of God will be constituted progressively throughout the course of the account. That they bear the name of elders is added: as the leaders of the synagogues and churches. Finally, to be sure, there are exegetes for whom they represent nothing at all: simply because the generality, the banality, of the description does not permit seeing something precise. Which is surely not the case, for everything in the text really denotes a meaning. It seems to me, but this is assuredly only a hypothesis, that the twenty-four elders have a still more general meaning, and in every case are established in a certain parallelism with the group of animals. They would then represent the totality of the history of men before God, the time of history (as, I believe, the Ancient of Days of Daniel 7:9 and 13). The symbolism of twenty-four is very often relative to the passage of time. And the fact that elders are presented is very clear. Of course, they could correspond to the twelve prophets and the twelve apostles, but then not as persons but as *pars pro toto,* representing all Israel and the whole Church, and more exactly the history of Israel and that of the Church, that is, the history of Salvation in the totality of the history of men. Their acts, the prostration, the throwing of crowns, imply those of the whole human species (4: 10 and 5: 14). They communicate to men a certain knowledge of historical connections (5: 5); they offer the prayers of the Saints (5: 8); they ask for the fulfillment of history. It could be said that they are in a way the totality of humanity in its historic reality, in the total flow of historical time, situated before God.

The other group, the four animals, is somewhat less enigmatic. It does not seem that "the four dominant animal species" (birds, wild beasts, tame beasts, men) can be seen here. An ancient tradition has seen the four Gospels, which is difficult to accept, since these animals correspond exactly to the description of chapter 1 of Ezekiel. It is probably more correct to see the signs of the Zodiac (referring then to space and time). On the other hand, the figure four is, we know, the number of creation, of the sensible universe. As for the choice of animals: the eagle is a symbol of eternity, the lion of glory, the bull of power, the man of wisdom. It can be said, on the one hand, that they are the whole creation situated before God; on the other hand, the whole action of God turned toward his creation. Turned toward the four cardinal points, they are, in a certain measure, the executive organs of the will of God. Their wings and their eyes manifest omnipresence. Their innumerable eyes are perhaps the expression of their communion with the knowledge of God. I would like to be able to say (but this is quite fragile) that these two groups represent history and creation, the relation between God and both the universe and humanity, in their double dimension. And in order to mark well the close relationship of the Creator to his creation, they are at the same time in the midst of the throne and around it.

The four animals proclaim God "Holy." This is the first declaration on the subject of the "one." And from this fact they have clearly the function of creation itself before the "fall." To proclaim the holiness of God, meaning "other" and "separate." God is *always* other than we can believe him, think him, imagine him, to be. The creation, before God, recognizes in this song that God is not the creation, nor in it; that he is both *recognized* by the creation (then by man also) but recognized as being the Wholly Other (Holy). The creation then recognizes itself as creation, because of that renounces its autonomy, and so attests its own dependence. We must never forget, that, very condensed, this is what we declare when we say that God is Holy. Next in their song the proclamation of power is affirmed, and the designation, "who was, and is, and is to come." This formula, often repeated in the Apocalypse, is also often presented in different ways. Thus in 1:4 the inaugural testimony of John is to the one "who *is* and who *was* and who *is to come.*" It is, then, "God in Christ": he is considered, first of all, as present: in the *contemporaneity* of Christ; then it is proclaimed of this present Christ that he *was,* from the beginning of the world. Finally, he is the one who comes (the Parousia). Insisting, as we have already, upon the precision of

the term: he is not the one who *will be,* or who *will return;* but
the one who actually is in process of coming.

On the contrary, here, concerning God the Father, what
matters is the stress upon *duration.* The past comes before the
present. But he also comes, which is to say that God and Christ
are the same; they are one, who come from eternity toward the
present, the actuality of man.

Finally, at the glorification, the animals add thanksgiving
(4:9) for, representing the whole creation, they are witnesses
of the love of God and know that God saves. When the creation thus manifests itself before God, the twenty-four elders
act as witnesses of what human history ought to be or should
have been: they carry out the adoration through the work of
man, who is linked to the role of creation in giving glory
(manifesting God). The creation was made to give glory and
to attest the holiness of God. The work of man in history was
intended to be the offering and the voluntary sacrifice of
power, which is freedom. The role of the work of man is then
linked to this vocation of the creation to give glory. If they
were silent, the stones would cry out. As for the political character of this act, it is directed more against the Seleucid kings
than against the Roman emperor (and this is something generally too often forgotten, in many biblical texts). The two acts
(prostration and the throwing of crowns) and the beginning of
the formula seem to correspond to the ritual established by
Alexander to affirm his own supremacy *(proskynesis)* over the
kings and taken up by the Seleucids, with the titles of *Sōtēr*
(Saviour) and *Euergetēs* (Distributor of Good). Kissing the hem
of the imperial garment was added. Therefore, this text attributes to God what the king (Seleucid) claims for himself. And
obviously, for the author, Caesar is always Caesar; whether it
is the kings of Asia Minor or the Roman emperor makes no
difference: there is no reason to prefer one over the others!
Then already, in a sense, this is a declaration of war against the
political power, as we have seen. The Church proclaims here
that God is the master of the Caesars, that she obeys God and
that the Caesars are the creations of God ("for Thou didst
create all things," in the midst of the reproduction of the

proskynesis). And it is at the same time the proclamation that all are equal before God, that there is no hierarchy or nobility, because all the glory and power of the world redounds to God alone. Here the Creator is sharply contrasted with the *Euergetēs*.

The Vision of History (5:8–14; 7:11–17)

In the third doxology, which begins the vision of history (5: 8–14), we find the same personages, but, in addition, angels and men. It is not addressed, as the preceding, to God the Creator, but to Christ, Lord of history, because he has been the immolated servant. This doxology is divided into three parts according to the three groups of actors. First, the group of elders and animals: they play music, and this is doubtlessly the "sigh of the whole creation," which corresponds exactly to the smoke of incense in the bowls that they hold, the prayer of the saints. The music and the incense here represent the unity of Nature and Faith, which is recovered: but *here*, and *here alone*, in the hands of those who are before God. They sing "a new song." Many think that this is an allusion to a Jewish ceremony: the rabbis sing the *shirot*, the songs of expectation before the coming of the Messiah, waiting to be able to begin singing the *shir*, the new song of messianic fulfillment. Then in the Jewish perspective this denotes the coming of the Messiah. But in any case, at the very interior of the text there is a new song, for, addressed to the Lamb, it is different from the one the elders and animals sang to God the Father. It is the great proclamation that only the Lamb can receive the Book of History (the Lordship) and disclose, reveal it. Because he has been perfectly faithful to God (in history) and because of that crucified. Because, in addition, he has obtained for God, in the course of history, men, a specific people, drawn from all the races, all the nations, who will be as a wire conductor through the events, powers, disorders, structures: in this history from now on there will be kings and priests without end attesting the presence of God in the midst of men (and not only the promise or the idea). Sacred history is then mixed with history. And the latter does not unfold according to a naturalistic mode, but not either as an object directed abstractly by God. It is impregnated in every tribe, every language, every nation, by this special people of God.

Then comes the proclamation of the divinity of Jesus Christ by all the angels. He is worthy not only of opening the book of history but of receiving the seven attributes of God: power and wealth and wisdom and might and honor and glory and blessing (5:12). There is, moreover, at the same time, the transfer to Jesus Christ of all that which humanity ever tries to seize for itself, which also includes the glories of men. Finally comes the proclamation of all creatures, in heaven, on earth, under the earth, and in the sea. Some say that man is not mentioned here, but "nature precedes man in adoration and in this sense already recognizes and praises the Lamb." It seems to me that the mention of all creatures, on the contrary, obviously indicates that man is included here. But without being different. Here he is not the creature of election: the salvation won by Jesus Christ is directed to all creatures and not only to man, who thinks himself a king. And I even believe, on the contrary, that because of the fact of his attitude toward creation, his abuse, his pitiless exploitation of things and animals, man is no longer the king of creation before God; in his history he did not at all accomplish what was announced in Genesis 2 and Psalm 8. He is a fallen king, reduced to the level of the other creatures, and his praise addressed to God is not more than that of the humblest living being. So all creatures join their praise *de profundis* to that of the angels *in excelsis;* for, the Lamb of God having intervened, the praise of God can be taken up in all creation. But we must comprehend well the difference between the four animals and all the creatures. The former represent, before God and permanently, the symbols of creation; in short, they are the abstract creation which, whatever be its condition, fallen or saved, cannot be absent from the presence of God, from glory. But the others are the creation (and not only its symbol) in its concrete, carnal, living, and perishable reality. All the creatures can render thanks and glory since the coming of the Lamb, not before: beginning with the moment that the Lamb, both put to death and risen, takes history in hand. Moreover, their praise is different from that of the angels. The first had seven terms, the second (the creatures') does not include more than four (the number of creation): blessing, honor, glory, and might (5:13). The creation *reflects* the Creator in its exterior manifestation and its creative force: the three elements (wisdom, power, wealth) that the creation cannot express are lacking, because only the revelation of God can do that. This trilogy of doxology shows us, first, the fullness of God's action in Jesus Christ, then that this action, disclosing history, can fully unite the creatures (and man) with the angels and the symbols of the divine world in praise.

The end of the period having to do with history is a bit different: after the vision of the people of God as a factor of history (7:1–10), immediately after the seer has been able to consider this multitude clothed in white robes who give glory to the Lamb, we find a brief doxology, in which the four animals, the twenty-four elders, and all the angels are united. Here there is no difference among them: all express the same joy and the same praise; these are the same as in the scene described at the end of the sequence on the Church and at the beginning of that on history, but now their role is more dissociated. The act is an act of adoration. Because finally history is revealed; we know that it is not sound and fury; we know that it is not the furious gallop of unchained forces (which it is also), but that it contains more, something else: the vision of history is ended not by disaster but by the gathering of the people of God. We apprehend that there is an orientation and a signification: that history is not closed around the powers who are endlessly renewed, but that it also contains the testimony of the love of God, of his presence by means of his people; that there is a sacred history hidden in the collective history, which supports and gives meaning to that history. The doxology is addressed to God who, we remember, is here distinct from the Lamb. But precisely what is interesting to observe is that the seven terms here employed are the same as

those found in the song addressed to the Lamb in the introduction to this sequence, except one. For the Lamb we have
wealth (or abundance); and here we have in its place thanksgiving. The six others are the same. Then it is important to show
that it is the same doxology which is addressed first to the
Lamb, worthy of receiving the book and opening it, then to
God the Father, who has permitted the work of the Lamb (and
this is why thanksgiving is addressed to him). In this passage
the song is situated exactly between the vision (the people
clothed in white) and its explanation. The work of God *is*. It
does not depend upon any explanation, any comprehension
by man, any faith or attitude of man. It is, by itself. And it is
because of what God has done that thanksgiving is directed to
him. There is the miracle of this people of God, the most
surprising of all mysteries, and incomprehensible for man.
Nothing can change that. Whether man knows it or not,
whether he believes it or not. There is in history a presence
that nothing can remove. It is the presence of the people of
God, the beginning of the Kingdom. Already the Kingdom of
Heaven, as strange and unbelievable as that can appear. *After*
praise has been addressed to God by these who alone can
penetrate the depth of the mystery of the will of God, then the
matter is *explained* to the seer, the witness. He apprehends what
this mysterious multitude is. Its relation to the sacrificed Lamb
(they have washed their robes in the blood of the Lamb). He
learns that they have passed through the great tribulation.

This "great tribulation" is also a "crux" for the interpreters.
If we adopt a historical perspective, it could be said that this
is an allusion to persecutions. But how would it be possible to
call some few martyrs of the first and second persecution innumerable people? How assimilate the 144,000 of the tribes of
Israel, and the "rest" to these martyrs? If we adopt an eschatological interpretation of the fifth seal, then it could be said that
this is the multitude that has passed through the eschatological
tribulation. But this supposes, first, that the septenary of the
seals is broken up: four seals concerning the horses, and three
others . . . incoherent: one on catastrophes, another on the
Church, another . . . . We are then incapable of explaining the

relation between this view of the Church and the catastrophes: unless we suppose that there has already been a judgment. But then we are led into saying that there are two or three or four repeated (redundant) descriptions of the judgment, of the eschatological tribulation, etc. Which appears to me unsound. Finally, we cannot explain how the whole people of God is composed of those who have passed through the eschatological tribulation. For after all, the Church is not permanently in this situation. Therefore, the only coherent explanation appears to me to be: the people are those who have passed through the tribulation (how terrible!) of history itself. They are this hidden people, constantly threatened by all the forces of history—sociological, economic, political, spiritual. They are put in question as people of God: that is the tribulation. It is this continuance in the time of human invention, of disobedience, of independence, of rupture, of laceration. They are the leaven, which can be smothered by the dough; the light, which can be put under a bushel: the people of God pass through the tribulation of history as Israel had traversed the Red Sea, the act which, very precisely, had made them enter into history. And finally the explanation given to the seer suggests the future of this people who will be the Kingdom of God, the celestial Jerusalem. The very sober verses 16 and 17 of chapter 7, which will be taken up again in the vision of the New Jerusalem are, once more, an example of what we have called "the preliminary allusion." An announcement of what will come later is woven into the midst of the development, an attachment of one section to another.

The Mystery of the Incarnation (12:10–12)

Coming to the fifth doxology (12:10–12), we recall that it is situated in the midst of the disclosure of the incarnational Mystery.[4] The text includes four very distinct parts: the praise to God and to Christ, the destruction of Satan, the victory of the people of God, and the joy in heaven; the whole is announced by "Now is the time," or "Now begins," this being expressed by the verb *ginomai*, "to come into being." These verses are found just after the vision of the woman who bears a child. It is difficult not to see in this birth the very time that is here announced. At the moment of the birth of Jesus, at Christmas, the "loud voice" that speaks in heaven, but that does not come from any mouth, proclaims that now, on the one hand, is the moment of salvation and of the power and reign of God; on the other, the moment of the authority of Christ. In other words, salvation is decided, effected, in the Christmas Incarnation, by God. It is the expression of the power of God (which is *true* power because it is "nonpower") and of his reign: only the absolute sovereign who is inaccessible and Wholly Other, only the Transcendent, can adopt this way. All the rest is literature. But it is also the moment when Christ puts on the *exousia,* which is to say that all those who bear this name—the *exousiai* in heaven and on earth, who pretend to exercise authority—are now dispossessed. The authority is given to Christ at the moment of the Incarnation (and not only after the crucifixion). The mark of this reversal is precisely the fact that there is no longer an accuser; there is no longer an accusation before God. We reach here a profound vision: the accuser had existed as long as God reigned as the Almighty, as long as he was a kind of arbiter of good and evil objectives, as long as the destiny of man depended upon a word from his mouth, as long as he could appear as the judge who is objectively indifferent to what he judges. Then there was an accusation that could be made, that could be heard. But when God has chosen to strip himself of his omnipotence, there can no longer be any meaning to the accusation. When God has taken the side of man, has established a covenant so profound, the covenant of Being itself, that it can no longer be broken by anything, then the accuser can no longer bring an accusation. And his word just falls in the void. There is no longer any accusation at all against men. Then there is no longer any accuser before God. But we must not forget that the time of the Incarnation continues. And if God is now with men, then the accuser in a way follows God and will be found in the midst of men: the principle of hatred, of reciprocal accusation and autojustification. In this danger, therefore, the doxology reminds us of the importance of the Church, the people of God: they can conquer the accusation and the accuser in the world and in the midst of men. Such is the admirable vocation of Christians, such is the role of the Church: not organization, nor the creation of orthodoxies, nor "political involvement," but the conquest of the mechanism of accusations and justifications (which is the same as the celebrated dialectic of Master and Slave), the work of Satan among men. This victory (of reconciliation) cannot be the work of intelligence, of tactics, of a well-applied psychology, nor of techniques and certainly not of sentimentality, piety, morality, or politics. The text is very precise: the blood of Jesus, the testimony rendered to the word, the imitation of God in Jesus. And there is nothing else. Reconciliation, the opposite of the work of Satan, is obtained by the blood of Jesus Christ, is created in each by the creative word announced in the testimony. But the issue here, now (since Satan is in the midst of men) and from now on (since reconciliation with God is accomplished definitively upon the cross once for all) is not reconciliation with God but with men and among men. We must be aware that this reconciliation can be carried out only according to the imitation of Jesus Christ: they loved not their lives even unto death. This phrase, which immediately evokes for us "the one who would save his life shall lose it," is not applied exactly to the question of individual salvation but, rather, to that of testimony to others: it means then that they have borne testimony *according* to Jesus Christ, so in establishing reconciliation between enemies and with those that can be considered enemies. It is, in other words, the opposite of the political option that implies the condemnation of oppressors, exploiters, etc., and so the intensification of conflict against them. Here is the question of reconciliation! Every political action is in this sense equally satanic; it inevitably proceeds by accusation. Finally, the last proclamation of this doxology refers to joy in heaven (related to the hymn of the angels at Christmas; we have spoken of how rarely this joy in heaven is mentioned in the New Testament) and, by contrast, to the woe upon the earth and sea. But here we must take care: once more the sea is a symbol of the aggressive Nothingness. The earth is the symbol of the "terrestrial," opposed to the "celestial," equivalent to the "world" (in the negative sense) and to the "flesh." These words surely cannot be interpreted in a simplistic fashion: heaven has got rid of the devil; he has been sent elsewhere, and it is men who are going to pay for the damage and meet the expenses of the operation. This is absolutely not the meaning. But rather, now the power of division, of destruction, of condemnation has been sent *into* the world of Nothingness and of the terrestrial; and it is going to be active there. It is precisely the kingdom divided against itself that is described in these verses. It is the beginning of "the destruction of destruction" (the negation of negation) by the work of Satan himself.

The Song of the Conquerors (15:1–5)

The sixth doxological text is situated at the beginning of the fourth section (15:1–5), before the seven bowls. It is connected with what has been said up to now of the innumerable elect people: they are now called conquerors of the beast, of his image, and of his number. And they sing the song of Moses, the liberator. Three remarks on these verses should be made here. First, they are a proclamation concerning the "works" accomplished by God. The works of the Lord are great and admirable: meaning that the people of God because they are saved, reconciled, because they have received (first) the attestation of the love of God, can proclaim that he is the Almighty and that his works are wonderful. But once more, the biblical God does not reveal himself initially as the Almighty: he is the Almighty for those who, knowing him as the Saviour, *then* discern his works and see that his works are admirable and extraordinary. But this is not discovered outside of faith, and the objective view of this or that marvel of creation does not enable us to apprehend anything: that could denote for us a God who is Almighty in himself, then inaccessible and terrible, but who is not the God of Jesus Christ. For this reason the text, when it announces the song of Moses adds immediately that it is at the same time the song of the Lamb. But just after "deeds" comes a declaration on the "ways" of the Lord. Of course, we could attach no importance to these verses, saying that it is simply a matter of the poetic reduplication dear to Israel—a couplet on works, a couplet on ways. But even admitting the correctness of this remark (it is obvious), we must at least observe that thus nothing is explained and that the existence of this reduplication does not obviate the question of meaning. The meaning appears to me very clear: there is first the designation of *works* (what is accomplished, the results, the ends obtained) and then that of *means:* the "ways" *(hodoi)* must be understood in the sense of "ways and means" of the procedure. The means employed by God, the processes in which he engages are "just and true": that is, they conform to justice and truth. This is quite fundamental. We find once more the importance of means. The end does not justify the means. It is necessary that the latter, as those employed by God, be in themselves just and truthful. Now we know what the justice of God is. We know what the truth of God is. It is exactly according to that measure and to no other that we have to measure our own means. And it is in this *grandeur* of the work accomplished by the *justice* of the means that consists, proclaims this song, the glory of the Lord and his holiness. Nothing except that! And this is announced to us at the beginning, in full, as a preface to the series of judgments and condemnations.

Finally, the last remark to be made is that "the nations shall come and worship thee, *for* thy judgments have been revealed." We have here again a "preliminary allusion": in fact, we must not interpret this as a too simple expression: the judgments of God are terrible; men are going to be very fearful, so they fall down before God in repentance, etc. Unfortunately, here there is no question of repentance, nor of the terrible character of the judgment, nor of the fact that the nations are terror-stricken. On the contrary. The text begins: "the nations shall come" (of themselves). And we must not forget that just after this verse, the seer beholds the Tabernacle of the Covenant. It is not first of all a vision of wrath. In reality, this verse serves as a connecting point for the later development: it leaps over the whole section concerning the judgments and condemnations and brings us immediately to the celestial Jerusalem, where, we have seen, the nations will come to carry in their glory and walk in the very light of the Lord. It is not unimportant to observe that the term employed is indeed "nations." They who will be subjected to judgment and who will then come. Therefore the judgment liberates the nations from their servitude, which prevents them from coming to God and keeps them from recognizing him as God. "The nations will come because thy judgments have been revealed." The judgment destroys the powers which alienate the nations from the Lord and they will find him when they have their liberty: this is the process that is here announced to us in two verses and described in the whole section to follow in order to emerge in the last part, that of the new creation.

The Song of the Great Multitude (19:1–8)

Finally, we have said the last doxology is situated after the judgments concerning men and the condemnations falling upon the historic incarnations of the powers, but before the condemnation and destruction of the powers themselves, the latter being inseparable from the new creation. This song (19:1–8) is altogether the most complex of those we have seen up to here, being entirely limited to taking up and synthesizing what we have already encountered. We find three participants. A great multitude (which speaks twice), the elders and animals, who only sanction what is said by this multitude (amen, hallelujah); and we have already emphasized the considerable displacement of center that implies: at the beginning the doxology is proclaimed by the celestial creatures; at the end it is proclaimed by the multitude. Then there is the mysterious "voice," already heard (12:10), which comes from the throne but which is not the voice of God (it is indescribable, like thunder), since it calls to "praise *our* God." We have said that the great multitude speaks twice: at the beginning of this sequence (vss. 1–2) and at the end (vss. 6–8). These two declarations, separated by the celestial choirs and the voice are in reality the exact articulation between the two parts: one ends the section concerning the judgments and one inaugurates the section of the new creation. Actually, we could consider verses 6–8 the doxology of introduction for the last part, which it really is. But this ensemble cannot be divided; it must be examined as a whole. Verses 1 and 2 are interesting in that we again find the central declaration (12:10): "Now the salvation and the power and the kingdom of our God," which becomes here, at the end of the judgments: "Salvation and glory and power belong to our God." What was spoken first by the mysterious voice from heaven is now *taken up* as the song of glory *of the innumerable multitude of men.* But it is important to emphasize that this comes after the judgments, while the first declaration is situated at the moment of the Incarnation: there could not be a better reminder that the decisive judgment falls back upon Jesus Christ himself. It is unnecessary to insist once more on the fact that the author of the Apocalypse adopts the essential theological orientations of the Gospels and Paul. And this acclamation made by the multitude of men attests that the judgments of God are full of truth and justice. The word employed here for "judgment" is *krisis.* Which confirms the interpretation that we gave of judgment as separation. But now that men have been "separated" from the powers that blind them, now that they see what in truth the judgments of God are, they apprehend what they have never seen before: that the judgments are actually full of truth and justice and that there is no arbitrariness, no negativity, no hatred, no despotism in these interventions which, viewed from the exterior, outside of Jesus Christ, could appear as such. That which is judged is only what corrupted the earth, what made this creation "earthly"; and this is only violence and hate against what testifies of love, what appears with the weakness of the Lamb: when we have seen that such is the meaning, the only meaning, of the judgment, then we can join in the glory rendered by the great multitude even if the temporal tribulation in which we are plunged can appear terrible in the moment. And once more we must admire the precision of this construction: in the doxology which comes immediately after the Incarnation

(12:10) we find the proclamation: here is the time of salvation, etc., because Satan has been thrown down; this inaugurates the period of the judgments. "Just and true are your ways" (15:3): and we are here (*after* the terrestrial judgment of the power) in the presence of the exact combination of the two formulas: the judgments are the "ways" [the means] of the Lord, and salvation belongs to God because "his judgments are true and just" (19:2).

Finally, the innumerable multitude, whose voice is like the sound of the ocean in its immensity, its infinite renewal, its calm and its fury, its majesty. But also like the roll of mighty thunder: it echoes the voice of the one who speaks as seven thunders; and this voice of men gathered before God then unites the depth of what was the abyss t.; .ne height of the inaccessible, celestial, wonderful image of what humanity becomes in its ultimate reconciliation with God; the great multitude with *this voice* sings the marriage song of the Lamb. The words seem obsolete and insignificant (here is the wedding of the Lamb; his bride is prepared; she is clothed in pure linen): but we must remember that they are spoken *with this voice.* We should recall, for the lovers of the cultural, that marriage was not generally, in the Greco-Roman world, a particularly solemn occasion. There were no pipe organs. Then this signifies a transposition: the marriage of the Lamb is not an ordinary cultural image. The fact that it is so announced transposes completely the comparison with weddings. In fact, what is proclaimed is the marriage of a king (which actually was solemn). It is the King who is married.

But here a problem of translation is posed. The Greek text says exclusively: "The Lord our God, the Almighty, has reigned" (19:6). This formulation appears impossible to translators. In fact, all think that God continues to reign, which is obvious. Then the text is modified by writing: has assumed the reign, has established his reign, has manifested his reign, has taken possession of his reign—all adding something that is not in the text. And the worst (Stierlin) projects into the future (finally reigns) that which is past. Nevertheless it seems to me that the meaning is quite clear: the Almighty (as such) *has* reigned: this reign is, as we have seen, the judgment and condemnation of the historical powers. It is there, at this moment, that the reign has manifested itself, has taken place, as royal reign. And now what is substituted for the reign is the marriage. Another radically new relation is established: the Lord has reigned as Almighty and now he becomes the Bridegroom. This is not only the appearance of a new mode of proximity of God to man. He was the Father, had been designated by Jesus as the Father, and now the Son becomes the Bridegroom of the Church (the traditional interpretation). I will not develop the well-known theme of the Husband: God had been called this (for example, in Isaiah 54 and Hosea 2) in the Old Testament. Then Paul had expounded this theme to interpret the relation of Jesus to the Church. I will not draw the consequences of this comparison. A thousand writers have done it. I only wish to note that there is probably progression here. We have seen several times that in the Apocalypse the Old Testament and what will constitute the New a little later are alike taken up together. In other words, God, the husband of Israel, and Jesus, the husband of the Church, are here alike resumed in these nuptials. So well that it is not a matter of repeating what Paul said, but the fulfillment of the espousals between God and the entire people of God, which we have also seen ultimately is the totality of humanity. This therefore signifies that the Incarnation has not been a fleeting instant in history; it is the "from now on" for all. And I could be confirmed in this interpretation by the singular final phrase (we can admit that it was an explanatory gloss): the white resplendent linen is "the righteous deeds of the saints." If the people were only the Church, it would have no need of being clothed in the righteous deeds of the *Saints,* since the Saints are the Church. In reality this immense people is clothed with the works (holy, in reality sanctified by Christ, but because of this holy) of the Church: and here is situated the end of the separation between the Church and the rest of the people— the unbelievers, the infidels, the ignorant, men. Just as the Church is clothed in white linen by her Lord (they have washed their robes in the blood of the Lamb), so humanity is clothed in white linen by the Church. And this indeed takes place at the end of the liberation from the powers, and *before* the final resurrection: here in fact the resurrection of the Church first, of the Saints who have not received the mark of the Beast (20:4) is distinguished from the resurrection of all (20:5). With this the song ends, the seventh and last doxology of the Apocalypse. The *Seventh*. Of course, we must not press things too far; that there are seven doxologies does not perhaps signify anything; it may be simply chance. But we should not disregard the hypothesis of an explicit decision of the writer, which would confirm the precision of this construction.

The Testimony of the Seer and the Testimony of the Son (22:6–21)

And now we are left in the presence of the last verses of this revelation, so moving and disturbing. The last word is that of appeal and encounter: "Come." Appeal from two sides: the Spirit and the Bride call to man, the whole of humanity: come, then come. The gate of heaven is open. Now the return of Adam is possible. The cherubim no longer guard the gate. For heaven and Eden are no more. The work of man, magnified, glorified, transcended (and nothing has meaning in the history of man if there is not a Transcendent) awaits only man himself for its fulfillment. And the witness who hears this appeal of the Lord repeats in his turn: "Come." He says it to this humanity; he echoes the word of the Lord; and he says it also in response to the Lord himself: "Come soon" to accomplish what we have just seen, to realize it, to make it real, after it has been revealed as *true*. "Come," says God to man. "Come," responds man to God.[5] But these two appeals are not like the tragic "cry" of Edvard Münch which goes off into the void and calls to no one. This double appeal is crossed and exchanged, and the hearer receives it. And the witness opens wide the ways of coming, of the return; it is enough to be thirsty, to be among the poor, the hungry, the naked, the excluded (not because this situation has the least value in itself, but because they alone are thirsty.

Only the one who is hungry has a longing for justice). It is enough, but necessary. All those who live in want (and writing that, how can I fail to think also of the miserable ones enslaved to drugs, and the alcoholics, who know better than anyone the agonies of want; how thirsty they are, how they need that which will completely fill up the terrible absence). All those who live in oppression and know the thirst for liberty. All those who live in separation (in themselves, or against others, or in mourning . . . , unfathomable) and know the thirst for reunion. All those who live in uncertainty and doubt, the tragic agnostics, the uneasy scientists, who are thirsty for truth. It is enough to be thirsty. It is enough to desire this lifegiving water and to find here freely that which is exactly the response and measure, the birth and fullness (at the same time), corresponding to the thirst of each.

But also the appeal spoken by God, the prophetic word, must be carried. It is no longer a matter of distinguishing learnedly between apocalypse and prophecy. The word here is prophetic because it is *complete* proclamation of the word of God, because it is existential, because it discloses the total fulfillment of the will of God. The witness, he who has seen these things, John, personally vouches for the authenticity of this whole revelation.[6] Of course, his warning does not mean, literally, that one does not have the right to reflect, to comment, upon this book itself of the Apocalypse, but that one cannot claim to add anything to the work of God in Jesus Christ.[7] To add whatever it may be is to deny the totality. And in the same way, nothing can be taken away. To take away whatever it may be is to destroy. The work of God the Father accomplished in Jesus Christ is infinitely simple. What more simple than this double appeal that is met with, "Come," or than the fulfillment of the nuptials of man and God? Infinitely incomprehensible and perfect. What perfection is to be sought beyond the Incarnation and the assumption of the work of men in the celestial Jerusalem? But this warning must be given by the witness himself, who has transmitted his vision. It is the word of a prophetic man, but which must be heard from man to man. The one who adds to or diminishes the Incarnation manifests thereby that he is not truly thirsty. He is still satisfied with all the drinks of the world and looks for a cocktail of Revelation and Culture. He is not yet brought to a standstill at this single and last prayer: "Come, Lord Jesus, come soon." But when this prayer is spoken, in simplicity of heart, in the acceptance of mystery revealed (but the revelation itself is mystery and is revealed as mystery) in the absoluteness of this thirst, then indeed the Lord responds: "Yes, I am coming soon." And when he so answers, he in his turn declares himself as witness. Jesus, the faithful and true witness. He comes first to attest what his prophet, his witness, has said. He comes to affirm that this witness has spoken truly, that he is right in proclaiming the appeal and the warning. To the testimony of man responds the testimony of the Son, who guarantees the word of man (who makes it true: it is this which makes true, not linguistics) and who in his turn bears witness, from the Father and for the Father, with every dimension that we have recognized to the testimony, "I am coming soon." This soon includes all temporal dimensions, not only the future but also the present. Not only the spiritual but also the existential. Not only the individual but also the galactic. Not only the true but also the real. And so that should be what we have glimpsed; in other words, "Come, Lord Jesus." What we say is only the response and the repetition and the stammering of the promise itself. And if we can still pray this after two thousand years of absence and havoc, how can we fail to know the truth, Amen: that we pray because grace is already the fulfillment. "The grace of the Lord Jesus be with all." For all is grace.[8] There is the central message of this Apocalypse.

NOTES

Introduction

[1]It is necessary to note concerning the term "apocalypse" the very intelligent résumé made by J. M. Saint in regard to Tillich (Bulletin Centre Protestant d'Etudes et de Documentation, 1970): The Apocalypse as revelation takes a particular meaning in the Christian tradition, providing above all an interpretation of reality. It presupposes that the hearers are already believers. It does not enter into the network of objective knowledge of things, it is not the disclosure of a solid physical law, it brings to view a mystery. And, like the miracle, it develops something that remains a mystery even after appearing. But it is not an enigma (because the mystery escapes objective knowledge). There is, like the narratives of the miracles, an ensemble of symbols.

[2]If I speak of the importance of the structure of the text, and of the meaning that derives from that structure itself, if I speak of the necessity of taking the text in its final totality, this is not at all in the manner and under the influence of structuralism. I have always had this position in regard to the biblical texts; I have always held that the interpretation was tied to comprehension of the structure. This can be seen in my commentary

on the book of Jonah (1950): I know well that by date and
perhaps by origin the four chapters are different, but the
meaning of the book appears only if they are put in relation
to each other, if they are put in motion, and if the reason for
this construction is sought (I do not say the psychological
motive of the author); it is this, then, that I have tried to do.
In other words, I am simply convinced that the author is not
an imbecile, that he had had a purpose in establishing this text
thus (another purpose than merely to keep on putting end to
end some texts vaguely related to the same subject), that he
has signified something in constructing this totality, and that
it is the totality which reveals its profound reality, and not at
all a certain fragment separated from the others.

[3]See the study of P. Le Guillou (*Le Mystère du Père,* 1973)
showing that the writings of the New Testament cannot be
interpreted according to Jewish thought alone, as too often is
done today, but that the Greek contribution, which is particularly important for the Apocalypse, cannot be neglected. He
is equally right in emphasizing that the political interpretation,
legitimate for the Old Testament, is transcended by the chris-
tological vision. The Apocalypse is not first and uniquely a
political book, but "today the political easily gives rise to the
hermeneutic of the Revelation"!

[4]J. Comblin, in *Théologie de la Ville* (1968), gives an excellent
note concerning the contrast between the Apocalypse of John
and the others, first showing that John radicalized the most
radical ideas of apocalypticism, then pointing out that the
notion of the end of history is not an idea unique to apocalyptic and by this fact denoting a movement of thought, but that
on the contrary it is the result of the *whole* conception of the
world and of history in Israel, the product of the long theological history of Israel.

[5]Bibliographical summary: I refer for the essential to what is
found in the book by C. Brütsch (see below). Among the
innumerable old commentaries, I will note one of the least
known, the least fantastic, and the most theologically pro-

found, that of Thomas Campanella, *De Dictis Christi prophetiae,* republished in Italian as *La profezia di Cristo* (1973). It is a very remarkable theological analysis of the Apocalypse *as prophecy.* It is obviously necessary to refer to the two great classics: *L'Apocalypse* by E. B. Allo (1933); *Clarté de l'Apocalypse* by Brütsch (5th ed., 1966); to which can be added M. Rissi, *Die Zukunft der Welt: Eine Exegetische Studie über Johannes Offenbarung* (1966). In the excellent precis by A. Feuillet, *The Apocalypse* (English trans. 1965), all the basic information for an actual study will be found, and a good bibliography, which completes that of Brütsch. The elementary book of Laepple, *L'Apocalypse de Jean* (1970) (historicizing, on the one hand, but weak as far as the commentary is concerned) can be useful for a simplified survey of Jewish apocalyptic and for the references to biblical texts upon the themes of the Apocalypse. M. H. Brunner, "Apokalyptik: Einige Überlegungen zu einem oft vergessenen Aspekt der Zukunft," *Reformatio,* 1972 (Nos. 11–12), is a very good classical study of the relationships between the Apocalypse and eschatology.

In my opinion many commentaries on the Apocalypse (modern at least, because the defects of the old commentaries are different, falling into a delirious gnosis against which a reaction had been necessary, but today this no longer concerns us) show three common defects: first, in order to become scientific they have practically abandoned the study of meaning and sense, adhering to the study of form, composition, style, genre. But it is an error of method in a book such as this to dissociate meaning and form: the latter is a servant, as in all poems, to explicate, illustrate, the meaning of the message. But to analyze endlessly the form in itself does not advance an inch the understanding of what the author intended to transmit, and especially of what he expresses concerning his purpose.

The second defect consists in merely ascribing the Apocalypse to a historical cultural milieu as a simple historical document. No longer is the attempt made to scrutinize the Apocalypse in order to know the future, which is good, but it is used only as a document instrumental in understanding early Christianity, the images, beliefs, formulas, liturgies, myths of Christians at the end of the first century, the cultural expression of the faith, possibly the taking of political positions. All this is obviously legitimate, but by no means exhausts the content of a text which implies a putting in question. In other words, all these studies are limited to an external and formal examination which does not enter into, and often does not clarify either, the intentional and transintentional meaning of the text that we now have in hand. It is certainly a dated historical text, but it is not merely a source for reconstituting a moment of church history or of Christian thought. And this represents a second current of interpretation.

Finally, the third error is perhaps still more serious; this is an internal contradiction of method: it is universally recognized that the Apocalypse proceeds by a symbolic mode of thought and that there is in apocalypses a dialectical movement. But this, which is true, once declared is no longer taken into account. A tip of the hat is given to something admitted, and then the text of the Apocalypse is treated as if it were neither dialectical nor symbolic. No search is made at all for the *way* in which it is dialectical (or else there is restriction to the very crude affirmation that it describes the combat of the forces of good and the forces of evil); how this dialectic comes into play, what the fundamental dialectical *movement* is that cuts across the whole text and structure—not at all; no attempt is made to show the planes of symbolization, nor the plurality of meanings that the symbol inevitably evokes and elicits. There is so great suspicion of allegory that after having said that symbol is present, it is avoided with horror. That a symbol is not interpreted in only *one* way (the woman = *a*, but not *b*), that on the contrary it includes a series of designations, each one related to the others, is immediately forgotten. Moreover, the contrary is done; that is to say, the attempt is made to interpret the text as if it were neither dialectical nor symbolic, applying to it a method of thought rational, linear, formalistic, univocal. It is said, for example, that "if the woman designates Mary, she cannot at the same time mean the Church or Israel." It is necessary to choose. And all this is dictated by concern for the exegetical method most closely related to the criteria for the study of texts: contradiction, unity of meaning, repetition, etc.—which is correct for a *modern* historical account, but not at all adequate for a poem or for a symbolic, dialectical work (and even for the historical books of the Bible!) It is a monumental error of methodology. I maintain that *all* the exegetical studies on the Apocalypse written during the last fifty years in applying this so-called scientific method are scientifically inexact because they have applied a method completely inappropriate to the object. The attempt has been made to measure the Brownian movement with the double decimeter of a schoolboy.

⁶There is also good reason to study the relationship between apocalypse, myth, and gnosis, but reference can be made to the good studies of Comblin and of Grant on this subject: J. Comblin (*Théologie de la Ville*) has an excellent development on the difference between apocalypse and myth: "It can be said that myth tends to reduce the god to his city, to his framework, to the ambitions of his kings . . . . Myth refers concrete situations to the absolute. It contains ideological elements in that it justifies situations of fact. On the other hand, . . . in apocalypse the mythical elements are incorporated in a vision which transcends myth. This means that myth is overcome, subordinated . . . , the myths have been stripped of their corrupt elements. They can serve to represent the design of God. . . ." But actually it is a matter of the design of God in a kind of reality that is not at all mythical. Myth is then an instrument, a vector, and does not itself give a meaning. And further: "Myth tends to reduce the city to the phenomena of the cosmos. It tends to refer phenomena back to cosmic phenomena. It thus flees the mystery of liberty. If the city is a cosmos in miniature (in the myth) it would be possible to ward off dangers by rites, exorcisms, recourse to the gods . . . thanks to the myths men could seek to persuade themselves that the city was a phenomenon of nature. . . . In the Apocalypse, on the contrary, in the city it is the cosmos which is reduced to the estate of matter, which is put at the ser ice of the people of God. The

city is the people, not a people who believes itself subject to the mysterious laws of a mysterious being who embraces it, but a people defined by the covenant and consistent in itself. That is why the architectural elements of the city are from now on only decorative elements. They no longer have magic or ritual meaning." This is excellent.

Neither must the possibility be overlooked that the Apocalypse had been written as a kind of *reaction* to the gnostic tendency which developed as a refuge in myth, the mystical, the metaphysical, in opposition to the historical: the disastrous events of the first century produced doubt in regard to the intervention of God in history, and consequently in regard to the apocalyptic promises. The attempt is made to leave the world, and to be liberated by knowledge. On the other hand, the Apocalypse of John would then be the total and rigorous affirmation of a faith in that intervention of God, a return to the historical and to the decision in history, with an amplitude never yet attained. Cf. by example: R. M. Grant, *Gnosticism and Early Christianity* (1959).

[7]Finally, we must emphasize a very important last aspect of the attitude to take before a text such as this: one can in fact consider that the formulas we know too well are simple "rituals," that it is a matter of liturgies, which in our thinking too often presuppose words without great significance. On the contrary, I believe it necessary to take very seriously these phrases which can seem ready-made, and that it is even starting from them that all the rest must be understood. Thus the doxologies must be analyzed carefully, noting the differences that can exist among them, and which are not the result of chance. In the same way declarations such as: "there will be no more delay" (10:6), or even: "the kingdom of the world is *now* the kingdom of our Lord" (11:15), must be considered as the point of departure for the pericopes which precede and follow. There is a kind of recognition of "cores" around which the totality of the text is organized. These cores are constituted by formulas that inevitably must appear to us ready-made or stylistic, although their banality is in reality only the expression of the permanent certitude of the Church.

Chapter 1

[1]However, a difficulty exists concerning the septenary of the fourth part: it is redoubled. In fact, we have a first septenary of angels (14:6–20) followed by the septenary of bowls. Then the question of knowing whether a new division must be introduced is posed: that is to say, a separate septenary for these fourteen verses. I think not, and here is why: this part would not be constructed like the others; it would, to be sure, have an opening vision (14:1–5), but no doxology; and reciprocally, the septenary of bowls would certainly have a doxology but no introductory vision, since it would begin abruptly with 15:1: "Seven angels bore seven plagues . . . ." But in addition, verses 6 to 20 of chapter 14 include a vision and no symbol. In this series we are on the plane of the action-symbol relation; however, there is precisely no action but proclamations (and even vs. 16, "the land was reaped," and vs. 19, "he gathered the vintage," are proclamations and not at all realizations). Then to my thinking the unity of chapters 14–19 must be maintained. But then is there not a doublet? And are not verses 6 to 20 of chapter 14 simply a repetition of the seven bowls? Is there not a judgment and final plague twice, with simply different images? I do not think that either. But we are in the presence of a key interpretation of the Apocalypse: in fact, precisely because it is a matter of "revelation," it reveals to us at the same time what happens in heaven and on earth. At least in chapters 8–14 and 15–19. We are before an extraordinary intention to relate earth to heaven, time to eternity, etc. And we observe (as in the prologue of Job) a kind of "council" in heaven before the event takes place on the earth. Thus verses 6 to 20 are in reality the making of the decision for the last judgment, with an astonishing construction: we have three angels (vss. 6–13), the Son of Man (vs. 14), and three angels (vss. 15–20). That constitutes a kind of "celestial tribunal." We will see in a closer investigation the meaning of its intervention. But what then is decided takes its reality when the bowls are overturned upon the earth: thus the two septenaries form the obverse and reverse of the same event.

[2]I am in complete agreement with A. Feuillet (*Johannine Studies*, English trans. 1965, second part) in considering that the center of the Apocalypse is constituted by the passion and the resurrection of Jesus (but I do not believe that that refers to the bringing forth of the Messiah by the woman nor that the woman is the people of God. On the other hand, his interpretation according to which chapters 5–11 represent the time of the Jews and chapters 12–15 the time of the Church or of the nations appears to me very insufficient, and among other things supposes the rejection of the first part, the letters to the churches, which seems strange. Nothing in the symbolism implies that division.

[3]We keep for convenience this word "heaven," though of course biblically, and above all, when in the Old Testament it is a question of the "heaven of heavens," that does not designate the "starry vault," the "above our heads," the "ether," etc. but, rather, the "place-nonplace" of God, the specific environment of God, the "nonworld" where God is all, the "Wholly Other" and the "Beyond," which is to say that which is not the creation but at the interior of which the whole creation is situated, although, obviously, "interior" being still spatial and inadequate, is a simple figurative image.

[4]For example, according to the introduction to the Apocalypse of *Traduction Oecuménique de la Bible.*

[5]See our critique in *Foi et Vie* (1973).

Chapter 2

[1]See the interesting study and interpretation of F. Montagnini, "Le 'Signe' d'Apocalypse XII à la lumière de la Christologie du N.T.," *Nouvelle Revue Théologique* (1967).

[2]That cannot in the least be assimilated to or even compared to the cosmic dramas of myths and gnosis: here the cosmic serves as a support for a more profound truth; it has no reality by itself. It is a means to designate something else.

[3]This is why I cannot accept the current interpretations of these passages: for verse 2, the references to bears, lions, etc. are simply other signs of power, and that has nothing to do with the four beasts of Daniel 7. Neither the symbolism nor the context permits any comparison. But this is attractive for those who wish to see here the empire of Rome according to the image of the four animals of Daniel, which are four particular empires. In the same way for verse 3, we cannot infer from the use of the same word to speak of the immolated Lamb and of the wound on the head of the beast that there is an imitation of the death and resurrection of Jesus.

[4]As for the importance of the political and the temptation toward the primacy of the political during the epoch when John was writing, certain exegetes seem to think that there was no longer any "political life" in the empire at this time. All historians of institutions know that the opposite is true; and I have recalled some important facts on this subject in my study, "Les chrétiens et la politique" in *Contrepoint* (1973), and in the collective work *Les chrétiens et l'État* (1973).

[5]It is also known that, in order to arrive at giving a meaning by this method, the number has sometimes been reduced to 616.

[6]It is perhaps also necessary to take account of the fact that the number six was particularly important in certain pagan religions, for example, the Chaldean.

Chapter 3

[1]See F. Bovon, "Le Christ de l'Apocalypse," *Revue de Théologie et de Philosophie* (1972).

[2]Although it has been held that for that epoch the words "Son of Man" mean simply "man." But given the fact that there was also the word "man," pure and simple, since another term is employed, there must have been a certain distinction between the two! According to the Aramaic, Son of Man, which is a familiar term, means apparently "man" or "I." But J. C. Re-

nard (*Notes sur la Foi,* 1973) makes a series of very judicious remarks on that formula. On the one hand, Jesus by that term marked his identification with the servant of the Lord of Isaiah (chapter 53); in fact, we find this term employed to designate the suffering servant (Mark 8:31–10:45). As man he leads men to a new covenant, which will make him the new man, the triumphant servant. The Son of Man in the glory of his Father: this appears in the opposition that Renard notes between the Son of Man already come and the Son of Man still to come. On the other hand, he calls our attention to the fact that to the question of the crowd, "Who is this son of man?" (John 12:34) (which would prove that for John it was obvious that Jesus had taken this word in a slightly different sense from that of the ordinary vocabulary), Jesus responds in an enigmatic fashion: "Walk while you have the light . . . while you have the light, believe in the light that you may be sons of light," which would signify that Jesus is not only a man born of the human species, but that having become the man that he is, he is no longer Son of the old man, but Son of the new man, to which all are called in becoming sons of light. Of course, in order to examine more deeply this question of the Son of Man, we must refer to the decisive studies of Th. Preiss.

[3]We find here an example of the geometric simplism of Stierlin (*Vérité de l'Apocalypse,* 1973). He thinks that this passage is incoherent because the horseman *is named* Faithful and True (vs. 11) while "his name is *unknown* to all." But here the exegete already makes an extrapolation: the text says: "a name which he alone knows," while subsequently we are told that he is called Word of God (vs. 13), and Lord of Lords (vs. 16), a name that he bears written upon his robe. Stierlin thinks that we are in the presence of two texts, since one says that the horseman has a name that is known, the other that his name is unknown. These are two different fragments. We notice once more that one starts with the idea that the compiler of the Apocalypse was the worst of imbeciles, since he has not even seen that from verse 11 to verse 12 there is a contradiction. Too bad. I would suggest to M. S. that there are not two

independent fragments but four, since the horseman is called Faithful, and Word of God, and Lord. Three *different* names, you see! These are obviously three different conceptions of the Messiah. In reality, M. S. comprehends absolutely nothing of the text. To say that the Messiah is called Truth or Word of God is one thing. But is M. S. so good a theologian that he can tell me what the content of these words is in itself, their total Reality, their absolute significance? What is the Truth, absolutely? What is the Word of God, absolutely? If I cannot answer these questions, then I do not know the *name* of this horseman. I know his designation. But how would I express the ultimate, spiritual, essential content? This very simple reflection shows how serious the apparently weighty scientific logic of M. S. really is.

[4]See my study on "Le Relatif comme catégorie éthique de la liberté chrétienne," in *Éthique de la Liberté* (English trans., *The Ethics of Freedom*, 1976).

[5]I know well all the aspects of "moral judgment" that can be found in the text, and all the references to individual salvation; they obviously should not be excluded: "Happy are those who wash their robe in order to have a right to the tree of life . . ." (though this is not exactly a moral work: it is faith); but this is only part of the revelation and because it has been so much exaggerated that it has become nearly the only question, for that reason I put it here in the margin. Not that it is for me less important. I am attempting to reestablish equilibrium by showing that for the Apocalypse it is not the central and decisive question.

[6]But there is also a naturalistic element, which has always seemed to me to be of great importance for the choice of the lamb, among the other sacrificial animals of the Old Testament, to designate Jesus Christ: of all the animals whose death I have observed, the lamb and the ewe are the only ones who do not struggle when they are struck: at the moment when the knife cuts the jugular, the ewe relaxes and does not try to flee or kick. It gives way perfectly. It dies with a sort of acceptance.

Another animal cannot be found which signifies in the same way the acceptance of death. This is why it is the only one that corresponds to Jesus: "I lay down my life . . . ."

[7]We will not enter here into the ethical consequences of what this signifies; see our *Ethics of Freedom*.

[8]This single observation ought then to cut short all foolish speculations founded upon aberrant interpretations precisely of the Apocalypse in order to calculate the dates of the "end of the world," and the time of history!

I will cite the very beautiful page of P. Le Guillou (*Le Mystère du Père*, p. 245) upon that which he calls "the paschal theanthropism of Christ," which corresponds to what we can comprehend here of the Incarnation. "The whole deployment of history has for its function only to make possible the perfect Amen of humanity to . . . the covenant made by the Father. This same Christ who is 'the lamb without reproach and without spot discerned before the end of the world,' the First of the creation according to the design of the Father, is also the one who can say, 'I am the Amen, the true and faithful witness, the First of the creation of God.' The paschal Amen in whom the filial adoption is consummated in the free collaboration of man with God, contains the beginning and the end of the benevolent act of God. In him are tied together in the theanthropic covenant human history and the divine economy; the liberty of God who has situated his creation in the mystery of the Lamb and the liberty of man whom he adopts and whom he saves. . . . The Amen is the *hour (kairos),* in the Johannine meaning of the word, the paschal moment when the divine act is consummated in the perfect human obedience of the Son. This paschal hour does not constitute solely the eschatological moment for which the Christ has come and which he accomplishes upon the cross in saying, 'It is finished.' It is originally the celestial *hour* which is at the beginning of the divine work. . . . From this moment, when the Son responds for men to the will of the Father and recapitulates his design, the economy of the fullness of time unfolds . . . ; the paschal hour is the moment when the covenant is sealed between God and man

in the Spirit, the covenant that Christ, obedient even unto the
Cross, put back between the hands of the Father and transmitted to the Church. From now on the Spirit and the Bride say,
'Come.' Because the Spirit is the Spirit of adoption who cries
in man: 'Abba, Father' and witnesses with him to his filial
condition. Beginning with the sonship in the Spirit man can be
opened to the eschatology of the Presence who delivers the
world to him in its reality, without plundering it in a titanic
manner. . . ." This remarkable page denotes exactly what the
heart of the Revelation of the Apocalypse is.

Chapter 4

[1]See the beautiful study by E. Käsemann (Bochum Confer-
ence, 1962; translation, Bulletin Centre Protestant d'Etudes et
de Documentation, 1970). A community that desires to be
Christian of itself has not the least authority. It must be called
to order when it makes its own piety the basis of the message
and derives a theology from it. It is destroyed when it makes
itself master of the Word. It is Regnum Christi only because
it is edified by the Word. A Christian is free only insofar as he
belongs not to himself but to his Lord.

[2]A detail on the subject of this tree of life: it is perhaps chosen
here as the opposite of the sacred tree that was worshiped at
Ephesus.

[3]Her bishop, Polycarp, died at the beginning of the second
century in a persecution and denounced by the Jews. This
detail has led certain historians to take this as proof that the
text dates from the epoch of the martyr Polycarp, a very cava-
lier use of a factual reference!

[4]I believe that for the whole first Christian generation the
relationship with civilization had nothing to do with the doctrine of Paul Tillich!

[5]Upon the factual details of this letter, and very particularly the
meaning of the hidden manna, read the excellent note that is
found for this text in the *Traduction Oecuménique de la Bible*.

[6]See the very interesting study of E. Haulotte on the garment, symbol of spiritual realities, which clarifies well all the texts of the Apocalypse where there is question of wearing the white robe: *Symbolique du vêtement selon la Bible* (1966).

[7]On the Epistle to the Church of Laodicea, one will profit from the remarkable study made by a group of authors (Maigret, Devambez, Leconte, Besnard) in the special number of *Bible et Terre Sainte* (1966) on Laodicea. It is a model of convergent studies, as would have to be necessary, and clarifies this letter perfectly from the historical point of view.

Chapter 5

[1]A simple indication to show the fragility of historical scientific studies in these domains, and reference to cultural elements: Everyone considers that this book sealed with seven seals is a testament. For some, reference is made to the "testament" of which Jeremiah 32:6–14 speaks (which is inexact because it is a matter of an act of purchase), and we are told that it is a double book (in use *at Babylon*) to attest a sale, one being sealed (but probably not with seven seals), the other deposited with the public administration permitting redemption by the one who has the right during a certain interval, after which the sale was held to be complete. But these formalities do not apply to a testament; they date from the seventh century B.C. at Babylon and this has no relationship with what we know of the law practiced in the Near East in the first century.

Other exegetes have then affirmed very emphatically that it is a matter of the Roman testament. Unfortunately, there again we are in the presence of a totally incorrect assimilation. In the first century the customary Roman testament is either the non-cupative testament or the praetorian testament, written upon two tablets closed one upon the other with the seals of seven witnesses. But nothing is written on the *exterior* except the name of the testator and perhaps those of the witnesses. According to a lawyer of the time of Nero, there were quittances and other probative acts that had to be written on the interior and the exterior: two tablets of wax, joined in the form of a codex and with the *same* text at the interior and exterior and then sealed, but this time there is neither seven witnesses nor seven seals. In any case we are not before a scroll which seems evoked by our text. It will be only in 439 that there will appear the testament upon a scroll with the text of the testament at the interior, with the signature *(subscriptio)* of the witnesses, and then the scroll is sealed with seven seals and on the exterior the *superscriptiones* bear the formal signs and in particular the designations of the witnesses. Consequently nothing permits the assimilation of this "sealed book" to a testament. Avatars of historical imprecision!

[2]Those who wish to see in the white horseman war have to be satisfied with civil wars for the red horseman. This appears to me absurd: there is not such a difference. And still more ridiculous is the affirmation that these civil wars were a considerable scourge in the empire, which was not true at this epoch. That developed much later.

[3]See the very remarkable book of Vendryes, *Le hasard dans l'histoire* (1950), and the study of Leo Hamon, *Acteurs et données de l'Histoire* (2 vols. 1970).

[4]After all, when psychoanalysis evokes Eros and Thanatos in order to specify the most fundamental instincts or impulses, it does nothing other than this "personalization" in Mammon or in the Horsemen.

[5]Our interpretation then denies radically the affirmation prevalent in most commentaries that the horsemen are eschatological signs: in the true sense that means nothing.

[6]Perhaps we must here allude to a problem that presents an interest only to curiosity: the lot of the dead before (insofar as "before" has meaning outside of time) the resurrection and the last judgment (to keep the traditional vocabulary). According to the Jews of the first century before Christ, the souls of the righteous are preserved under the throne of the divine glory and are found in an intermediary state, in expectation

(which already is not very consistent with the tendency that seemed the strongest in early Jewish theology according to which the dead are totally dead and have no survival at all). This text seems directly inspired by the former image. But what is this "soul"? It seems that it is hardly in the line of Jewish thought and very strongly influenced by the Greeks. There is going to be drawn from this text innumerable heresies about the immortality of the soul: the existence of an intermediate life in limbo, etc., and also the custom of putting the remains of the martyrs under the altars in the churches, consistent with the idea that the altar where transsubstantiation takes place is the altar of the very glory of God. All this is of the order of simple curiosity. I will recall briefly that that which returns to God is the spirit that he has given (not the soul in itself) and which is found in God, in the spirit itself which is God. But this spirit which has been incarnate is not a sort of neutral fluid: it has *lived* with "the body and the soul." It has had a history. When it returns to God, it is not a vague and unformed current of air; but it carries with it, and by the very power of the Spirit of God, the identity of the being where it had been incarnate, his historical and psychic identity: it is in this sense that we can speak of "the soul of the just."

[7]We must notice that the whole movement of this text reveals to us an exact replica of the departure of Israel from Egypt: there is the slavery, the putting to death, the place of the double anguish (history), the plagues of Egypt (equivalent to the troubles of nature described here), the mark of the blood of the lamb upon the sons of Israel, the gathering of the people by election, the judgment upon Egypt and its king, the journey of Israel by faith alone, the journey to the promised land across the desert, which is the time of testing.

[8]See the commentary on this psalm by A. Maillot and A. Lelievre.

[9]This revelation upon history contains no kind of possible allusions to a revelation of God in and by history. This current of contemporary theology appears to me in exact contradic-

tion to the Apocalypse. History has no particular virtue. "The apocalyptic Advent of the will of the Father in the love of the Risen One," as P. Le Guillou correctly says, is the key of the revelation. And nothing else. "The hermeneutic historicity of Christianity is an apocalyptic of the will of the Father in the paschal advent of Christ," and there is no other possible meaning of history, which is there embraced, assumed, synthesized, but never revelatory.

Chapter 6

[1]A. Feuillet, "La Moisson et la Vendange de l'Apocalypse (chapitre XIV): Signification chrétienne de la Révélation johannique," *Nouvelle Revue Théologique* (1972).

[2]Verse 3, concerning the sea, is very difficult. But if we consider that the sea is the origin of all life, which is biologically agreed upon, and that which was said already in Genesis 1: 20–21, this verse can mean sterility: that which man does nevertheless engages himself and engages creation in the way of sterility; not death, but the impossibility of reproducing and transmitting life.

[3]Cf. my book *The Meaning of the City* (1972).

[4]We observe that the Apocalypse exercises extreme discretion on the subject of hell. There is not even any question of it at all! How did hell with its traditional imagery come into being? Why has it now disappeared? One can read with interest on the subject of these beliefs the article by Caillois, "Sur l'Histoire et les avatars de l'Enfer," *Diogène* (1974), No. 1.

[5]As a symptom of the lack of seriousness of the exegetes I could cite the phrase of one of them; in order to arrive at the figure seven for the desired epoch he indicates that it is necessary "to restrict oneself to the *principal* Roman Emperors"! But for a scientist what is the criteria for "principal"? Duration, I suppose, which means that Galla, Othon, and even Vitellius are not principal because their reign is not long enough! As for the "kings," they could be the "sovereigns of

nations that are vassals of Rome": unfortunately, at this epoch there were not ten "vassal" kings. (And what does this term mean? Strictly nothing in the Roman organization!) While we are at it, why would the seven first kings not be the seven kings of Rome? All this does not hold up.

[6]I have, however, employed this same argument to show that the white horseman cannot designate two different things. But the important factor, I believe, is that for the horseman there are explanations in the text which relate the two in an identity, while here that which relates the two is the total contradiction that is present.

[7]We must recall the whole biblical theology of the City, which I cannot do here. I limit myself to referring to my work *The Meaning of the City.*

[8]In a word: thus we refer to the fact that the first Christians believed (probably) and Jesus himself had believed (perhaps) that the return of the Son of Man would take place immediately after the resurrection. Then the first generation passed: the return left Christians waiting; the second generation had to adapt themselves, revise the notions of the immediacy of the return and install themselves in an intermediate period, that of the Church. The expectation became less fervent while the organization appeared. The Parousia became less and less an event expected immediately: an explanation was sought for this delay.

[9]Concerning the delay of the judgment, I put aside the most current explanation, doubtlessly correct but very insufficient, according to which the eschatological temporality is characterized by a distension between the realization of the design of God at Easter and its full manifestation. It is the classic opposition between the "for the time *(kairos)* is near" of Apocalypse 1:3 and "I gave her time" *(chronos)* of Apocalypse 2:21. The opposition between kairos and chronos has been carefully studied in these last years but we always return for that which occupies us here to the explanation of the Second Epistle of Peter 3: 8–10 ("not wishing that any . . ."). Which is one of the

aspects of the delay, but not the only one! On this subject see Von Allmen, "L'Apocalyptique juive et la retour de la Parousie dans la 2e Épître de Pierre," *Revue de Théologie et de Philosophie* (1966).

[10]Upon the importance of separation in the creation see the very essential book of P. Beauchamp, *Création et séparation,* an exegetical study of chapter I of Genesis (1969).

[11]Of course I leave aside completely the innumerable fantastic, delirious, and dangerous speculations of the millennialists, who from Joachim of Fiore to Hitler have really understood nothing of this text by taking it literally.

[12]Therefore, we comprehend well why the "second death" is spoken of here: it is not at all, as most commentators think, the "definitive" and "spiritual" death, which would be opposed to simple corporal death: it is a matter of the death of Death. Death with its action, its whole action, upon earth is the first. But when it itself is condemned to the nothingness of the fire, to the abyss of fire, this is a new phenomenon; it is the Second Death. That which acts upon Death itself.

[13]In any case that implies: if we remain in the schema of predestination, one single predestination, that to salvation, and not double predestination.

[14]And of course in this condemnation of destruction are included *all the works* of men participating in destruction: war, the exploitation of man by man, every negation against man or against God.

[15]Of course I do not pretend in two pages to solve the unfathomable theological problem of universal salvation or of predestination, simple or double (who could do better here than the extraordinary volume of the *Dogmatics* of Karl Barth?). I know all the texts that can be advanced to "prove" the existence of the damnation of certain men. I wish only to show that here, in the Apocalypse, that interpretation is not imposed; and that it even goes counter to the revelation as a whole furnished in this book. For the other texts I wish also to em-

phasize that we must be very prudent: for example, we must not confound condemnation of men with that of their works or that of the nations. We must not either interpret the parables as descriptions of reality (curiously, there is general agreement in saying that a parable is interpreted by its "point;" but when it comes to the three parables of Matthew 25, and above all the last, they are interpreted as if it were a matter of concrete reality).

One final precaution: we must not confound the warnings and the exhortation with an objective fact: that is, the one to whom the Word of God is addressed is at the same time addressed the warning of the possibility (beginning from this moment) of a condemnation. I would say that then the threat becomes one of the elements of the pedagogy of God, but does not at all imply a realization of this threat for the totality of humanity. It is a possibility opened before the one to whom the Gospel is announced and consequently to whom grace has already been given. It is not an objective theological discourse, and we do not have the right to transform it into one.

Chapter 7

[1]This chapter will be very brief because I have analyzed at length the symbolism of the New Jerusalem in *The Meaning of the City,* to which I refer. I limit myself here to summing up the main lines of this book. See also the very beautiful study of Brunner, *Von der Schöpfung im Anfang zur Apokalyptischen Neuschöpfung, Zeitwende die Neue Furche* (1968).

[2]In former times this was the great difference between Catholic and Reformed Theology. Péguy has admirably characterized Catholic theology: the carnal cities . . . because they are the image, and the beginning, and the body and the model of the House of God. This was repeated today by Teilhard de Chardin. And now a great number of Protestant theologians and the Ecumenical Council have in their turn fallen into this error.

[3]And inevitably there are here the principal sexual "sins" which, since sex participates in the sacred universe, are not in the moral but in the spiritual domain.

[4]Here then I would be very tempted for this last section of the Apocalypse to present another septenary, which is not explicitly stated in the text but which is nevertheless found. The septenary of the divine New: in fact we find: (1) the resurrection (20: 12–13); (2) the appearance of the new heaven and the new earth (21:1); (3) the appearance of the dwelling of God with men (21: 3); (4) the symbolic description of the heavenly Jerusalem (21: 10–23); (5) the bringing of the works of man into this Jerusalem (21: 24–26); (6) the river of living water (22: 1); (7) the tree of life (22: 2). Indisputably a septenary which includes the *totality* of the New.

[5]We even think we find, parallel to what we wrote of chapters 6–7, that the plagues unleashed by the seals which accompany in history the setting apart of the people of God (cf. chapter 4 of this study) correspond exactly to the plagues unleashed by the bowls which accompany the appearance of the New of God.

[6]Once more I limit myself to summing up in these five lines the very good note of the *Traduction Oecuménique de la Bible* upon this verse.

[7]I am in complete disagreement with Rissi *(Die Zukunft der Welt)* when he supposes, concerning the relationship between the historic Jerusalem and the celestial Jerusalem, that the New Jerusalem refers uniquely to the Jerusalem of the Old Testament and to the prophecies of restoration. See my book on *The Meaning of the City*.

[8]I had expounded this for the first time in an article in *Foi et Vie* (1948) and an article in *Dieu Vivant*, No. 16 (1950).

[9]Certainly we must not read the text in order to be able to write as the annotator of the Centenary Bible has done: "Many descriptions of this last chapter are inspired by the history of paradise. That which was at the origin of the world returns at

the end of time. The last page of the Bible rejoins the first. The sacred cycle is closed"! This because of the river and the tree: the city and the fact that the tree in question is situated in the square of the city are simply forgotten. A little negligence!

[10]In this city there is no trace of "savage" nature. There is only the tree. "Nature" has disappeared. In reality it has been omitted to the profit of the cultural work of man. The God of Israel thereby totally completes his revelation: from the beginning he was not the God of nature; he was not the God of natural forces, mountains and waters; but in an ultimate way he associates himself with the work of man in order to attest in this last revelation what he was from the beginning.

[11]J. Comblin is certainly right in relating the vision of the gathering of the nations to the festival of pilgrimage and showing the importance of the festive element—here light, gift (consumption superior to production) (and Comblin's analysis of the opposition between the pagan festival and the Jewish festival is good). And more precisely the Feast of Tabernacles, feast of water and of light, where the rites had an eschatological meaning, which receives its fulfillment in the absolute light of God which is the light of the City and of the River of Life. We refer to the good study of Comblin on this subject. But this feast, instead of being a rupture of daily life and passage to an unreal world, is, on the contrary, the feast of the integration of the daily into the total reconciliation of man with man and with God.

[12]Here again I may be permitted to refer to the detailed study in my book already cited.

[13]Rissi *(Zukunft der Welt)* holds the opinion that the city is a cube, recalling the Holy of Holies of the Temple of Solomon. In favor of the ziggurat there has been insistence above all on the inverse image of Jerusalem/Babylon. But I believe this to be an error because the ziggurat implies precisely the ascensional movement toward God, which is denied here. On the other hand, it supports a temple, while in the heavenly Jerusalem, which is a habitation, there is no longer a temple. The transition from the ziggurat, a monument, to the City, habita-

tion and place of man (not of the gods) appears to me unthinkable.

[14]Of course, outside the symbolic factor, we must also keep the splendor of the city and its precious stones, the aesthetic and nonutilitarian value noted by many commentators. "Matter has become ornament. Utility is transcended. Matter has become beauty; as such it is the revelation of God, of that which God manifests of himself in his gift to creation . . ." (Comblin).

[15]Of course I do not accept the idea of the Centenary Bible according to which the mention of the Lamb is an interpolation added to a primitive Jewish text. There is simply original rank prejudice, but entirely without demonstration.

[16]But a very judicious remark made by Comblin must be added: "In reserving secularization for the world after the resurrection, John denies it for the present time: we have not transcended paganism. . . . We can foresee that a present tentative surpassing of the dualism (profane-sacred) can only lead to a return of paganism." It is this renaissance of the sacred, of secular religions, etc., in a world which wants to get rid of God and of the religions that I have attempted to show in *The New Demons*.

[17]This abolition of the political power appears to me irrefutable and I have never understood how Karl Barth could say that in the heavenly Jerusalem, if the Church has disappeared, on the other hand the *exousia* of the political power remains. I do not see any trace of it. On the contrary, everything that was political power has disappeared. But Comblin presents a wise reflection: since the disappearance of the political power is promised exclusively in the heavenly Jerusalem, this means that, on the contrary, it will remain in one form or another upon earth up to the end. No anarchist society is realizable or possible upon earth.

[18]The absence of Church and of Power must not be interpreted in modern terms as "laicity and democracy," which Comblin does. This is a profound error and a little demagogic. For

these words are charged with a passionate potential and a meaning not found in the Apocalypse. No, there is no laicity, since there is a transcendence of the sacred. There is no democracy, since there is no longer any "political power" at all. Democracy is not the reign of Love, but a constitutional form of the State.

[19]This is what the strange little phrase means at the end of this passage: "and they shall worship him." Though spontaneously we cannot comprehend how worship arises again in this heavenly Jerusalem where there is no longer a temple and where there exists a total association between God and man (vs. 3).

"The purpose of the vision of the New Jerusalem is not to furnish speculative knowledge about the beyond but to reveal the dynamism in which humanity is involved. The vision of the New Jerusalem is a projection of the movement which draws humanity along. . . . It is then already visible in the present movement, at least for the one who knows its secret. The revelation of John consists in the manifestation of this invisible and which already brings about the movement . . ." (J. Comblin, *Théologie de la Ville*). It is therefore evident that the vision of John cannot be assimilated to utopias. The latter always include designs of ideal cities, which serve as a pretext to expose social or political ideas. "Utopias are born of the awareness of the insurmountable distance which separates morality from reality," J. Comblin remarks correctly, and his whole analysis on the opposition between utopia and the Apocalypse is excellent; I simply refer to it. He emphasizes very well that the Apocalypse is not a protest emanating from conscience. It is a testimony concerning the action of God. It is not a matter of ideas that a man could have concerning justice, or the organization of the just society, but of another world where present conditions are transcended.

Chapter 8

[1]P. Le Guillou formulates very profoundly the meaning of these doxologies in the following passage: "We will attempt to give a faithful account of the *presence of the Being who gives mean-*

ing to the world. Then, on a plane of interpretation more formally theological, we will consider the *eschatology of meaning*, which is the Passover of Christ. Finally we will show that the manifestation of the name of the Father by the Son (the glorification), whether man receives it or whether he rejects it, decides the meaning or nonmeaning of the world, the meaning of man and his destiny, in a system which is fundamentally Apocalypse."

[2]Of course, we read with the greatest profit the studies of P. Prigent on the liturgical elements of the primitive Church revealed to us by the Apocalypse: in particular his book *Apocalypse et Liturgie* (1964) where he attempts to show the liturgical fragments of baptism and the Lord's Supper in the letters to the churches, fragments which would then be inscribed in a paschal liturgy (which is certainly possible: I have never denied that the author of the Apocalypse could have borrowed and utilized preformed texts). Chapters 4 and 5 could contain a Christian paschal liturgy adopted from a Jewish liturgy, but this appears to me less evident. However, given the competence of Prigent in these matters, I would have confidence in him. In the same connection: P. Prigent, "Une trace de Liturgie Judéo-chrétienne dans le chapitre XXI de l'Apocalypse," *Recherches de Sciences Religieuses,* vol. 60 (1972).

[3]Of course, with all the commentators, we must emphasize that there is a close kinship between this vision and that of Ezekiel; but we must then ask if the seer is subject only to some stereotypes or if we are not in the presence of a confirmation of the vision of the Old Testament by the newness of God known in Christ.

[4]We can even divert ourselves by observing that these verses are located *exactly* in the middle of the Apocalypse as a whole: 205 verses before, 207 after. This is clearly the center. But obviously an argument must not be drawn from this kind of observation.

[5]With many others, we could consider that each time it is a prayer ("Come") addressed to God the Father: it would have only a single direction. The Spirit asks the Father for the

return of Jesus. The Church asks ..., the one who hears says, "Come," and verse 20 would respond to all these requests: Jesus answers, "I am coming soon." But we would no longer understand at all vs. 17b: "and let him who is thirsty come." This no longer has meaning. On the contrary, the "crossed" explanation must be adopted: the Spirit addresses himself not to God (he is himself God, even if he bears our prayers before God) but to man. And the Bride addresses herself to God. As for the witness (the one who hears), he is evidently the one who, on the one hand, witnesses before men and calls them, and who prays to God and asks him for the return of his Son. Then there is a double line from 17b to 20a.

⁶There is the witness of verse 18a and that of verse 20a. It is remarkable that some commentators have affirmed on the subject of the first: "It is evident that it is Jesus who speaks as verse 20 shows." But this evidence must be suspected! The text must be read: the change from "I" to "he" is significant. With the "I warn" we are no longer in the presence, for what follows, of the discourse in the first person of verse 16, which is interrupted by verse 17. It is John who here takes up the word; he is the witness for the whole. As this is said explicitly in 1: 1–2 (the warning given here is the exact replica of 1: 3). And then there is the one who attests this attestation, who comes to confirm the word of his witness. The text is very exact in its unfolding but it must be read as it is. We can also note (a little cultural detail) that this mechanism of a witness, a powerful personage, who comes to attest the value and validity of what another witness (of less weight) says, is an essential juridicial practice in Roman law: it was applied in the whole Roman empire at this epoch (the process of the *Auctoritas*).

⁷As Roland de Pury said at another time: "as soon as 'and' is added to Jesus Christ, Jesus Christ is no more." Jesus Christ *and* morality or politics or justice or country or socialism or revolution or Zen or values, to say nothing of money and work, etc. It is that which falls under this condemnation. The work of God *less* something: mythological resurrection, death of God, disappearance of the Father, rejection of God as Being, etc. It is that which falls under this exclusion from Life.

[8]We must always remember that grace means freely given. That the one who desires it receives freely. Which implies not only the classic opposition of works of the law and grace (but on condition of knowing well that the grace which evokes faith can be expressed only in works), but above all, and this is less theological but, I believe, much more important, the opposition of the world of the free gift to that of payment, of balance, of owe and must: the world of the free gift is the opposite of that of measure and of reckoning (I would say, carrying this further, of money and technique).